NOUGHT TO THIRTY
IN TWO SEGMENTS

For David

NOUGHT TO THIRTY IN TWO SEGMENTS

STORIES AND MEMOIR

with best wishes

Peter Lloyd

30/5/2023

PETER LLOYD

Matador
Unit E2 Airfield Business Park,
Harrison Road, Market Harborough,
Leicestershire. LE16 7UL
Tel: 0116 2792299
Email: books@troubador.co.uk
Web: www.troubador.co.uk/matador
Twitter: @matadorbooks

ISBN 978 1803136 479

British Library Cataloguing in Publication Data.
A catalogue record for this book is available from the British Library.

Printed and bound in the UK by TJ Books Limited, Padstow, Cornwall
Typeset in 11pt Minion Pro by Troubador Publishing Ltd, Leicester, UK

Matador is an imprint of Troubador Publishing Ltd

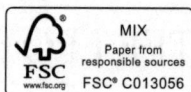

For Nick, Georgie and Jez

Contents

Preface

This work is addressed to my children, Nick, Georgie and Jez, with the intention of giving them an idea of my life before they were around and before I had even met their mother. I hope it is more than an ego trip. It gives me the opportunity of understanding myself a little better but also tells them about a world that may seem very foreign to them – the 1940s, '50s and '60s. Much has been written about the post war period in Britain, and especially the so-called swinging sixties. I lived through the latter as a teenager and in my twenties. They can judge for themselves the extent to which this was a critical epoch in our history.

Since we are all the product of our inheritance and environment, further insights into the background of one of their parents should provide my children with a broader sense of who they are. It may even prove of interest, in time, to Milly, Lois, Ben and Marcel and other grandchildren should they emerge. If it occasions exclamations such as: "Oh, so that was what Dad was really like. That explains a lot about me", I suppose I cannot complain. However, I would like to think a more complex picture will emerge in which they can look beyond this account to a totality that involves grandparents and the circumstances that obtained at the time. This is to leave out the influence of their mother and her rich inheritance and background. There is plenty of fertile ground to be ploughed there but I shall not be mounting a tractor to pursue that course.

I think of myself as a private person and so there is a fair degree of trepidation involved in producing a work of this sort. But I also enjoy writing and, lacking much imagination, the main source of writing is therefore one's own experiences. Nevertheless, I began to find the autobiographical form somewhat restrictive and this is why this book is in two parts. I felt the need to stretch out into a fictional or factional format, to produce stories that had their origin in my own life. Often, the difference between fact and fiction is minimal but the advantage of the fictional approach is that it allows you to plot and dramatize the action and hopefully make it more entertaining. The *Tales from Torrington*, for example, are pretty much a straightforward account of a peculiar period of my life as a small boy in a boarding school. But this time was also shared by my brother Allan and it will be an example of the fallibility of memory if his recollection is rather different.

Another example is what I call my war story and, undoubtedly, my earliest memory. The memory is of the flashbulb type in that I have a picture of myself rushing outside holding some cutlery. On a number of occasions I recounted this incident to my mother and received only a look of incomprehension. Eventually I gave up asking and so it was with some astonishment that, on the occasion of a party to celebrate my 60th birthday, I heard my mother recounting the time that I was blown out of the house from the kitchen, through the hall, and out into the middle of the road. This event had been precipitated by the explosion of a V bomb in the vicinity of our house in Clapham. The Prologue to this book recalls this episode in the form of a short story.

I will forebear from discussing the content further. It is here; it can speak for itself. But I should say a word about my parents who, by implication, may not always come across as paragons. This is just how it is. No one is perfect and by and large we do our best in the circumstances and my parents' situation was often far from easy. What they provided was support and encouragement for me to go my own way and for this I'm profoundly grateful. An example was the foreign adventures I undertook alone from the age of sixteen. Although I was instrumental in setting them up, they never discouraged me which perhaps stemmed from their own love of the Continent and their pioneering camping holidays in France, Switzerland and Spain. I wonder if they would have been so blasé if I had been a girl.

I wish to acknowledge the help of two friends who are experienced authors and who have read and commented on the manuscript. Heather Pollitt has been the source of wise counsel and numerous practical suggestions. John White has provided constant support and pertinent advice. I am very grateful to them both and, of course, neither is responsible for any imperfection in the book. I'd also like to thank the members of the Heatons and Reddish U3A Writing Group who have listened to me read many of the stories included here and kindly encouraged me. Finally, I must thank my wife and life partner, Virginia, who acted as a diligent second proof reader and produced digital versions of the pictures that appear in the book. The material she had to work with was frequently substandard, being photographs taken many years ago on inferior equipment by amateurs. This caused me to question whether to include such illustrations, but on grounds of immediacy and interest they are here for your edification, or otherwise. Returning to my wife, I am sure she must have often wondered what I was doing in my study. The answer 'writing' was not one she probably regarded sympathetically being herself a 'doer' rather than a contemplative sort. Nevertheless, she put no obstacles in my way, and even though this 'life' contains few references to her, she does have a star walk-on part towards the end.

Although this book is principally addressed to my children, I will not object should anyone else find it of interest. On the contrary, I would be flattered to learn that this modest offering had an audience wider than the immediate Lloyd family.

Any proceeds from the sale of this work will go to the charity 'Mind'.

P.L. March, 2023

Looking Back

My name is Evelyn Winter and I live in a 'home' in Bromley, which still thinks it's in Kent but is really South London. I never thought I'd end up in a home. It brings to mind my son when he used to get impatient with me, probably because I refused to wear my hearing aids: "You don't want to end up in a home, do you?" Well, I have and as well as not hearing anything, I don't see very well. To be blunt, I'm almost blind. So, I need looking after.

The staff are very kind but insist on calling me Eve, or worse, Evie. I tried telling them that my name was Evelyn but they wouldn't listen. In fact, when I was first admitted I said I was Mrs Winter but they wouldn't hear of that. "We use first names here, Eve. We're all friends in Summerland." I gave up after a while. Life's too short, or, in my case, too long. Yes, the home is called Summerland. Who'd have thought that Evelyn Summer would end up in Summerland. But then who'd have thought that Evelyn Summer would marry Edward Winter. Certainly not my father who was dead against it. But I did and we were more or less happily married for 55 years.

Now, would you believe it, we're in 2021. Last October I celebrated my 101st birthday. The word 'celebrate' is an exaggeration. There was a cake and they sang Happy Birthday but that was about it. Not that I minded. There's not a lot to celebrate at my age. When I clocked up the century the previous year they

made more of a fuss and a couple of my grandchildren turned up.
And I was pleased to get the Queen's telegram even if I couldn't
read it.

And now we're in the middle of the pandemic. Coronavirus
I believe it's called. Sounds like something from outer space but I
don't think it is. I do know it's carried off a few from Summerland.
I still like listening to the wireless and I heard our prime minister,
Mr Johnson, telling us only yesterday that we all had to stand
together to get through the last lap. Of course, I can't see him but
they tell me he still looks like he did when he was London Mayor
which I do remember. In other words, he still looks as though he
sleeps in his clothes. And that hair! Can't the man afford a comb?
I confess I didn't take to his bumptious manner. It was said that he
fancied himself as a reincarnation of Winston Churchill. If only. I
once met Churchill when he was visiting the site of bomb damage
in Clapham. There was a man. He inspired us to get through
something a lot worse than coronavirus.

I spend a lot of time these days thinking back, especially to
the war years. I was in London throughout the war. Got married,
had two kids. It was a grim time but the community spirit was
genuine. We rallied round and helped one another. They talk on
the wireless today about the blitz spirit helping us to get through
coronavirus. I hope it does but I'm not sure. The London blitz
was truly terrible. Daily bombing, often at night which meant
we had to sleep in a shelter. My Edward, who was in a protected
occupation, got caught in a bomb blast just as he was coming out
of the tube. It rearranged his face somewhat and he lost his front
teeth. Didn't make him look any better unfortunately.

We got through the blitz but the deprivation for the next few
years began to grind you down. Barely enough to eat, curfews,
blackouts. It was grim. And then finally we heard about the D Day
landings on the Normandy beaches. This gave us a big lift. We'd
begun to dare to think that the end was in sight. At last we were
taking the fight to the enemy. Then my brother George, who'd
been part of the invasion force, got injured and was repatriated.

His leg was a mess. That made me realise that while there was still fighting, the war was far from over. We had another nasty shock when the Germans started bombing us again. If this was an enemy on the run, how come they were able to mount a big bombing campaign that was particularly evident south of the capital where we lived.

The new bombing threat came from the V1 flying bombs that we called doodlebugs. They were little unmanned aircraft that came skimming across the Channel and delivered a huge explosion. After a while our lads got the measure of the doodlebug and were able to shoot them down so that only about a quarter of them got through. We were beginning to think that we may have survived this latest blitz, especially when Mr Sandys, the Minister of Works, announced that the latest Battle of London was over. He spoke too soon. The next day there was a huge explosion at Chiswick, by the river, which killed three and injured a number of others. But this wasn't a V1. It was a V2. This was a rocket and unlike the doodlebug, it came down from space. It was an enormous thing, the height of three London buses and travelled at thousands of miles an hour. There was no question of shooting it down. And they said that you got no warning. The one that fell on Woolworth's in New Cross before Christmas killed over a hundred and fifty. My friend Pat was nearly caught in the blast. Well, she was a few hundred yards away but she said the force of the blast nearly knocked her over. She'd been in Woolworth's only half an hour previously.

This third bombing campaign was just about the last straw. These huge new bombs seemed to be giving the Germans the edge again. We were downcast. But somehow we got through another Christmas and New Year and into 1945 still daring to hope for peace. I missed my period for a second time and realised I was pregnant again. Little Roger was now a toddling two-year-old and talking non-stop. He loved to answer the phone and give his name and our number which amused callers. He liked to help me in the house as well. One morning, it was a Friday in late January,

I was washing up after breakfast, Edward had gone to work, and Roger was drying the cutlery. We were rather late, I remember, since I'd begun to feel some morning sickness in the early months of pregnancy.

I'd just given Roger a couple of spoons to dry when there was a huge bang as the front door of the house blew off. At more or less the same moment, Roger was lifted off the floor and hurtled out of the kitchen, down the hall and into the road outside. I screamed and remember thinking as I ran down the hall, surely I wasn't going to lose him when the end of the war began to seem in sight. When I got to him, he was sitting in the middle of the road looking a little bemused and still holding the spoons and the cloth he was using to dry up. He seemed completely unharmed. As I picked him up and hugged him, I was astonished that he'd suffered no injury. I then saw that there was an enormous cloud of dust and smoke at the end of the street on the other side of Poynders Road. It could only be a V2.

PART ONE

STORIES

Tales From Torrington

*Being the adventures of Roger Sanders and his
pals in a small preparatory boarding school in
West Kent in the 1950s*

Starting Out

He came bounding down the stairs to meet them, a tall, bespectacled figure with thinning hair. He reminded Roger of Reginald Christie, the multiple murderer of Rillington Place, whose picture had been in all the papers recently.

"Good afternoon, Mrs Sanders," he boomed as he came across the hall proffering his hand. "And these young gentlemen will be Roger and John," he added, ruffling their hair. "Righty ho, the first thing is to see Matron and let her know you've arrived. She will tell you which dormitory you are in," he thundered.

"Mrs Sanders, would you like a cup of tea?"

'Thank you," said their mother.

"Come this way then."

The boys made to follow but were checked by the teacher.

"You stay here boys. Matron will be along presently."

The boys looked at one another nervously, standing by their ancient leather suitcases.

"Why does Mr Jakeways shout when he speaks?' demanded John.

'Because he's deaf, I suppose. Didn't you see his deaf aid?" said Roger.

John shook his head and then turned when he heard someone coming along the corridor. To John she looked like a nurse with a starched white uniform, including a cap.

"Hello boys, I'm Mrs Jakeways but you must call me Matron." She smiled, revealing dimples in her large, soft, round, pink face. "Come with me and I'll show you your dormitory."

Roger went to pick up his case.

"No, leave that. Laker will bring your cases up."

Roger was feeling uncomfortable in his new, scarlet uniform. The blazer itched and so did the grey shirt. And he didn't know what to do with the cap that his mother had told him to remove when they entered the school. He now held it self-consciously in his hand.

Matron bustled along the corridor from which she'd come and then down a small flight of stairs.

"Those are the heads," she called out as they passed some cubicles. "And that is the dining room." She gestured towards a large wooden door. She then mounted a larger staircase to the first floor and turned into the third room on the left side.

"Right, you'll both be in Dormitory 2. Take these two beds," she pointed. "I'll go and find Davis and he can show you the ropes."

They were left alone in a long room with eight beds, four on either side. All had iron headboards and were identically made up with navy blankets. There was a small chest of painted, apple-green drawers beside each bed.

"I wonder where Mummy is," said John.

They never saw their mother again that day and for another three weeks. Mr Jakeways explained that it was for the best if she just slipped away. Parting could sometimes be 'a messy business' and in their experience the boarders coped better if emotional scenes could be avoided.

A red-headed boy with a friendly grin came into the dormitory.

"Hello, you must be Sanders Major and Minor, I'm Toby Davis. Matron asked me to show you the ropes. When Laker brings up your bags you must unpack and put your clothes in the drawers next to your bed. Shoes and coats must go in that cupboard." He pointed to a large wardrobe near the door.

"And your sponge bag should be left on the top of the chest of drawers and your slippers under the bed. By the way, we don't wear blazers after school so you can take those off and hang them on the hook in the wardrobe. And change your shoes – we wear black plimsolls in the house."

At that moment a slightly stooped figure wearing something approximating a butcher's apron stepped across the threshold carrying the two leather suitcases.

"Thank you," said Roger. Laker nodded and withdrew.

"Right, I'll leave you to unpack. Supper is at five thirty." Toby left them, calling as he went, "you know where the refectory is, don't you?"

Two hours later the brothers were in their pyjamas ready for bed but not ready. They were not used to going to bed at 7.00 at home. John went to bed at 8 o' clock and Roger at 8.30. And they also felt hungry. Supper had been bread and cold sardines with bread and jam and a glass of cold milk to follow. Mr Jakeways presided at the head of one table and Matron at the other though the adults didn't appear to eat.

Before putting on their pyjamas they had to go to the washroom in their vest and pants and wash in cold water as well as visit 'the heads' as the lavatories were called. While they were putting on their pyjamas Mr Jakeways came in to the dormitory and told them they had fifteen minutes before lights out and not to forget to say their prayers. Roger and John saw the other boys kneeling by their beds with their hands together and, though it was not their practice, decided that it was appropriate to follow suit.

Then it was into bed and a return visit from Mr Jakeways. His ritual at this juncture was to go to each bed and say goodnight individually. When he got to John's bed, Roger saw him ruffle his brother's hair and place his hand underneath the sheet.

"Hope you're nice and warm in there, Sanders Minor," he whispered in a voice loud enough for Roger to hear. When he got to Roger's bed, he ruffled his hair and said, "Sleep well Sanders." Finally, he paused at the door and, turning out the light, called "Good night, boys."

"Good night, sir," was the answering chorus.

Within a couple of minutes of Jakeways's departure there were whisperings in the dormitory and some giggling.

"Do you know any jokes, Sanders?" someone called out. When there was no answer, a boy called Cropper said:

"I know a dirty rhyme."

"Let's hear it then," shouted someone else.

Cropper began, in a sing-song voice:

"Not last night but the night before,
Three tom cats came knocking at the door.
One had a fiddle, one had a drum,
And one had a pancake stuck to his bum."

Howls of laughter greeted this masterpiece and prompted Davis to add one of his own.

"Fatty and Skinny went down to the bay
Fatty blew off and blew Skinny away."

More mirth. Roger thought it would endear him to the dorm if he could contribute a rhyme of his own. "'I've got one," he called out.

"My Uncle Billy
Had a three foot willy
And he showed it to the lady next door.

She thought it was a snake
And hit it with a rake
And now it's only two foot four."

The response that this induced was music to the ears of Roger and for the first time since arriving at Torrington House the anxiety he had been suffering slightly abated. But then the door burst open, light flooded the room and the angry face of the headmaster could be seen.

"Who is responsible for this dreadful racket?" he bellowed.

Silence.

"I'll ask you once more, who is responsible for this shocking noise?"

No one spoke.

"Very well," said Mr Jakeways. "Davis and Sanders Major, get up, put on your dressing gowns and come with me."

The boys did as they were told and followed the Head to his room. There, Jakeways looked at them severely.

"As the two oldest boys in the dormitory I hold you responsible for setting an example and maintaining good order. Since you have singularly failed to do this, I have no other recourse but to punish you."

He speaks like Pontius Pilate, thought Roger. Jakeways was still talking.

"Take off your dressing gowns. Davis, bend over the arm of the chair." The headmaster then selected a large gym shoe from a shelf by the door and pulled down Davis's pyjama trousers. He hit him on the buttocks with four mighty smacks of the shoe. Davis cried out and continued crying "Oh, Daddy!" after the beating ceased and he hopped around the room, hauling up his pyjama bottoms. Then it was Roger's turn. The pain caused by the descending slipper was worse than he expected – a terrible burning sensation. It got worse with each blow and he was unable to inhibit tears. He felt the absence of his mother dreadfully at this moment and as he sobbed he called out, "Mummy, ooh Mummy!"

They were told to go back to bed and entered a very hushed dormitory.

"Are you OK Rog?" John whispered.

"Yes," said Roger. "Shush, go to sleep."

But he wasn't OK. He felt humiliated and unfairly treated. That he should get a beating for talking after lights out on his first day in the school seemed a completely disproportionate punishment. He lost any respect he felt for the headmaster. He would have to let his mother know how he felt. He was sure that she wouldn't allow them to stay in a place that dispensed such harshness.

Next morning at breakfast, Roger avoided the eye of Mr Jakeways. To his surprise, the headmaster seemed cheerful as he recounted something to his wife. Then Roger realised that the topic of conversation was last night's incident involving him and Davis.

"You should have heard them, Matron. One shouting for his mother and the other for his father. Ooh, Daddy, ooh, Mummy."

Roger flushed when he heard what was being said and it reawakened the bitterness of the previous night. The man was not only a sadist but a heartless bully, enjoying the torment of his victims.

After breakfast, on his way back to the dormitory, he fell into step alongside Davis. "Did you hear the Head talking about us to Matron?" asked Roger.

"Yes," Davis replied.

"Didn't you think it was terrible?" Roger protested.

Davis thought for a moment. His frank, cheerful, freckled face clouded and then he said,

"I suppose so but that's the way he is. You need to keep on his right side."

"But he wasn't in the right," persisted Roger. "He should not have beaten us like that and he shouldn't find our pain amusing."

"Well," replied Davis, "he's the Head, he's in charge. What he says goes and you can't do anything about that. That's why it's sensible to keep on his right side."

Roger realised that Davis was not amenable to his argument and decided to drop the subject. But he was puzzled about something.

"Can I ask you a question, Davis?"

"Of course."

"Why did you shout for your Dad when Jakeways was hitting you?"

"Oh, that," said Davis a little sheepishly. "It's simple, my mother's dead."

"Oh dear, I'm sorry," said Roger.

"It's OK. You didn't know. That's why I'm here." It's too much for my father to look after me on his own when his work takes up so much time. How about you, why are you and John here?"

This was a question that Roger had wondered himself but there was a logical answer.

"Daddy is working abroad and our mother also works and so it is better if we are boarders."

"It's a familiar story," said Davis. "You'll find that most of the boys have only one parent at home, usually mother. Don't feel too down. It's not so bad here. Matron's OK and so is Miss Johnsson."

Bowel Movements

Robert Lionel Jakeways rocked back and forth on the balls of his feet at the top of the stairs. Dressed in a navy vest and similarly coloured long shorts, he was checking the boys out of the dormitories as they made their way down to the quad for morning PT. He enjoyed this moment of the day, observing his young charges as they hurried past him saying 'Good morning sir' as they passed. It reminded him of his navy days where he had learned the vital lessons of discipline, order and team spirit. No one needed to tell him that a healthy mind required a healthy body and he knew of no healthier start to the day than fifteen minutes vigorous PT. He followed the last boy, Hodge, down the stairs to the quad. He noted that Hodge's shorts were rather skimpy and a little frayed and made a mental note to mention it to Matron.

When he got to the quad he found that the boys were sheltering in the lobby because it was raining. Jakeways seldom allowed the boys to exercise inside but since he did not fancy getting wet himself he ordered them to the gym. There he stood at the front of two lines of boys and started the routine.

"Deep breathing exercise. Legs apart, hands at low cross!" he bawled like a sergeant major.

The boys placed their hands together, one across the back of the other, over their private parts.

"Deep breathing commence, bringing your arms up and rising on the balls of your feet," he shouted.

The boys all raised their arms above their heads and out like a star shape. They did this a dozen times breathing in and out exaggeratedly as they had been taught. They then went through a series of drills involving the vigorous movement of the four limbs mostly in their assigned place. They finished with running and then jumping on the spot before doing three laps of the gym. Jakeways then ordered them back to their positions and carried out an inspection. He went down the two lines stopping at Hodge.

"Your shorts are too tight, Hodge, and they are worn. See Matron after breakfast."

He touched the last boy on the shoulder as he got to the end of the second line and that boy marched off with the line following him. Jakeways loved to see boys march and he had persuaded Mrs Brent, the principal, that they should have marching to music once a week. This proved popular as the parade ground came into a cleared classroom and lines of boys performed a series of manoeuvres while Mrs Bonnett played the piano. It was noticeable that the boys enjoyed the activity, recognising the pleasure to be gained from performing, say, a particular diagonal criss-crossing pattern successfully. It was not long before the activity transferred to daily assembly so that pupils would march out at the conclusion of assembly as Mrs Bonnett thumped out the Vicar of Bray.

After breakfast, typically bullet hard boiled eggs, cold toast, butter and marmalade, and hot milk, the practice was to go to the heads to relieve themselves, and wash hands and clean teeth. It was essential to have a 'proper sit-down job' as Jakeways called it. He made a point of hovering around the heads during this time. This was because he had an important role. All boys were required to let Mr Jakeways know when they had finished their toilet before they pulled the chain. When a boy signalled to Mr Jakeways that he had finished, the Head marched along the line of six WCs to the appropriate cubicle and stared down the pan, removing paper if necessary. He then put his head back out of the cubicle and made a signal to the boy who by now was standing by the entrance where hung a clipboard with a chart and a pencil on a piece of string. Jakeways's signal consisted of a raised hand with either one finger in the air, known as "a one", crossed fingers, known as "an X", or index finger and thumb forming a circle, known as "a nought". The boys getting the raised finger felt pleased as they put a "1" against their name on the clipboard chart since they knew they had a done a good job. "X" was not quite so pleasing as it meant that only one or two miserable 'plops' had been produced but it was not so bad as the dreaded "nought" for that meant a visit to Matron.

Every boy had to see Matron after breakfast and supper. She would dispense medicine to any boy in need of medication and also see to any domestic matters concerning a particular boy. Since everyone was administered a large tablespoonful of cod liver oil and malt, this meant there was always a line to see her. In the evening she would have the 1-X-0 chart to hand and as each boy reached her she consulted the chart. A 'zero' was automatically given a spoonful of syrup of figs as was a boy who had had two consecutive Xs. Being regular was a further part of the Jakeways creed with constipation being regarded as something approaching a sin; hence the feelings of dejection occasioned in the boy given the circular signal.

Tradition was another favoured feature of life under Jakeways. He was conservative with a small and a large "C". He had personally felt the insult when Churchill was voted out of office after the war and was relieved that Attlee and his red cronies were back where they belonged, on the opposition benches. One of his traditions had been to train the boys in his various needs. In some sense, each could be regarded as miniature batman, there to ensure that his life, hard as it was, might be ameliorated a little. One tradition was the break time cup of tea. Various rosters existed, one of them being to take Mr Jakeways a cup of tea at morning and afternoon break. This week, Sanders Major was doing the morning break. He went to the kitchen and received the Headmaster's cup complete with two sugar lumps and a biscuit in the saucer. Jakeways's custom was to take his tea on the landing outside his classroom at the top of the stairs. On this particular morning, the Head was sitting on the top stair and Sanders carried the cup up to him.

"Thank you Sanders."

He seemed in a good mood. Sanders waited to be dismissed while Mr Jakeways stirred his tea. Suddenly, Sanders gave a jump and cried out. Jakeways laughed. The reason for Sanders's discomfiture was that Jakeways had placed the spoon that had come out of the hot tea on the back of Roger's knee. The fact that the "ouch!" caused by the momentary pain amused Jakeways was not lost on Roger. He stored it away in the account he was mentally compiling of this man's sadistic profile.

Bodily Functions

The school only had two classrooms, one for five- to seven-year-olds and the other for eight years and over. The younger class was taken by Mrs Brent who owned the school and whose name was on the board at the entrance as principal. She seemed kindly to Roger, with a friendly smile, but since he was in the class of older children she made little impression on him. Mr Jakeways was in charge of the older children and had somehow to keep different levels of work going simultaneously. The eight-year-olds were still developing their basic skills in the three Rs while the ten-year olds were preparing for examinations which would hopefully take them to good private schools or grammar schools. This meant dealing with advanced composition and maths as well as elementary history, geography, biology and French.

Jakeways's practice was to bring the class together once a day for a plenary teaching session. One day he announced that a communal biology lesson would take place. He was going to talk about the human digestive system. A chart depicting the human body was pinned up and caused a giggle because a penis was depicted. Unusually, Jakeways ignored this and started with a question.

"How do human beings stay alive? Streeter?"

The boy who had put his hand up answered, "By eating food, sir."

"Yes, and what else? Davis?"

"Drinking, sir."

"Yes. Anything else?"

No more hands were raised.

"Well, we all need air to breathe, don't we, to stay alive?"

For some reason that had not occurred to Roger but he did not doubt the truth of Jakeways's claim. The teacher then began to discuss the digestive system. He talked about the ingestion of foodstuffs including liquids. How they entered the mouth, went down the gullet into the stomach where they were processed. This processing provided energy for the muscles and nutrients for the blood and, in the case of children, growth for the body.

"But," barked Jakeways, "we do not absorb all the food and liquid we consume, do we?" He paused theatrically. "What happens to the material that is unwanted?" This question hung in the air as the class wondered, and perhaps feared, what was coming next. There was another nervous snigger on the back row which comprised Davis, Streeter and Sanders Major.

Jakeways directed his attention to the rear of class as he said, "Our everyday behaviour makes it clear to us that there is a process of elimination involved in the intake and digestion of foodstuffs. The waste material goes to the bladder in the case of liquids and the bowel in the case of solid stuff." As he was talking he pointed to the chart with a stick, making movements between the bowels and the genital and anal area.

Roger was wondering what the eight-year-olds made of this lesson when he heard the teacher saying:

"... and what happens is that you rid the body of waste matter when you go to the toilet," and he made a sign of pulling an imaginary chain.

An explosion of muffled laughter issued forth again from the back row.

"There, in a nutshell, is the digestive system of the human body," said Jakeways.

As Roger contemplated the undesirability of that particular nutshell, he was conscious of the lesson ending and Jakeways taking down his chart. Before he left the room he announced:

"I want Davis, Streeter and Sanders Major to come to my room after school today."

An hour later, the three boys knocked on the door of the Head's room. He admitted them and eyed them ominously.

"I've been aware of the filth that pervades your minds for some time. I've heard your smutty jokes and your sniggers at unintended innuendo. That is why today's lesson was no accident. I wanted to bring out into the open the cesspits that are your minds. As I expected, reference to bodily parts and bodily functions would be regarded as a laughing matter by you. Since you are the older boys, required to set an example to the younger ones, I cannot let this pass without severe action. You will each receive six strokes of the cane."

One by one the boys dutifully took down their trousers, bent over the chair arm and received six strikes from the slender, whippy stick that was Jakeways's cane. Roger noted how the Head placed his hand across the bottom of each boy before delivering the punishment. The pain was dreadful, a stinging sensation that would not go away and would not allow you to sit down without even more hurt. Again, Roger felt a terrible sense of injustice. Why should a bit of sniggering over bodily functions elicit this harsh treatment? What was wrong with a bit of nervous laughter considering that it was a subject that was generally regarded as taboo? And the fact that Jakeways had deliberately engineered the situation made it worse. He was fully aware of the effect that his approach to the topic would have and yet he chose to deliver the lesson in that way. It was actually his fault that the so-called bad example had been set. But, far from being held responsible he would escape Scot free, as his father used to say. Not only did he escape punishment, he actually meted it out.

These questions went round and round in Roger's mind and only succeeded in prolonging the torment. He realised that he would have to tell his mother. In fact, he did not need to mention it to his mother because she saw the wheals on his bottom which were still present when he was at home more than a week later. She had seen them when he was undressing for bed and he told her what happened. His mother was thoughtful and then said she would have to talk to someone.

Moving House

Excitement was in the air. It had been announced that the boarders were to move from Torrington House to Woodley Grange, a house some three miles away. This was because space had become a problem at Torrington and the removal of the boarders would allow some expansion of classrooms. The boys were required to pack their belongings in their cases and deposit them on the landing. From there they were taken by Laker and another man to a van which was to transport their clothes, furniture, kitchen equipment and much else besides to the new boarding school.

The move was on a Saturday and Roger and Toby and Streeter were allowed to travel in Mr Jakeways's car while the rest of the boarders went with Matron and Miss Johnnsen in the coach driven by Mr Burton. Roger knew that Jakeways regarded it as a privilege to be taken in the car but Roger never felt comfortable being too close to Jakeways. He would have preferred to be in the coach. He liked Mr Burton who was entertaining and often made remarks with a wink that were mildly to the detriment of the Headmaster. He called him, behind his back, Old Jake, a nickname which was picked up by the boys. Besides, Mr Burton smoked Turf cigarettes and he passed the cigarette cards that accompanied the packet to the boys.

When they saw the new place, Roger and Toby were not impressed. Woodley Grange was considerably smaller than Torrington with no playing field only a garden with a few trees and hedges and a sloping lawn. The ground floor contained a dining room, play room and conservatory and, they observed, had heads and washing arrangements similar to the old place. The dormitories were smaller with four beds each rather than eight. Nevertheless, when the rest arrived, the thrill associated with exploring and discovering a new environment made the boys light-headed and there was still a high degree of animation when they sat down to high tea.

Jakeways and Matron were in a good mood and Jakeways was musing as to how Trooper, the dog, would take to the new place. Roger, noticing that Mr Jakeways had taken a slice of bread, deduced what he would want next and called out

"Butter to Old Jake!"

There was a shriek of laughter which even Matron joined in but the Head was not amused.

"See me after, Sanders," he said. This took some of the euphoria out of the group and it was not helped when a small boy named Potter dropped his knife on the floor. As he went to pick it up, Jakeways shouted,

"Leave it Potter. If you cannot be more careful you will have to manage without a knife."

Potter looked dismayed and wondered how he was going to spread butter and jam onto his bread.

"Use your finger!" thundered Jakeways.

Watching Potter try to spread his butter with his finger was a pathetic sight especially when he started snivelling.

"I hope that will teach you to be more careful when you are at table. Clumsiness and bad manners will not be tolerated during meal times."

Boiled eggs, a school staple, were also being consumed at high tea and diners were required to pass their 'empty' egg to the top of the table after they had finished so that Jakeways could inspect it. If he found any egg white stuck to the shell, he worked a spoon round loosening it and then returned it to the perpetrator with a reprimand.

"Don't you realise that there are children starving in the world while you let good food go to waste?"

When he had drunk his mug of tea, Jakeways wiped his mouth on his napkin and stood up although everybody had not finished the meal. He walked down the side of the form on which boys were sitting and tapped Roger on the shoulder.

"Follow me, Sanders."

He was taken to a room that he had not seen in his exploration of the new house, a room used by the Head.

"I am disappointed in you Sanders. You know that I like a joke as much as the next person but I will not tolerate impertinence. Take your trousers down and bend over."

Once again, it was not so much the physical pain of the slippering that upset Roger as the over-reaction of the man. Roger had not intended rudeness. He had got carried away in the excitement of what had been a special day. He even thought there was some affection in the term 'Old Jake', a belief clearly not shared by his headmaster. The trouble was, each time such an incident happened, instead of bringing Roger into line, making him feel regretful for his action, it had the opposite effect. It made him resentful and determined to seek an opportunity for revenge.

The opportunity came about a week later. Jakeways persisted in taking a group of the older boys over to Torrington House each morning in his car while the remainder took the school bus. The excuse was that there was not room for everyone on the coach but it was apparent that the coach was never full. Roger sat with Toby and Clive Simons in the hall watching Trooper licking his penis while waiting for the Head to take them over to Torrington.

"Do you wish you could do that?" said Simons, who had a weird sense of humour.

They sniggered. Then they heard a shout from deep in the bowels of the house. It was Jakeways asking them to open the garage door. They went out and started to do as requested when Roger noticed some long rusty nails in the driveway in front of the garage. He pointed them out to his friends and then picked one up. Jakeways then appeared with his battered brown briefcase. He started up the old Morris and slowly edged it out of the garage.

"Shut the doors boys and get in."

They set off for the short journey to Torrington House, just over two miles. They had just turned right into George Road, less than half a mile from their destination when there was a terrible bumping sound from the car.

"Blast!" said Jakeways. "I think I've got a puncture." He stopped the car and got out and verified his diagnosis.

"Come on you lot, don't sit in there," he shouted to the boys. They obediently got out and surveyed the sad looking flat tyre.

"I'm going to need some help. I want you boys to walk on to school, it's not far. Tell Mr Laker, or Mr Burton, to come down and give me a hand. Explain where I am. Go on, hurry up. I don't want you to be late for school."

They started off in the appropriate direction when Jakeways called out again.

"And explain to Mrs Brent what has happened. Tell her I will be back as soon as possible."

As soon as they were out of sight of Jakeways, they stopped hurrying and Roger started to chortle. The others joined in.

"That was bad luck wasn't it," said Toby, "getting a puncture."

"Yeah," said Roger grinning.

Three days later, the Morris suffered another puncture and the following week a third. By this time, Mr Jakeways was angry and frustrated. At supper that evening the boys overheard him talking to his wife.

"And the funny thing is that each time it has been a three-inch nail. I wonder where I am picking them up."

"Well, it's only started happening since we moved here," said Matron. "Perhaps they are in the drive or the road outside. Why don't you get the boys to have a look round."

And this is how the boys came to discover that there were indeed a number of long nails in the drive. Roger brought a couple of them to Mr Jakeways.

"Ah, that's the culprit. Where did you find them?"

"Lying in the drive, sir."

"Well done, boys. Make sure you pick them all up. I shouldn't have any more problems with punctures."

The boys went outside and found that were only a couple of more nails to be found. But instead of throwing them in the bin, Roger hid them under an old brick. You never knew when they might be called for again.

Trooper

Jakeways's pride and joy was Trooper, a black Labrador. Normally the boys would not have minded Trooper even though he was occasionally slobbery and usually smelly. Trooper's problem, however, was that he not only belonged to Jakeways, he was positively adored by him. Anybody or anything in this position would not be popular in Torrington House.

Quite why Jakeways was so enamoured of Trooper was unclear. It was partly a male thing as Jakeways thought it masculine to have a large dog at his heel while out on walks. It also accorded with his strong disciplinary trait. The dog was something else he was able to control and to shout at. Something about Jakeways's murky military background was also implicated in the presence of his canine friend. The Head had a collection of children's books about a black Labrador called Bruce who was attached to a scout group. Bruce was something like Lassie in that he was constantly being the hero in a tale involving children and a ne're-do-well. Jakeways often used to fantasise that Trooper acted as a guardian to the boys, keeping them out of trouble whenever they were out on country walks. Of this there was no evidence whatsoever. If anything, the contrary was true.

Despite all the shouting and bellowing of his name, Trooper was not a particularly obedient dog. He had a tendency to run away and get lost. This didn't surprise Roger since it was a feeling he consistently had himself in the company of Mr Jakeways. The exasperation on the face of a red and expostulating Jakeways when Trooper did one of his disappearing acts was always worth seeing. It represented one of the small victories that a group of the senior boys began to conspire to achieve in the light of the constant bullying and humiliation they received at the hands of the Head.

At weekends the older boys were allowed to walk in the local woods

"Would you like us to take Trooper, sir?" said Davis.

At first this suggestion annoyed the other boys as the presence of the animal might hamper their activity. Since they were indeed saddled with Trooper after Jakeways 'allowed' the dog to go with them, Davis was not popular as they set off with the Labrador on a lead.

"Why did you want to take Trooper?" wailed Streeter.

"You'll see," said Davis.

Once they were off the main road and into the field that led to the woods, Toby let Trooper off his lead and he bounded off at a great pace.

"Careful, he might get lost," Streeter cried.

"Exactly," said Toby. "We can but hope."

The other boys were startled at this deliberate ploy by Davis but also rather excited. They realised that Davis was deliberately trying to upset, if not provoke, the Head. They then enjoyed their walk in the woods, discovered the tree house that someone else had put up and spent some time in there sharing a bar of chocolate that Simons had smuggled from somewhere. Next they found an improvised swing and had goes pushing one another on this for a while. Roger noted that they had been out an hour and that they should start getting back. The others agreed and Toby solemnly said,

"Good gracious, has anyone seen Trooper?"

Everyone burst out laughing. They started calling out the dog's name in a fairly half-hearted way but without any reaction. Toby explained that they must get back a little bit late and look upset when announcing the bad news to Mr Jakeways.

The effect on the Head was all that they hoped.

"Oh, no! Not again. Why did you allow him to get away?" This statement contradicted Jakeways's conviction that it was the dog that looked after the boys, but at this moment that did enter his calculations. He shouted to his wife that he was going to look for the dog and ordered Davis and Sanders to accompany him. Davis led the way.

"I'll show you where we were when we last saw him, sir."

Roger smirked when he realised that Toby was heading in a completely different direction. The result was that they searched and shouted for half an hour without any joy with Jakeways getting increasingly hot and bothered.

"Oh, we'll have to give up. Matron will be expecting us for lunch."

The group wended its way back to the school with the two boys attempting to put on a show of sorrow as they told the other boys that they hadn't found Trooper.

Trooper did return after lunch. He announced himself by barking at the gate. Roger went to let him in and he was jumping up and wagging his tail and filthy dirty. Suddenly he spied his master and began whining and crouching as low as he could get. He knew what was coming: a good scolding and a good hiding. The boys should have felt guilty at allowing the dog to suffer this fate but they did not. As far as they were concerned, Trooper was one of them and had to take the rough with the smooth.

"Bad luck, Trooper," Davis said softly.

The Other Sex

The introduction of a girls boarding section at Torrington House was the cause of much excitement among the boys. Some of these girls were already known to the boys as day girls including Sandra Brent, the Principal's daughter, a beauty with long dark hair and a shy smile. Jill Cousins was another popular girl with fair, bouncy hair and high colouring. She owned a horse and it was easy to imagine her being at home in the country, dressed in jodhpurs on the back of her pony. Less attractive was the pudgy Doreen Winters but there was a reason to think that Doreen, too, had a sporting side.

Before the introduction of the small girls boarding group, the two sexes stayed pretty much apart. Now, gradually, they became more familiar through taking part in everyday activities like mealtimes. One evening Jakeways and Matron took half a dozen older pupils to see 'The Titfield Thunderbolt' at the local cinema. Sandra Brent and Jill Cousins joined Roger Sanders, Toby Davis and Streeter.

During an interval, a favourite pop song of the period called 'Sugar Bush' was playing. Davis started singing the song quietly so that the boys could hear him, substituting the name Sandra Brent for Sugar Bush:

"Sandra Brent come dance with me, let the other fellas be."

The boys found this both amusing and daring and looked down the row at the lovely Sandra who appeared completely oblivious of their excitement. The feel-good film, an Ealing comedy, had the desired effect and everyone came out of the fleapit a little heady and a closer-knit group with boys and girls sharing comments about the performance of John Gregson and Stanley Holloway. Doreen Winters was also there and she smiled at Roger as they walked back to the shooting brake together.

Next day, after school, was the weekly shoe cleaning routine. Mr Jakeways appeared in the area off the kitchens where this activity was carried out.

"I think it would be a decent gesture if some of you older boys cleaned the shoes of the girls."

This sexist remark might have met with little enthusiasm in the normal run of things but after the previous evening's cinema excursion, Sanders Major, Davis and Streeter were feeling warm towards the girls.

"OK sir, we'd be happy to do that," said Davis.

The girls' shoes were lined up outside their dormitory and it did not take long to clean and polish their sandals. When the time came to return their shoes, they had to pass the bathrooms where the girls were having their evening baths. The door was ajar and on an impulse Sanders went into the passage and then stepped inside the first bathroom and found himself confronting a naked Doreen Winters.

"Just checking that these are your shoes," he said, holding up a pair of brown sandals.

An unabashed Doreen said from the bath, "I think so but put them all together outside our dormitory and we'll sort them out."

When the boys heard what Roger had done they were horrified but envious.

"What did you see?" asked Streeter

"What do you mean?" replied Sanders.

"Well did you see her wotsit?"

"Not really. I only saw the top half of her body."

"Cor," said Davis. "Pity it wasn't Sandra or Jill though."

The following Saturday Roger was enjoying free play time in the gardens of Torrington House when he found himself alone with Doreen Winters among some bushes in an isolated part of the grounds. It seemed like an accident but Roger knew it wasn't. Jackie came up and took Roger's hand.

"Would you like to kiss me?"

"All right." Awkwardly he put his mouth against hers.

"Let me see your thing," she now demanded.

"Not unless you show me yours," said Roger.

"OK." She lifted her skirt and pulled down her navy knickers. Roger stared, heart racing. "'Now watch," she said and squatted down and urinated. "Now it's your turn."

Roger did as he was bid but struggled to produce any urine.

"Go on, wee," ordered Doreen.

What a strange ceremony Roger thought as they wondered back to the house a short time after. Is this the sort of initiation that girls expect he wondered and, not having any sisters and certainly not willing to ask his mother, it remained an unanswered question.

The Last Refuge

To say that Jakeways was a conservative and a royalist was almost to insult the man. He was a fanatical patriot, a proud lover of king and country. One day in the classroom he pinned up a huge map of the world.

"What do you notice about this map, class?"

Silence.

"Come on, isn't it obvious?" Still no reaction. "What about the colour? What strikes you about the colour, Davis?"

"There are a lot of different colours, sir."

"Yes, but one colour stands out, doesn't it?"

He got impatient when there was still no reaction.

"Goodness me, you cannot fail to notice that this is everywhere." He jabbed his finger over different parts of the map. "What colour is that?"

"Red, sir," shouted a few of the class.

"Exactly. The world is covered with red and that red is the British Empire. The British Empire is the largest and most powerful empire the world has ever seen."

He glared at the class, almost daring them to dispute his claim.

"You can all be proud to be British and know that this country and its values have been sent round the world." He rocked on his heels with a smug smile of self-satisfaction, looking as if he had been personally responsible for distributing this largesse.

"And it is thanks to the Royal Navy, and you all know that I used to be in the Royal Navy, that we maintain peace in our empire and indeed the rest of the world."

He had not been in the navy only the Royal Naval Volunteer Reserve but as far as he was concerned there was no difference.

After break, Jakeways entered the class looking very solemn.

"Stand up class." There was the sound of chairs being pushed back as the class got to its feet.

"I have a sad announcement to make. We have just heard that His Majesty King George the Sixth has passed away. Please bow your heads and pray for his soul and our new Queen, Elizabeth the Second." He looked at the class with a wild gleam in his eye.

"God Save the Queen." The class seemed slightly embarrassed. "Did you hear me, God Save the Queen!" he thundered.

There was a ragged response of God Save the Queen from the class which, while not entirely satisfying Jakeways, at least allowed the class to sit down.

"Right, as a mark of respect, there will be no further lessons today. After lunch I want you to assemble in the library."

In the afternoon, Jakeways, now wearing a black tie, was self-importantly examining a sheet of paper. He called for quiet.

"As you know, the nation has suffered a dreadful loss today. Our king and head of state has died and left the responsibility of leading the nation to his young daughter, Elizabeth. It is important that our new queen knows that this school is very saddened at the death of her father, our king. How should we let her know our concern?"

"Send her some sweets," someone suggested.

"Don't be fatuous," Jakeways retorted.

"Write a letter to her," came another suggestion.

"An excellent idea," said Jakeways. "As it happens I have drafted a letter that you might send. Sanders, you have the best writing, you can copy the letter."

Sanders was given the letter in Jakeways's flowing script:

Your Majesty,

It is with great sadness that we learned of the passing of His Majesty King George VI today. We wish you to know that the staff and pupils of Torrington House School send their deepest sympathy to you and your family.

We remain your loyal subjects.

Yours faithfully,

Sanders dutifully copied it out on the headed notepaper provided. Unfortunately he was distracted by Davis pondering aloud on what sort of sweets the queen might like – jelly babies, dolly mixture, gobstoppers, acid drops… This caused Sanders to giggle and smudge the letter. Jakeways was not amused and told him to do it again. When it was completed, it was placed on the desk at the front of the library and each child was required to go up and sign it.

A week later Jakeways came into the senior classroom bearing an envelope. It had a black border round it and he waved it in the air.

"We've had a reply from Her Majesty." He said the words with a hushed respect. "I didn't expect it to come this quickly. I'll read out what it says. It is typed but it comes from Her Majesty herself.

"Dear pupils of Torrington House School. I am very grateful for your letter of condolence. It is some comfort to me at this difficult time. I am also pleased that I can count on your loyalty in the years to come. With best wishes. And it is signed, Elizabeth R," he finished triumphantly.

During break, Sanders and Davis discussed the turn of events. "Gosh, wasn't he like the cat that got the cream," said Davis.

"Yeah," replied Sanders. "That's really all he wanted, all along. A letter from the palace. He'll be bragging about it for weeks."

Jonny

There were a few compensations in the life at Torrington House, the main one being the comradeship of the other pupils. Another was the kindness of Matron who seemed to be a genuinely caring person which made her partnership with Jakeways all the more puzzling. But Roger retained most affection for Miss Johnnsen. The young Norwegian woman was presumably there to improve her English and received board and lodging in exchange for acting as Matron's assistant. She assisted at the dispensation of medicines and at mealtimes and one evening found her seated in a chair in the upstairs sitting room darning socks. They called her Jonny behind her back and she was popular. Plain and without airs, she was unfailingly good humoured in her quiet way. Everybody liked Jonny.

One evening as Roger and Davis were going to their dormitory they passed Miss Johnnsen's door which was slightly open with the light on. They heard a sound which seemed like crying which disturbed them. Of one accord, Roger and Toby knocked softly on her door.

"What is it?" a voice called from within.

"Are you all right, Miss?"

Miss Johnnsen came to the door looking a little flushed. "Oh, Sanders and Davis. Yes, I am OK." She hesitated and then invited them in. It was not the first time they had been in her little room – she had once taught them a Norwegian folk song as she sang to her guitar. Now she invited them to sit on her two small chairs while she sat on the bed which seemed to occupy most of the space.

"Were you crying, Miss?" said Davis shyly.

"Yes, I'm afraid so," said Miss Johnnsen, "I've had a letter from home."

"Oh dear, is it bad news?" asked Roger.

"Well, no, not really. My friend Ingrid is telling me that she is getting married."

"That sounds like good news," said Davis who was still sensitive after the recent loss of his own mother.

"Of course it is." She hesitated again, wondering whether to take these two ten-year-olds into her confidence. "But it is complicated. Ingrid and I grew up like sisters. We are both single children and we have a very close relationship. And then we met Lars and Olaf, two brothers and started going out with them. Ingrid is getting married to Olaf. I am pleased for her but it also feels like I am losing her."

"What about Lars?" Roger asked.

"Oh, well, I don't know. He has stopped writing to me."

Miss Johnnsen looked pensive and sad. Poor woman, thought Roger. She is always so cheerful and kind to us but we give no thought to her personal situation, in a foreign land, miles from home. In a way, his thought process continued, we are all in the same boat, obliged to live apart from our loved ones in a place that is, at best, a weak substitute for a secure, loving home.

Some days later Miss Johnnsen was assisting at the swimming pool, a small private indoor pool only twenty minutes walk from the school. It was run by a man called Holder who, like Jakeways, derived pleasure from bullying little boys. He marched around the pool in gum boots, armed with a long wooden pole with which he would hit boys on the head when it suited him. Roger, who was the best swimmer in the school, was allowed in the deep end with a couple of other boys to practise his diving. While about to take a dive off the spring board he noticed an incident at the other end of the pool. Since the pool was so short, he was able to hear as well as see what was going on.

A Persian boy named Hassan Ahmed, who had arrived at the school at the start of the term, was having a confrontation with Jakeways. Ahmed had poor English and had been finding it difficult to adapt to the ways of an English boarding school. He had a habit of marching around the playground, during breaks, like a soldier exaggeratedly bringing his legs up high, almost goose stepping, and, every now and then, throwing in a salute. He even found a piece of wood which he used as a pretend rifle. For obvious reasons he had failed to make any friends and had become a figure of fun. It was impossible to know if his situation was compounded by a learning difficulty but it would not have been surprising.

"I told you to get in the pool, Ahmed," Jakeways was shouting.

"I no swim, sir," said Ahmed, who looked at the water with terror.

"For the last time Ahmed, get in the pool or I'll throw you in."

"No," said Ahmed, backing away.

Jakeways quickly seized Ahmed by an arm and a leg and held him over the pool. By this time the Persian boy was screaming. "In you go!" boomed Jakeways and chucked the horrified boy into the water.

All this was witnessed by Miss Johnnsen who seemed appalled by what she was seeing. She rushed to the pool edge and tried to calm the child who was threshing about and shouting. Because they were at the shallow end, there was little danger of Ahmed coming to any physical harm but Miss Johnnsen saw that he had been traumatized by the experience.

"Just what he needed," said Holder with a grin.

"I don't think so," said Miss Johnnsen.

"Don't mollycoddle the boy, Miss Johnnsen," said Jakeways.

She had helped Hassan out of the pool and wrapped him in a towel.

"I don't know what 'mollycoddle' is. I am just showing him some respect and consideration."

"Well, I'm afraid you are undoing all the good I have done by behaving in this way," said Jakeways and tried to take Hassan from her grasp. There then followed an unseemly tug-of-war between Miss Johnnsen and Jakeways with Ahmed in the middle. Eventually, Jakeways, aware that the whole of the senior school was watching, shrugged and gave up.

"Very well. Have it your way for now but you and I will have words when we get back to school."

"I don't think so," said Miss Johnnsen. "I've had enough of your bullying ways. I want no more words from you. Call yourself a teacher? You are a disgrace to the profession and should not be allowed near children. I will take this boy back to the school and I will be gone before you return." With that she took Hassan to the changing room.

Jonny was true to her word. There was no sign when the boys returned nearly an hour later. Had she identified with the other foreigner in a strange environment in taking sides with Ahmed? Probably not, thought Roger. He was discussing the incident with Davis and Streeter.

"Gosh, wasn't she wonderful?" said Streeter.

"Fantastic," said Davis. "She can't be much more than twenty herself. To take on Jakeways like that. "Fantastic," he repeated.

"Well, I think it's dreadful that she's gone," said Sanders. "She's practically the only decent adult here." They were quiet as the implications of this sank in. What made it worse is that they hadn't even been able to say goodbye to Jonny.

Three weeks later a new Scandinavian assistant appeared at the school. Miss Bjorn was unlike Miss Johnnsen in appearance, being petite, blond and slightly simpering. She was nice enough but would never replace Jonny in the affections of the boarders.

Carlsen and Dancy See It Through

Roger was back in Torrington after the Christmas holidays. He was in bed but wide awake and excited. All day, and for some days, the nation had been gripped by an adventure on the high seas. An American ship called the *Flying Enterprise* was in the Western Approaches to the English Channel and was fighting to stay afloat. It left Hamburg bound for New York on December 21st and was hit by a storm on Christmas Night that caused severe structural damage. It was a cargo vessel but carrying ten passengers and by the 28th December the ship was listing at 45 degrees. The captain, Kurt Carlsen, made the decision to have the passengers taken off by lifeboats belonging to ships that had come to the aid of the stricken craft. One passenger died in the operation. Carlsen stayed aboard his boat in the hope that it could be towed into the nearest port.

A tug based in Falmouth, the *Turmoil*, had arrived at the scene in order to salvage the valuable cargo and perhaps the vessel itself. The operation was proceeding successfully, even though the list was now at 60 degrees, until another storm struck the ships. All day long the pupils had been trying to do normal lessons but the radio carried regular reports from the Falmouth coastguard about the fate of the *Flying Enterprise* and it was all Roger and his pals could talk about.

The storm caused the tow line to snap and it looked like the end for the *Flying Enterprise* and the intrepid Captain Carlsen. Another hero now emerged, the first mate of the *Turmoil*, a young man called Ken Dancy. It was early evening and the coastguard were in touch with the *Turmoil*. The reporter on the radio announced that Ken Dancy was to undertake a dangerous mission to try to board the *Flying Enterprise* to assist Captain Carlsen to attach a new tow line to the tug in the midst of a howling storm.

After supper, a group of the senior boys were allowed to sit by the radio in the common room to listen to the drama as it unfolded. The tension was almost unbearable as the two men battled to try to secure the line. The Head came in and told them that it was time to go to bed. The boys were crestfallen but obliged to do as they were told. Matron came into the senior dormitory to wish the senior boys good night and they asked her what the latest news was. She told them, realising how caught up in the drama they had become. Roger heard her talking to her husband, the Head.

"Can't we give the boys a radio, Bob, so that they can listen to the drama? They are incredibly excited by it all."

He couldn't hear the Head's reply but a few minutes later Jakeways came in with a radio and plugged it in. It was not in his nature to be particularly kind but he came from Cornwall and was in the Naval Reserve and so he had some sympathy for the situation and the children's excitement.

Tucked up in bed but still wide awake they listened to the account of the attempted rescue. Dancy had managed to get aboard the *Flying Enterprise* but the extent of the storm was making the attachment of the tow line almost impossible. Meanwhile the ship continued to list. Captain Carlsen had been alone on his stricken vessel for thirteen days and clearly any decision to abandon ship was a difficult one for any Master to make but even more difficult given his long vigil.

It became apparent that there was no hope; the storm was worsening and a freak wave sent the vessel even further under. The concern now was whether Carlsen and Dancy could be saved. The *Turmoil* tried to come alongside. By now the ship was half under and the two men could only stay above water by standing on the funnel. The decision was made to abandon ship and Carlsen and Dancy, wearing life jackets, jumped into the sea from the ship's smoke stack. No one would last long in January seas in the English Channel. Fortunately, the men were picked up by the *Turmoil* which then set off for Falmouth. The last thing the boys heard before they drifted off to sleep was that the *Flying Enterprise* had gone down about 30 miles off Cornwall.

Next day all anyone can talk about was Kurt Carlsen and Ken Dancy. Carlsen was a Dane while Ken Dancy was a young

Cornish seaman. They had become the school's heroes as well as the nation's. Like all good heroes they were incredibly modest and self-effacing when interviewed the following day as they arrived in Falmouth to be met by the Mayor and other dignitaries. Captain Parker, the master of the tug *Turmoil,* was first to be interviewed as he talked about the rescue and the sea conditions. But everyone was impatient to hear from the main figures. Carlsen, his voice sometimes cracking with emotion, thanked everyone who had assisted in the rescue, especially Captain Parker and Ken Dancy but also the boats that rescued the passengers, something that had happened a fortnight ago. Ken Dancy was a soft-spoken west countryman and talked as though it had all been in a day's work.

The older pupils were again allowed to interrupt lessons to listen to the live broadcast from Falmouth but now the Head made it clear that normal service was to be resumed. School work seemed particularly humdrum after the excitement of the last few days but Roger and Co continued to follow the fortunes of the two men for some time and play games where they re-enacted the parts of Carlsen and Dancy. They learned that Kurt Carlsen, now living in the United States, returned to America by aeroplane and was given a tickertape parade and reception in New York to mark his heroic actions. Ken Dancy was given a medal by the Daily Herald newspaper.

Trouble in the Toilet

There was a rumour going round that someone had been scribbling on the walls of one of the lavatories and that Jakeways had found it and hit the roof. The offending scribble was not in the bogs but in one of the lavs near the main entrance. Normally boarders would not use such toilets but they were not forbidden to enter them. On learning which toilet it was, Roger managed to get inside to see for himself. It was blatant. Four words in red, childish crayon written one above the other. Starting from the top it read:

Silly, king, bum, shit.

What a peculiar collection of words thought Roger. 'Bum' and 'shit' might be appropriate scatological vocabulary for the particular location but 'silly' was rather tame next to those words and the significance of 'king' was unfathomable. There was no boy or teacher by the name of 'King' in the school and so this line of enquiry did not seem promising.

At the next lesson an announcement was made that Mr Jakeways would address the whole school in the assembly room at 3.30. Roger knew what it would be about and mentioned it to Davis and Streeter during the lunch break. When he indicated that he had visited the scene of the crime, Davis and Streeter were keen to see it as well.

"Come on then. I'll show you," said Roger. However, when he tried the handle he found it locked.

"What are you doing Sanders?" a loud voice enquired.

"Nothing sir," said Roger.

"Nothing? How can carrying out an action, in this case trying to open a door, be nothing?" Jakeways said sarcastically.

"I was just going to show Davis and Reader, sir," said Roger.

"Show them what?" said Jakeways.

Roger felt himself redden. He didn't want to reveal what he had seen in the lavatory but he had fallen into a trap which Jakeways was evidently enjoying.

"Come on Sanders, I want to know what it is you wish to show them."

Roger had a bright idea.

"If we can open the door, sir, I can show you as well. I think you might want to see it."

This momentarily unsettled Jakeways but he quickly recovered his poise.

"That lavatory," he said, "is currently out of bounds. It will be locked until further notice. You will all find out what has happened when I speak to the whole school at half past three." With that he went off along the corridor towards his office.

Later the whole school was gathered in the Assembly Hall, the pupils nervously whispering to one another and the adults, including Matron and Mrs Brent, the principal, also looking uncomfortable. After a few minutes Mr Jakeways swept into the hall, his gown flowing behind him. He quickly got to the point.

"I've called you all here because there has been an extremely serious infringement of school discipline. This morning, at approximately 11.15, Mr Laker directed my attention to some disgusting writing that he had found in the toilet near the school entrance. Such is the nature of the words written on the walls, that I am unable to utter them in the presence of women and children." He waited a moment to enjoy the effect his words were having.

"I am sure I do not need to emphasise the gravity of this situation. Not only has someone defaced school property, they have done so in an obscene manner." Jakeways stopped to let this sink in. He continued, "I want the perpetrator of this outrage to own up to the crime by coming to see me in my room at four o' clock. If no-one owns up, the consequences for the entire school will be extremely unpleasant." With that, Jakeways turned on his heel and left the hall.

By the time that supper had been and gone, it became apparent that no-one had owned up. No formal announcement of this was made but the grapevine was working assiduously and the word was that nobody had been to see Jakeways. What would happen now was the question in everyone's mind. The atmosphere was full of foreboding and there was not even much enthusiasm for Davis's jokes.

What happened next was revealed at morning assembly. Mr Jakeways again addressed the school.

"I am disappointed, but not entirely surprised, to tell you that no-one came forward yesterday afternoon to admit to the filth in the toilet. This means that the whole school will have to be punished." A ripple of disquiet was heard in the room. "However," Jakeways continued, "I propose to carry out my own enquiry before taking any further action. This requires that I see every pupil individually during the course of the day. You will come at five minute intervals to my office, in register order and starting with the senior class. I will set work for the senior class before these interviews commence."

All that day, a small line of children was to be seen outside Mr Jakeways's office as they queued to take their turn in the inquisition. Roger got his turn in the late morning. "Come in Sanders." Jakeways was standing beside his desk, rocking back and forth on the balls of his feet in familiar style. There was some paper and a crayon on the desk. "Right, I'm going to ask you some questions and I want the God's honest truth. Did you use the toilet near the school entrance yesterday morning?"

"No, sir."

"I think you are lying, Sanders," said the Head.

"No, sir," Roger repeated.

"How come, then, that I found you trying the door during the lunch break and saying that you wished to show something to Davis and Reader?"

"Well, I had been in the toilet earlier, sir."

"So, you *were* lying," Jakeways barked.

"No sir. You asked me if I had used the toilet in the morning. I did not use the toilet but I did go into toilet before lunch."

"Stop trying to be clever, Sanders. Why did you go into the toilet?"

"Because I had heard that there was some writing on the wall."

"Who told you?" asked Jakeways.

"I don't remember sir. There were quite a few boys talking about it."

Jakeways continued to rock on his feet and now added tapping on the desk with his knuckles to the repertoire.

"Look, Sanders, this is looking serious for you. You are the only person who has admitted to entering that place yesterday morning and further you have admitted that you knew about the outrage on the walls."

Roger was not convinced that he had admitted any such thing but he remained silent.

"I will ask you once more. Did you deface the lavatory wall?"

"No sir," said Roger.

"Very well. Now come here to the table and sit on the chair. I want you to write down, in your own handwriting, each word as I tell you." Roger wondered if Jakeways seriously thought that boys of his age, and younger, would try to disguise their handwriting.

"Silly." Jakeways called out the first word and Roger wrote it down.

"King." Jakeways was hovering over him as he wrote, and he could smell the sickly soap that the Head favoured.

"Bump." Roger smiled grimly to himself as he heard the way that Jakeways avoided the taboo word.

"Shirt." Another master stroke, thought Roger. I wonder how many options he discarded before he came up with that. A childish rhyme came into his head;

Shakespeare was a man of wit
And on his shirt he had some shit.

Was that where he had got it from? As Roger left the room he saw the Head look eagerly at the paper and then transfer it to one of two piles that were on his desk.

Towards the end of the school day it was announced that Mr Jakeways once more would address the whole school in the Assembly Hall at the end of lessons. At the appointed time, the Head entered the room, flanked by Mrs Brent, and began to address the children.

"As you know, the school was violated yesterday when one of our number desecrated one of the school lavatories. I am pleased to say that the culprit has been found and admitted the offence and severely punished. Sanders Minor, John Sanders, is the boy concerned. In my opinion the fitting punishment for such a crime is expulsion but Mrs Brent convinced me that we should be lenient. I have therefore administered a severe thrashing to

Sanders Minor and taught him a lesson that I doubt he will forget. Let this also be a warning to you all."

Roger was horrified at this news and felt a mixture of shame and anger. As John's older brother he felt he should have been called into the interview with John to give him some support. But he knew that this was not Jakeways's approach. He had not spoken much to his brother about the incident. Everything had happened so quickly but the previous night they had talked a little and it was clear that his brother knew nothing about the graffiti. As soon as the teachers had left the room, Roger rushed out to look for John. He found him crying on his bed. He was shaking and looked very pale.

"Oh John. What has he done?" Realising the futility of his rhetorical question, Roger gave his brother a hug.

"We can't stay here, John. This place is worse than a prison. We must get in touch with Mummy."

John continued whimpering. Later, when he had calmed somewhat, Roger asked him what had happened.

"I got six of the best," said John.

"Yes, but what happened before that?" Roger persisted.

"Well, he called me in after he'd seen everybody and he held up my bit of paper what I had written those words on and said he knew that I had scribbled in the toilet."

"You didn't, did you?" said Roger.

"No, I told you yesterday."

"Jakeways said that you admitted it."

"Yes, I did," said John.

"Why?"

"'Cos he went on and on, saying he knew I'd done it. He had the evidence – my writing – and it was no good saying I hadn't. In the end I had to say yes."

Next morning at assembly Jakeways looked particularly self-satisfied, singing the hymn lustily and intoning prayers in the low, 'sacred' voice he adopted, mimicking the vicar at the local church they attended. At the end of assembly Jakeways announced that the toilet near the school entrance would remain out of bounds to all pupils. It was for staff and visitors only.

"And I hope that anyone else thinking of writing filth on school property will bear the example of the miserable John Sanders in mind."

"He didn't do it," a voice called out from the hall.

"What was that?" said Jakeways.

"He didn't do it."

Roger looked round and saw that the voice came from Lance Dangerfield, perhaps the cleverest boy in the school.

"What are you talking about Dangerfield?" spluttered Jakeways.

"He didn't do it," Dangerfield repeated for the second time. "Sanders Minor is innocent."

"Nonsense," said Jakeways, "he admitted it."

"He only admitted it because you bullied him into a confession." Dangerfield spoke calmly.

"But I have the evidence," said the head triumphantly. "His handwriting matches that on the wall of the lavatory."

"That evidence would not stand up in a court of law. You would need the testimony of a graphologist, at least, to support your claim."

Jakeways paled a little. He knew that Dangerfield's father was a distinguished barrister.

"Anyway, I know he didn't do it," said Dangerfield, "because I did."

There was an audible gasp in the Hall. Was Dangerfield mad? Having got away with his crime, here he was exposing himself to worse punishment since he had made a fool of the Head. Dangerfield continued:

"I want to say sorry to Sanders Minor. I feel very bad that he got caned for something I did. I thought I might get away with it but it was too late by the time that I realised that I must own up."

"Well," said Jakeways, "you must come with me, right now."

"No," said Dangerfield. "I'm not coming with you now or ever again. My father is coming to collect me at 9.30. He's probably waiting outside now. I telephoned him last night from the caretaker's flat. I have had enough of the intimidation that passes for education in this place. What I did was wrong but the only surprise is that it didn't happen earlier given the provocation that I and everyone else has had to put up with."

Jakeways looked stunned. The eloquence issuing from the mouth of this 10-year-old only made his humiliation greater. As Dangerfield left the hall, a low rumble started which soon erupted into a full-throated cheer. Roger wondered if the school would ever be the same again.

Summer Holiday

They were at the seaside staying on a large campsite on the south Devon coast near Exmouth. The journey from Kent had taken all day. An early breakfast was followed by the loading of the coach and then departure: sixteen boys, the Jordan brothers, Jakeways, Matron and Mrs Thompson, mother of the Thompson twins. The Jordan brothers were the teenage sons of Mrs Jordan, the school secretary. They were getting a free holiday in return for helping with the running of the summer camp.

Devon seemed like a foreign country. Winchester, Salisbury, Crewkerne, Chard, Honiton; mile after mile in a hot bus with only the odd stop to eat soggy sandwiches and drink orange squash and answer calls of nature. Jakeways shouted for everyone to look out of the window and admire the red earth which signalled arrival in Devon. When they eventually reached their destination, all bags had to be transferred from the coach to a smaller vehicle which relayed them, seven at a time, down a grassy track to the camp site. The excitement at discovering the canvas home for two weeks helped to offset the hunger and tiredness but it was a weary group that finally sat cross-legged on a ground sheet to a meal prepared by Matron and Mrs Thompson. Luncheon meat, potatoes and beans followed by stewed apple (complete with core and pips) and custard.

The older children were allowed to explore the site while the younger ones made ready for bed. Accommodation was in two large bell tents with two smaller tents for Matron and Mr J and for Mrs Thompson. Sandy Bay was a large site in a good position on cliffs overlooking the sea. A steep path, partly of steps, wound down to the beach and Jakeways issued a warning not to go down to the beach unaccompanied. Roger and his friends familiarised themselves with the heads and shower blocks and the camp shop.

Next morning, they were roused at six and told to put on swimming costumes and plimsolls and take a towel. The complement was then marched down to the beach in a crocodile with Jakeways at the head and the Jordan brothers bringing up the rear. The sun was starting to get up but it was cold and the idea of a swim at this early hour was not appealing. But there was no escape. On arriving at the empty beach, Jakeways put the group through their normal early morning exercise routine; hands at low cross, and so on. After ten minutes of this he ordered the boys to run into the sea for a quick bathe. An unenthusiastic rabble trotted down to the sea and ran in the shallows, screaming.

"Go on, get in," Jakeways shouted from the sidelines and the Jordan brothers were urged to set an example.

Everybody got more or less wet and then ran out again, shivering. They were then instructed to towel themselves dry, vigorously, and then do a few more exercises, including running on the spot. The group then lined up two by two again and marched back to the camp. By this time many more campers were emerging from their tents. The crocodile was a source of amusement and wonder to the onlookers.

So the routine was established. Early morning exercises and dip followed by ablutions and getting dressed. By this time breakfast was ready. Various jobs had to be carried out after breakfast. Making beds and tidying up; shopping at the camp shop; preparing lunch. Shopping was the favourite activity since it meant the chance of meeting other campers, including girls, and seeing, if not exactly sampling, the sort of camping holiday that normal people enjoyed. A jolly campers PA system operated for about an hour in the morning and marked the opening hours of the camp shop and site office. The announcements did not interest Roger but the music was striking. In particular, two records were played to announce that the camp shop and camp radio were soon to close down. The first was Vera Lynn singing 'We'll Meet Again'. Much more rousing was Joseph Locke's rendering of 'Goodbye'. Once you heard the Irish tenor start up with: 'Goodbyee, goodbye, I wish you all the luck, goodbye', you knew that you had just a couple of minutes before the shop closed.

One morning Roger's brother, John, always difficult to arouse from slumber, failed to get up for the morning dip even after repeated shakings. The crocodile eventually set off without him and Roger knew there would be a terrible price to pay. Sure enough, when they returned and Sanders Minor was sitting dressed on his bed, Jakeways ordered the entire company to assemble outside the main tents. He formed them into a circle. Sanders Minor was then summoned and told to stand in the middle of the circle. Jakeways intoned the 'charge'.

"Sanders Minor has failed to attend the early morning bathe and beach exercise. Accordingly he will be punished. Take off your clothes."

Young Sanders took off his clothes, keeping on his pants.

"And your pants," shouted Jakeways.

By this time, Sanders Minor was beginning to snivel as he removed his pants. At this point Jakeways approached him with a large enamel jug and threw the contents of the jug, cold water, over Sanders. This actually had the effect of stopping his snivelling, so cold was the water.

"Now get dressed and never make the mistake off missing the early morning dip again."

Matron was standing by with a towel and the victim gathered up his clothes and disappeared into the tent to dry off and get dressed. Roger saw the look of concern on the face of Mrs Thompson and the Jordan brothers and wondered what action Jakeways might have taken if there had not been witnesses. Surely there would have been a beating for such a blatant challenge to his authority.

The boys were allowed a modest amount of pocket money, strictly controlled, of course, by Jakeways. The camp shop was virtually the only place that they could spend this 'rhino' though, in due course, other locations were discovered.

Once all the chores had been completed, the campers were assembled once more to make the walk down to the beach wearing their school shorts and shirts and carrying towels, swimming trunks, buckets and spades, balls and so on. Being the target of jeering children and their more sympathetic parents did not help to lessen their self-consciousness as they made the return journey at least twice a day from camp site to the beach and back. Jakeways, himself, cut a ludicrous figure in outsize khaki shorts and navy sweater and a floppy sunhat but he believed he was the envy of the campsite with his flock of well trained and well-behaved youngsters.

The routine was broken by the occasional trip out: a trip on a steamer down the River Exe and a visit to a concert party on the pier at Exmouth. The entertainment at the concert party was very much to the taste of Jakeways and Matron but the humour was rarely funny to the boys and the singing and dancing were not slick. Travers revealed his sophistication when announcing, in a stage whisper, that one of the dancers had not shaved under her arms. The significance of this remark, if it had any significance, was lost on the other boys.

The days went past with the usual activities on the beach: shrimping, sand castles, beach cricket, swimming and paddling. This was acceptable but not exactly gripping and failed to take Roger's mind off the constant hunger he felt. There never seemed to be enough to eat and the sweets obtained from the camp shop did not prevent the pangs from affecting them most of the time. Then, the fish and chip caravan was discovered. In fact, it was hardly a matter of discovery since it was passed every day, at least four times, and on two of those occasions it was open. The smells emanating from this tiny emporium were wonderful and yet torture. Then, one day, after lunch when it was the habit of Jakeways and Matron to have a snooze, Roger suggested to his friends that they nip up to the top of the cliff path and get some chips. Some of them had money and so this option was possible. Roger checked that the Head was thoroughly asleep. Roger nudged Toby Davis and pointed to Jakeways.

"Look what's peeping out," he whispered. Sure enough, one of Jakeways's balls was half exposed, where his trunks were slack. The boys struggled to contain their laughter then slipped off towards the cliff path. Two pennyworth of chips – ambrosia. They lay on the cliff top, looking out to sea, enjoying the best meal they'd ever had. After this, the trip to the chip caravan became a fairly regular event. The fact that it was an illicit activity made it doubly enjoyable and the fact that Jakeways was the target of mirth by those who passed him on the beach was an extra delight since the uncontained testicle was also a fairly regular event.

Another pleasure from these holidays was the friendly relationship established with the Jordan brothers. Being older, it would not have been surprising if they had barely tolerated Roger and Co. But, on the contrary, they were friendly and helpful and seemed to treat the boys as equals. One evening, while chatting about nothing in particular, one of the brothers excused himself and went off to the heads. You were allowed to take two sheets of toilet paper to the heads if your visit was one that required paper. Roger noticed that Jordan took four sheets and commented on this to him when he returned. He laughed.

"Yes, this is because I'm older and bigger than you. I need more paper." Roger laughed too but was not sure that he understood his logic.

Tea Leaves in
the Local Shop

The local shops in my Kent village in the 1950s were important to the community, and strange. The greengrocer was run by a mother and son, the latter being disabled. His disabilities were many, including spasticity, harelip and cleft palate. His speech was unintelligible and his shuffling gait and poor motor skills meant that he was achingly slow in weighing out fruit and vegetables. Another oddball was Mrs Belcher, wife of Colonel Belcher, who together ran the village post office. Mrs Belcher didn't get dressed until about midday but this didn't stop her appearing in the shop in her diaphanous mixture of night attire and house coat. She sounded far too posh to be running a village post-office and one had to assume that the Colonel's pension didn't cover his wife's needs, probably not even her drinks bill. It was evident that Mrs Belcher and the whiskey bottle were intimate companions. Another local shop was the newsagent, tobacconist and confectioners run by Mr and Mrs Canning. Harry Canning with his sandy hair, smudge of a moustache and soft voice was polite, friendly, even obsequious. I think some people took advantage of his self-deprecating approach to business and life in general. I know we did.

My brother and I worked for Harry Canning as paper boys.

Formerly we had worked for the Belchers at the post office but had increasingly found the Colonel and his wife too idiosyncratic to handle. For an army man his inefficiency and lack of punctuality were surprising. When you got to the shop on a dark, frosty morning, your natural irritability was only made worse when you found that your round hadn't been made up. And when the Colonel would cease assembling the papers because his wife was calling from upstairs for a cup of tea, your patience completely ran out. When we learned that the Cannings were looking for paperboys (papergirls were not invented then), we made enquiries. When we also learned that Canning was paying ten shillings a week, we needed no second bidding. Ten bob – a small fortune.

Working for the Cannings was a pleasure after life with the disorganised Belchers. After some months, Mr Canning asked me to shift to another round which involved collecting the paper money on Sundays. For this he was prepared to pay me seventeen and sixpence a week. I answered in the affirmative without a second thought only to realise in due course that collecting money took a very large chunk out of my Sunday morning. On the positive side, it meant that I got back too late to go to church. My next 'promotion' was the offer of more money in return for helping the boss to make up the paper rounds. In practice what I did was make up my own round and that of my brother. With rubber thimbles on our index fingers, we used to work from greasy ledgers in which were entered the names of the papers and magazines taken by each house. On some mornings a paper boy would ring in sick or was away for some reason in which case Harry himself would take out the round. Since the shop didn't open until eight o'clock this was not necessarily a problem but it did mean that, on occasions, my brother and I found ourselves alone in the shop.

Temptation was certainly there in the shape of the sort of treats to make schoolboys drool, but I'm still not certain how it began. I offer a version of events which puts me in a slightly better light than I probably deserve. My brother and I started our rounds together, pushing our bikes up Charnley Hill. One morning, just before we went our separate ways, my brother said, "Want a bit of chocolate?" He fished out from his paper bag a bar of chocolate and snapped off a lump for me. "Where did you get that?" I asked, since I knew he was skint. "Nicked it from Cannings," he said. My eyes widened but I took the proffered booty. As I cycled off, enjoying the sweetness in my mouth, I marvelled at my younger brother's cool approach while also feeling discomforted that he could swindle such a generous employer.

The next time we were in the shop alone, my brother said "What do you fancy?" pointing to the array of sweets and chocolate on display. I took a Kit-Kat and quickly shoved it in my paper bag. Later we got bolder and even when Harry was in the shop we waited until his back was turned and pinched a bar. But we had our eyes on a bigger prize. Like most boys in their early teens, we were fascinated by cigarettes. Smoking was a very desirable forbidden activity. It had started when we had taken a Woodbine from our Granddad while visiting him in the north. We had sneaked off to the fields to sample our illicit fag, breaking it in half and almost choking on the harsh smoke as it seared our lungs. We then took to roaming the streets, picking up dog ends from the gutter, sometimes emptying them out and making 'fresh' roll-ups using Rizla papers purchased for a penny. The taste of these appalling creations can be imagined but still we were not put off.

Back in the early morning village shop, the row upon row of cigarettes behind the counter took on the dimensions of Eldorado. Players, Senior Service, Park Drive, Capstan, Strand, Rothmans, Passing Cloud, State Express – all gloating at us from the safe haven of the cigarette shelves, well out of reach. But were they really so safe? When Harry was out of the shop, it took only a moment to duck under the counter and grab a pack of ten Weights. This was the first serious larceny. As we went up the hill, I got out the pack and handed my brother one. "Oh, no!" he shouted. What's happened, I wondered, have we been discovered? But his cry was one of frustration because we didn't have any matches between us.

The theft of cigarettes now became regular to the point where we had more than we could manage. As supply began to exceed demand, we kept the unused cigarettes in a shoe box hidden at home. One morning, Harry told us to keep an eye on things as he had to do a round since young Fletcher had failed to show up. Since we knew that Mrs Canning was away, we had a golden opportunity to stock up on fags and sweets. As soon as the coast was clear I nipped over the counter and began to toss packets of cigarettes at my brother who stashed them in his paper bag. I can't remember how many I took but it was a sizeable haul. As we trudged up the hill, we roared with laughter at our outrageous fortune and our outrageous behaviour. When we eventually got to deposit these cigarettes in the shoe box, we were thrilled and appalled to see that the box was nearly full. There were scores of cigarettes, different sizes, some with filter but most without, as was the fashion those days, and even some elliptically shaped ones with peculiar scented tobacco.

This is getting ridiculous, I thought. When are we ever going to smoke these? (It never occurred to us to sell them although we did give some away to friends). Whether this sane realisation would have stopped our nefarious activity in itself is doubtful. Our path down a road possibly leading to more serious crime was nipped in the bud by the victim of our theft. One day, as we were making up rounds, Harry was talking to his wife who also happened to be in the shop. He was referring to a shortfall in cigarettes and also in confectionery.

"Stuff seems to be going missing," he said to his wife. Apparently noticing us, he said casually: "Keep an eye out for me, boys. Someone seems to be pinching sweets and cigarettes. If you see anything, let me know."

Was he warning us? Probably. And fortunately we took the warning. We'd had a lucky escape and determined not to give in to temptation again. This was made easier by the fact that we were already knee deep in fags. What were we thinking of? Why did we rob this kind man? If he'd been a mean or callous employer, some mitigation for our behaviour might be possible but we had no such excuse. How to explain it therefore, since criminal behaviour didn't run in our family and there was nothing in our upbringing to indicate that we would engage in petty theft. It seemed to me to have something to do with daring and excitement as well as the lure of the weed. We were under age, of course, but this didn't stop us being attracted to cigarettes. Holding a cigarette, between forefinger and middle finger, and then coolly dragging on it was a sign of manhood, then and now. And, what's more, you were never alone with a Strand.

The New Arrival

Aunt Hilda was to blame. Her affectionate poodle, Fifi, fascinated me. As well as seeming to like me by wagging her tail and licking me, she did tricks such as barking on demand, whining and going into a crouch posture, and standing and walking on her hind legs. I failed to notice that she received a snack after each of these accomplishments but that wouldn't have worried me anyway. I wanted a clever dog like Fifi.

My constant requests finally wore my parents down and one day my brother and I came home from school to find a yellow Labrador puppy bouncing around in the kitchen.

"This is Sandy," said my mother. Sandy, I thought, how original but I was too excited to worry about the banality of the name. Sandy wasn't a poodle and he didn't do any tricks but these were early days. Indeed his first 'trick' was to get so excited at seeing my brother and me that he made a puddle in the kitchen.

"Naughty Sandy," said my mother. "I think he needs to go for a walk."

And that was the problem, Sandy often needed or wanted a walk. My parents made it clear that there were conditions to having a dog. Dogs, particularly young ones, needed regular exercise. It was our responsibility to take Sandy for a walk before we went to school and when we got home. At the weekends we should think about taking him out three times a day. We listened to this rigmarole impatiently. Of course we'd take him for a walk. He was *our* dog.

Initially all went well. If anything, too well as we were in competition for holding Sandy's lead.

"It's my turn to have the lead," said my brother as I was putting the lead on the dog one morning. Reluctantly I handed him over and we left the house together. Our routine was to do a circuit that included our road, left at Dryden Hill, then left again along the unadopted Tapster Road, and then through the footpath at the end which took us back to our house.

All was going well until we met Bill the Boxer at the end of our road. Bill wasn't an aggressive dog but he liked a game. Unusually his owner, who we called Mr Man for some peculiar reason, wasn't with Bill and therefore he wasn't on a lead. This led him to charge up to Sandy and challenge him to a play fight. Sandy didn't understand and tried to hide behind us. This only encouraged Bill who started barking loudly. Sandy now started shaking and wouldn't budge when we tried to move him along. Eventually Mr Man appeared and Bill backed off.

"Who's this little chap then?" asked Mr Man.

"Sandy," said my brother. "I think he's scared of Bill."

"Bill wouldn't hurt a fly," said Mr Man. Not intentionally, maybe, I thought, but he's big and boisterous and upsetting our dog. But I let that go and we carried on. As we entered Tapster Road, Sandy started pulling on the lead, almost throttling himself.

"I think we could let him off for a while," I said.

"I don't know," said my brother. "Suppose he runs away."

"No, he won't," I said.

We took the lead off his collar and he sat looking at us pathetically. Then, suddenly he realised he was free and bounded off back the way we'd come.

Oh, no, I thought, there's a busy road down there. By the time we caught up with him he was on the other side of Dryden Hill and barking at the traffic. On seeing us, he darted across the road, just missing a swerving car in one direction and a motor bike in the other. Fortunately, he came up to us and we were able to put him on the lead. Then I realised that one of the vehicles that had just missed him had stopped and the driver was approaching us.

"Is this your dog?" the driver asked unnecessarily. "For God's sake can't you keep control of him? He nearly caused a serious accident."

We mumbled apologies and after listening to a lecture about the responsibilities of dog owners, we were finally able to continue the walk. By now it was late and I was in danger of missing the school bus and so we retraced our steps and went back the way we had come hoping that Bill would not be on the scene.

"Has he done his business?" mother asked as we came in with the offending animal. We shook our heads.

"I'm not sure," I said.

"You're not sure. I would have thought it was pretty obvious," my mother retorted.

After that experience we were not quite as keen to take Sandy for his walk.

Two days later as I came out of school with some friends I noticed my mother by the gate, holding Sandy. Instead of rushing up and making a fuss of him I was embarrassed and pretended not to see them. My mother had to call out to me which just made it worse.

"Sorry, I've gotta go," I said to my friends.

"Yeah, go to your little doggy-woggy," I heard one of them say.

As we got into the car and drove home my mother said: "You made such a carry-on about having a dog and when I give you a nice surprise by meeting you with Sandy, you ignore me."

"Yeah, well mothers don't meet their sons when they come out of school. I'm not a little kid anymore."

"Thanks," said my mother, "I won't make that mistake again."

Next morning it was pouring with rain and neither my brother nor I were keen to take the dog out. We made some excuse about it being late and in the end my mother said she would take him. My mother joined us in taking him for a walk when we got home in the afternoon and my brother dropped his lead while running with him and Sandy rushed off into the road. Again, a car had to brake sharply to avoid him and we were all treated to a lecture from a shocked and angry motorist.

"He's not very obedient, is he?" my mother said. "I think he needs to attend dog training classes, and you as his owner," she looked at me, "should go with him."

"I'm not sure I fancy that," I responded. "Can't you go?"

"No, I can't," said my mother, "I've got enough to do."

I was the first one home the following day when I got in from school. I was surprised to be greeted by an excited Sandy leaping up at me. He was usually shut in the kitchen. Someone had forgotten to make sure the door was closed. Then he rushed off and came back, tail wagging, with something in his mouth. I took it from him. A chewed-up lump of rag covered in slobber. Then I recognised it as one of my father's slippers. Predictably he was not amused when he got in later that evening.

The next few days we missed taking the dog for his morning walk a couple of times and once in the evening when I had to stay late for a detention.

"Look," said my mother, "you fussed and fussed about having a dog and now we've got one you aren't taking your responsibilities seriously."

"Well I can't help it if old Monty puts me in detention," I said.

"So, it's not your fault, eh?" said my mother. "It's never your fault. Anyway, this is the final warning, if you don't pull your weight in looking after the dog, he goes."

The next day it was raining again and Sandy was whining to go out. I was running late and my brother had already gone to school as he was reading a lesson and had to practice.

"Sorry, I'll get wet through if I take him now, can you take him, please. I'm late anyway."

My mother shrugged and said nothing. When we got home at the end of the day the house seemed unnaturally quiet.

"What's happened?" asked my brother.

"What do you mean?" I said.

"He's not here, is he?"

Sure enough, the usual bark and leaping about by the excitable puppy was not in evidence. My mother came in.

"Where's Sandy?" I asked.

"Not here. I've taken him back to the people we got him from. They were very understanding and took him back."

"Oh dear," I said.

"Yes, well, you should have thought of that before. We warned you that it was primarily your responsibility to look after the dog that *you* wanted, that you pleaded for. Your father and I haven't the time to spend constantly taking him out, feeding him, not to mention attending dog training classes."

I was quiet, affecting an air of injured persecution. Secretly I was glad to see the back of Sandy. He'd become a liability.

"Perhaps we can get a cat," said my brother.

"Or a tortoise," I suggested.

"Mm," said my mother. "At least Dad's slippers would be safe."

A French Kiss

The moonlight glinted on the calm sea as we walked hand in hand on the soft, silver sand. It must be a dream. I couldn't really be in this romantic situation with this exotic foreign girl. Things like that didn't happen to me.

It had started when three lovely French girls accosted us on the beach and asked if we'd like to play volleyball with them. Would we? A difficult decision for six English lads who'd spent the first week of our Costa Brava holiday trying to attract girls. Reluctantly, we acquiesced, and then attempted to impress them with our athletic skills. Indeed, we then saw the girls, two sisters and their cousin, almost every day.

And now, on our last evening, I'd finally got some time alone with the cousin, Marie. I could have walked all night with her but the time came when she had to return to her friends. She permitted me a chaste kiss and we arranged to meet next morning before we set off for the drive back home.

When I got back to the tent where I was sleeping, I felt exhilarated but restless. It was a hot night and I couldn't sleep. I got up and announced that I was going to sleep on the beach. A couple of my friends said they would join me.

The slightly cooler air and the sound of the waves lapping on the shore was soothing as we lay in our sleeping bags. There are no prizes for guessing who was in my thoughts as I fell asleep.

I woke to an uncomfortable pain in my side. Something was prodding me. I heard a noise and looked up into the unshaven face of a member of the Guardia Civil. I saw that the thing that was prodding me was his rifle butt. The sun was up. It must have been about 7.30. The policemen were angry. My Spanish was good enough to understand that we were breaking the law by spending the night on the beach. It was 1964, Franco's Spain, and you knew not to mess with the dreaded fascist police. Apologising, we quickly got up and left the beach before any further unpleasant repercussions ensued.

Later, when we were all packed, we met the girls at our favourite bar in Aro. We said farewell to the friendly waiters and we each got a hug from the girls before we boarded our camper van. We found that they'd daubed a message in lipstick on the van that they had christened Hector. Just before we left I managed to get Marie to write down her address. I promised to write.

The dream that was Marie didn't end that summer. We corresponded regularly, she in French and I in English. I was getting interested in Sartre, Camus and De Beauvois and she directed me to Mauriac and Malraux. We disagreed about religion but empathised on much else. I was overjoyed when she wrote and said she was coming to England. The bad news was that she was visiting a family in Nelson, Lancashire and I lived in London.

I was determined to see her. I looked at the sensational photo she'd sent and wrote saying that I would collect her from the house where she was staying and bring her south for her final weekend with me in London. After some persuading, she agreed.

Some weeks later, I picked up a hire car after work on Friday and drove to my grandmother's house in Southport. After less than an hour on the road, I felt very sleepy. I pulled into the next services and had a black coffee. This worked wonders and I was able to spend the rest of the journey wide awake, dreaming of the reunion with Marie.

I hadn't appreciated how far north Nelson was but on the Saturday morning I managed to find the house on the hill by eleven o' clock as arranged. I mounted the steps to the severe looking red brick house. The elderly couple who were hosting Marie insisted on knowing where I was taking her and that I would be sure to get her on the coach from Victoria on Sunday. They didn't seem reassured but eventually they called up the stairs and the enthralling vision finally appeared. She was even more beautiful than I remembered. We shook hands awkwardly for the benefit of the old people and engaged in some small talk. Finally, we managed to get away and I put Marie's quaint, brown leather suitcase in the boot of the car. We drove off with a wave. Once we were out of sight, I stopped the car and told her how delighted I was to see her. She smiled and we embraced.

The rest of the weekend flew by. We went to an all-night party in Kensington and spent most of the evening exchanging passionate kisses, either while dancing or on a sofa. To coin a phrase, I was head over heels in love.

For some time afterwards, I was convinced we would settle down together, perhaps in France, perhaps in England. I didn't care where as long as we were together. Our letters touched on this possibility.

Of course, it never happened. She met someone called Yves whom I hated. She began to ask for my advice about the emotions she was feeling for Yves. Me!! Meanwhile I had begun the long saga that was Penny. Eventually the letters dried up and I realised that perhaps it had been a dream after all. I never saw her again.

Heinz's Varieties

He was small and dark with a wispy beard. Seated at the adjacent table, he was drinking Ricard, occasionally pouring water from a small jug which caused the anise to turn cloudy. I was drinking beer. He asked me where I was from.

"You're OK then, the French will tolerate you even though they resent you because you liberated them. Us, we Germans, it's simple – they just hate us." He chuckled.

His English was fluent though he spoke with an American accent. We continued chatting and I liked his dry sense of humour. We soon discovered we had shared interests in music and literature. He came from a small town in Bavaria and was travelling alone. I was seventeen and travelling in the south of France during the school holidays. Currently I was in the youth hostel in Nimes having just attended a UNESCO youth camp in Montpelier for two weeks. A few minutes' walk away was a bar and that was where I met Heinz.

I learned that he was due to start University in Innsbruck in six weeks but was worried because it would take him away from his girlfriend. She was American, the daughter of a US service man. Once he started talking about Laura, he couldn't stop and I suspected that the relationship was a little one-sided. He was crazy about her and had been with her in the States earlier in the summer. For this reason, he was currently without money.

"It all went over there. It was so expensive."

I asked him if he'd like another drink and he nodded at the Ricard. When I returned with the drinks we continued to chat and I discovered that his father owned a factory which manufactured brushes. He didn't seem very impressed; it was evident that he didn't get on with his father. Just then there was an announcement: the film starts in five minutes. It turned out that there was a small open-air cinema on the roof and they were showing a French comedy.

"Let's go and see it," I said.

"Well, that would be fun but I don't have any money."

"My treat," I said, "it's only a franc each."

The film was ridiculous, a farcical crime caper that the French do so well, full of slapstick and silly chases. I think Fernandel may have been in it. We laughed uproariously and by the end of the evening we had become firm friends. I had one more beer but Heinz declined another drink. The bar was beginning to close and I suggested we meet up the following evening.

"That would be swell but I have to get a train to Munich tomorrow. My folks won't send me any more money so I've got to get back home."

"That's a shame," I said.

We exchanged addresses and promised to write to one another. We shook hands and went our separate ways and I suspected that would be the last I'd see of Heinz.

I was wrong. A letter awaited me when I got home two weeks later. There then ensued a long correspondence over the next couple of years during which we repeatedly suggested ideas for meeting up. A favourite scheme for Heinz was to canoe down the Danube from Passau. I pretended to be enthusiastic but was never sure about the feasibility of it. Finally, two years after our first meeting, I found myself in Innsbruck where Heinz was at university.

I thought he might meet me at the station but he had told me to make my way to his digs if he wasn't there. I had no German but his landlady made me to understand that he was away and that there was a note for me.

Sorry I had to return to Dinkelsbuhl urgently as one of my closest friends has been killed in a road accident. I'll be back in a couple of days as soon as the funeral is done. Enjoy looking round Innsbruck, it's a great city.

Innsbruck is an attractive city but on my budget without the language and given my natural reticence, its pleasures soon began to pall. By the third day on my own I began to wonder if I should give it up as a bad job. But then the landlady called me to the telephone and it was Heinz saying he would be with me by tea time.

I was pleased to see him even if he was in a sombre mood after his good friend had wrapped his car round a tree killing himself outright and badly injuring his girlfriend. He cheered up in the evening after a few drinks and we talked about the trip we were going to make. He had it all planned.

His Skoda sports car was heavy, noisy and lively. I enjoyed driving it, being a big contrast to my sedate Morris Minor Coupe. The first part of the trip took in the spectacular Austrian Alps and Italian Dolomites. We went up to the glacier of the Gross Glockner and walked in snow even though it was August. The russet sun glinting on Marmolada in the Dolomites near Cortina was a magnificent sight and the switchback roads and the roar of the car as we drove through the small villages was exciting.

We went back into Austria and swum in the delightful warm Corinthian lakes and then on to Salzburg and some sophisticated music and food. From there we drove to Chiemsee where Heinz's family had a chalet on an island and a boat to reach it. This was the most relaxing part of the holiday as we sailed, swam and sunbathed. One evening we were having a drink in a tavern where some local men were engaged in loud conversation and occasional singing. I saw Heinz shake his head.

"What are they talking about?" I asked.

"They're regretting the passing of Hitler. Times were much better under him."

"Are they Nazis?" I asked incredulously.

"Oh, sure," said Heinz.

For the next few days we visited some of Mad King Ludwig's Bavarian castles. One of the most famous was on the island where we were staying, his replica of the palace of Versailles. Ludwig believed he had a divine mission to re-establish Bavarian greatness and he totally bankrupted the state in his futile building programme even if the results were sometimes remarkable in a fairy-tale way.

Hitler reared his head again when we visited Berchtesgaden, the Fuhrer's summer residence. Nearby was a salt mine which had become a tourist attraction. We had to dress in special overalls and wear fezzes and get aboard a little train which took us below ground. There we boarded a boat and crossed an underground lake. All very exciting though it was difficult to keep a straight face with everybody dressed like oompa loompas.

Our last night before we returned to Heinz's home town was spent in Munich. We met up with some of Heinz's student friends in what he called a downtown bar. It was a gorgeous warm evening, everybody seemed beautiful, friendly and happy and I fell under the spell of the Bavarian capital.

We arrived in Dinkelsbuhl about tea time and I was introduced to Frau Werner and shown to my room. It was a large house with a substantial garden and I realised I would be here for three days before returning to England with Heinz.

About seven, Heinz knocked on my door and said it was time to go down to dinner. A heavy, rather severe man came towards me and shook my hand vigorously. We sat down to trout, kartoffel and sauerkraut and a bottle of hock. The conversation was stilted as Heinz's parents spoke no English and everything had to be translated and Heinz was not the most enthusiastic of translators. I noticed that his mood had changed since he had been back with his parents.

After we had finished the meal, Herr Werner, reached down and produced a polished wooden box about the size of a small suitcase. He opened it with a flourish to reveal it was full of clothes brushes of different sizes and functions. He got the brushes out one by one and demonstrated their purpose; one was in the shape of a little hedgehog and it still resides in my mother's house. He accompanied this with a commentary which Heinz ignored. All he said was:

"He must think you're a real dusty person."

After the meal we walked into the pretty little town and into a cellar bar. There were one or two friends of Heinz there and I was introduced to Erich and Peter. Drinks were produced and I noticed that no-one was paying.

"Is it free, here?" I asked. Everyone laughed.

"This is Heinz's bar," said Erich.

I must have looked puzzled because Heinz explained.

"They were premises owned by my Dad. He had no further use for them and I persuaded him not to sell. I suggested they would make a nice club for me to meet up with my friends. We put a lot of work in didn't we guys?"

The others nodded assent. We had a nice evening and I got on well with Erich and Peter which was as well since they were travelling with us on the journey back to Kent.

Next day Heinz left me more or less to my own devices saying I was welcome to listen to music in his room. I found some jazz which was to my liking. He deplored my taste and couldn't understand why I wasn't into Bartok. He told me he had received a letter from Laura who wanted to finish their relationship. She was once more in the States. From what I had gathered, there was really no future in the affair but it was impossible to convince Heinz of this.

After another stiff, more or less silent, dinner, we again walked into the little town and down the steps into the cellar bar. Erich and Peter and a few others were there again. Heinz was in a bad mood and started drinking heavily. Eventually he began shouting and throwing bottles about. Erich and Peter indicated that we should leave.

"When he gets like this it's impossible to reason with him. Just leave him. We will walk with you to the Werners' house."

Next morning I was up early since we were driving to Ostend that day. Heinz appeared looking pale but said nothing about the previous evening's events. We packed the car, bade goodbye to Frau Werner, and drove round to Erich's house where he and Peter were waiting. It was a tight squeeze with luggage and four people in the Skoda but the car seemed to make light of the load.

We got the last ferry from Ostend which meant that we didn't reach my home in Kent until early morning. My mother had made up beds for the German visitors but I asked if anyone would like anything before we went to bed not expecting any requests since we were all very tired. However, Heinz had spotted an open bottle of brandy and asked if he could have a cognac. I duly poured him one and he sipped it suspiciously.

I was up before the guests next morning to find my younger brother excitedly holding the brandy bottle. After greeting me, and expressing envy at my deep tan, he asked,

"Someone's had some of this, haven't they?"

"Yes, Heinz had some."

"Great!" He chortled. "It was empty and I filled it up with cold tea." He was very amused that his practical joke had worked. I wasn't so sure it was a good idea to convey this to Heinz.

A First Date

The telephone was ringing. Someone answer it, thought Jane, too lazy to get up herself from the sofa where she was reading. Eventually she heard her mother talking and then:

"Jane, it's for you."

"Who is it?"

"Mark, I think he said."

Mark, who the hell is Mark? And then she remembered the tall, fair boy at the party last Saturday, a party she'd never wanted to go to. She finally gave in to Valerie's wheedling and went along as her unwilling companion. She was used to a lot of attention at parties because, although not naturally conceited, she knew she was a striking beauty. But she'd completely not been in the mood for socialising and warded off those who tried to engage her in conversation. She recalled that there was this one guy who wouldn't take no for an answer and persisted, even managing to get her on the dance floor. Despite herself, she knew that there was something about him she found appealing. Nevertheless, she was in the middle of a difficult relationship with an older man and any further complication in her life was simply out of the question. So how was it that, Mark – if that was his name – had managed to secure her phone number from her? What a mistake; she'd only done it to get rid of him. Well, she better get rid of him now.

"Hello," she breathed into the receiver.

"Hi, it's Mark. We met on Saturday at Jenny's party. You remember?"

"Yes," she said uncertainly.

"Well, how are you?"

"OK, I guess."

"I'd love to see you again. Could we meet up for a drink, this week?"

"No, I don't think so, I'm busy this week."

"Oh, that's a shame. Look, I tell you what, I've got a spare ticket for The Sound of Music at the Dominion on Friday. It's just opened, would you like to come?"

This was a dilemma, she really wanted to see the film. Most of the boys she knew wouldn't be seen dead at such a show. And she should really be seeing Edward on Friday. Perhaps this was a chance to move on from what she knew was always going to be a disastrous relationship.

"OK, I would like that. Where shall we meet?"

Wow, thought Mark. I've done it, this amazing girl is going to go out with me. He hadn't had high hopes. He'd spotted her at the party, looking miserable but gorgeous. He'd tried to engage her in conversation but she talked in monosyllables when she talked at all. He'd almost had to drag her onto the dance floor where she shuffled around like a lifeless rag doll. Yet, towards the end of the evening, he had managed to amuse her a little and discovered that they shared musical and literary interests. When she'd agreed to give him her telephone number, he was elated and said he would ring her the following week.

That was all he could think about for the next couple of days. It was her sheer physical perfection which stood out, of course. Her fair delicate skin, forget-me-not blue eyes, delicious full pink lips and light blonde hair, all aided by a minimum of cosmetics. When her friend Valerie told him she was a model, he was not surprised, given her lovely figure, but it added an extra frisson.

Me, going out with a model, he thought. He got excited at the idea but then remembered he only had her phone number. She hadn't agreed to anything. But now, it was reality. She was actually going to go out with him. He'd lied about the tickets for Sound of Music and immediately worried that he wouldn't be able to get any.

He was relieved when he went to the box office next day, which was only round the corner from his office, to find that tickets were available for the Friday. He'd arranged to meet her at the modelling school she was attending in Bond Street. He sat in reception and watched as a procession of beautiful women passed to and fro. Then she appeared coming down the stairs in a figure-hugging green sweater and mini kilt. She stood out even among these stunning visions and smiled shyly at him as he came towards her.

They dined in a little Italian restaurant in Marylebone and immediately she was a completely different person. She had a delightful, trilling laugh which he hadn't heard before. She put her hand on his arm as she told him about her dreams. She really wanted to be an actress but modelling represented the best way of earning a living at the moment. At the film, which they both loved, she allowed him to hold her hand, and they came out of the cinema full of shared, positive emotions. They parted at Victoria Station, as she went to Sutton and he went to Sevenoaks. They embraced and shared a modest kiss and he promised to ring her again over the weekend.

On the train home from Victoria, Jane wondered what she was doing. It turned out that she wouldn't have seen Edward on the Friday, in any case, as he had to go abroad at short notice on business. So the idea of 'moving on' had got nowhere. And now, was she not 'leading on' this nice young man called Mark? She admitted to herself that she'd enjoyed the evening and that he'd been good company and that he was also quite nice looking. But it was totally unfair to allow him to think that there was any future in a relationship when she was still so completely engaged with Edward. She had to sort that out before she could commit to anyone else. And yet, deep down, she was in emotional turmoil. She felt she hadn't seen the last of Mark.

Key of the Door

I knew it was a special day as soon as I woke up but couldn't quite remember why. Then it dawned on me. Halloween, my birthday. But not just any old birthday – my twenty-first birthday. Wow! Twenty-one. It seemed like I had been dreaming about being twenty-one for years. Coming of age. Key of the door. Grown up at last. Ready to take my place in the adult world.

Then I remembered I was already in the adult world. I had a job and I was due at work by 9.00 and if I didn't get a move on I was going to miss the 8.11 train. My parents had already left for work and I noticed a pile of cards on the breakfast table and a package. However, I didn't have time for that and left that pleasure for later in the evening.

The day went by in a bit of a whirl. They made a fuss of me in the office and Laura Graham, one of the account executives whom I particularly liked, said she wanted to take me to lunch. I had actually already arranged to meet Rodney for lunch, an old friend who was also in the PR business. But I didn't want to turn down an offer from Laura and so I rang Rod and asked if we could meet after work. I'd already decided that not a lot of work was going to get done after lunch. Tommy Russell, the boss, wandered in and greeted me.

"So, youngster, you're a man now, eh?"

He guffawed and I joined in the laughter though I wasn't sure of the joke.

"Come and see me at eleven. I've got a proposition for you." With that he took his bulk out of the room and I looked at Laura who had the next desk.

"He's got an account in line for you," she yawned. "You better accept it, whatever it is."

"Mm," I said. I had no intention of turning down any offer. It was one of the changes I was expecting now that I was a man. My own account portfolio.

Laura took me to the Connaught Rooms and we had a superb lunch. She introduced me to pork Ophelia, a Greek dish, and a luscious Rhone wine.

"Do you see your future in this business?" she asked as she lit up a cigarette between courses.

"Well, yes. Tommy has given me the Robson Lowe account and wants me to shadow Bill Bradley on Warner Hudnut with a view to taking it over, I think."

"I'm not sure you're cut out for this," she said, blowing a stream of smoke across the restaurant.

"You may be right. But I'm going to give it a go. Anyway, it's my birthday, my special birthday. And I don't want to think about Hallmark Public Relations right now. "

"Good," she said. "Because I've got a surprise for you after lunch."

The surprise was a visit to The Red Devil, our local pub which was hardly novel. However, the pub was full of most of the office and I got a nice cheer as we went in and was presented with a large brandy. It was pleasant being the centre of attention and I realised I was getting drunk as more and more drinks were pressed on me. People started drifting off back to their desks and eventually there was only me, Laura and Lance, another young executive, left. Laura was expertly tearing to bits each member of the organisation and Lance was trying to convince me to read Ian Fleming in whom I had no interest. Eventually we too returned to New Oxford Street.

I slumped into my chair and promptly fell asleep. No one

seemed to care and when I woke up it was five o'clock. God, I thought, I'm meeting Rod at five thirty, I better get off.

Well, that was a good day's work I said to myself as I splashed water on my face in the Gents. Rod was already in The Shaftesbury in our usual corner when I arrived and he had a pint waiting for me.

"Good day, good lunch?" he enquired.

"A tiring day but I managed to get through," I volunteered. "I need something to eat otherwise I'm going to fall over."

We ordered pie and chips and another pint. After the meal Rod produced some huge cigars and we lit up like a couple of old men. Unlike Rod, I wasn't a smoker but he knew I liked the occasional cigar. The trouble was I needed a whole box of matches to keep it going as my inexperience in the art of smoking meant it was constantly going out.

"I'm meeting some of the gang in the Queen's Head later. Can you join us?"

Rod said that he would come along for a quick one but he had to do some preparation for a meeting in the morning. We staggered down to the tube at Leicester Square both still sucking on our cigars. Smoking was forbidden on the tube even in those days but no-one seemed to take any notice and we got off at Charing Cross and took the train to Orpington. We passed the taxi queue on the way to the bus stop and I said to Rod.

"Sod the bus, let's get a cab. I'm a man now."

The usual gang were in the Queen's Head, including my brother. I realised I'd not been home and I wasn't sure if my parents were expecting me. My brother assured me that they hadn't planned anything since I was having a big party at the golf club at the weekend. Good, I thought, I'm not sure I am in a fit state to face my parents right now.

I forget whose idea it was, but when the bell sounded to signal chucking out time, those who were left all jumped into Reg's car and set off for the golf club where my party was taking place. The occupants of the car included two girls, Jenny and Helen, my old friend Dick and my brother and his mate Reg, that is six up in a car that was a squeeze for five.

We reached the golf club, which was, of course, closed and then some bright spark said let's go up to the airfield. The airfield was RAF Biggin Hill. The top car park of the golf club bordered Biggin Hill aerodrome. Prominent at the gate was a large sign saying Ministry of Defence – RAF Property – Keep Out. Perhaps it was the same bright spark that said: 'We're gonna have this sign' whereupon we jumped over the gate and started pushing on the post that held the sign. It gave way surprisingly quickly and in no time was stowed in the boot of Reg's car.

Sign looting now became our mission and the next target was the sign on the side of the road which said Jail Lane. This proved a harder nut to crack than the Air Ministry sign. I was happily sitting in the back of the car canoodling with Helen when the others shouted for me to come and give them a hand. Jail Lane eventually joined the RAF notice in the boot of the car. However, it was too big to be accommodated with the boot lid shut so that was left open with the sign partly hanging out. That was to prove a big mistake.

We next found ourselves back near the Queen's Head outside the newsagents that was owned by Rod's parents. There were some advertising signs on the road outside the shop and they were just being eyed up when someone shouted: "Look out, it's the cops."

Sure enough a police car was approaching and so we all jumped back into Reg's car and locked the doors. Of course, it was a completely futile gesture since the police simply stood outside the car telling us to open the doors and come out, though they didn't say: "With your hands up."

Sheepishly we crawled out of the car and noticed that someone was leaning out of an upstairs window in the newsagents. It was Rodney, calling out.

"It's OK, officer. These are friends of mine. They are just in high spirits. We won't press any charges."

"You may not, sir, but we certainly will," said one of the policemen.

We were instructed to go to the police station a couple of miles away at Locks Bottom including the girls who had their own car parked in the Queen's Head car park. At the police station we were charged with larceny, and statements were taken along with our finger prints. We were then put into the cells, the girls disappearing into another part of the building.

Meanwhile, the gallant Rodney had got dressed and driven up to my parents' house to tell them the dramatic news. They in turn also got dressed and drove to the police station to take delivery of their delinquent children.

Everyone was told by the police what a serious offence we'd committed and that we would be required to appear in Bromley Magistrates Court at ten the following morning. By now it was gone three and I was feeling remarkably sober.

Next morning all six of us we were in the dock of the magistrates' court dressed in our Sunday best. The clerk of court read out the charges and one of the policemen who had arrested us read out his account of the event. It seems the police had been tailing us for a mile or so once the car was spotted with a sign hanging out of the boot.

The chair of the magistrates asked if any evidence was forthcoming and two policemen came into court solemnly carrying the air ministry sign and the Jail Lane sign which had clods of earth attached, one of which dropped off onto the floor of the courtroom causing us to stifle a giggle.

After the police had finished giving their account, the chair of the magistrates looked at me.

"I understand it was your birthday. Did you think that gave you license to roam the county stealing other people's property? What have you to say for yourself? I address you because you are the oldest person charged and so should set an example."

I muttered something about being truly sorry for what we

had done and the trouble we had caused the police. It was not behaviour that we were accustomed to and that we had got carried away in our celebration of my birthday. I also pointed out that no blame should be attached to the young women since they had not taken part in the theft. This was not strictly true as I recalled that Jenny, in particular, had joined in with gusto.

The magistrate shook his head and said that we were all involved and that we had perpetrated a very serious crime. Stealing government property was a threat to the safety of the state and should be punished accordingly. We were all fined five pounds and warned as to our future conduct.

Outside the court I saw the two girls standing with their parents and I went over to apologise. Helen's mother immediately told me to go away and never to try to make any contact again with her daughter. Jenny's mother was more forgiving and said that she hoped there would be no further occurrence of such a happening.

My parents had engaged an official photographer for my 21st birthday party at the golf club the following Saturday and we particularly asked that he take a picture of the four desperados – the girls were not there. I later discovered that Dick, who was an articled accountant, was extremely worried that his firm would find out about the court case. He was convinced that he would have been dismissed and be in danger of being struck off if it had come to light.

Meanwhile, I mulled over the considerable demands of becoming a man.

Under the Hammer

Roger had been working for the Agency for nearly a year when he was called into the Director's office.

"Well Roger, are you ready to take on your very own account?' Before Roger had time to reply, the director continued. 'Yes, I'm sure you are. I'm going to start you with Robson Lowe and if that goes well you can also take over Spode. Are you familiar with these clients?"

"Well, I have had a look at Spode but I don't know Robson Lowe."

"No, of course you don't because Robson Lowe is a new client. I'm going to meet them tomorrow morning for the second time and you will come along. Robson Lowe are stamp auctioneers by the way."

At 10.45 the next day George and Roger alighted from a taxi in Pall Mall. Roger noticed that members of the agency never took the bus or tube, always a taxi. He could get used to this. Robson Lowe's premises resembled those of an exclusive London club which was hardly surprising as Pall Mall was the centre of London club land. They entered through an elegant portico and mounted a marble staircase to a reception area of comfortable leather armchairs and coffee tables. They were greeted by an attractive woman.

"Hello, I'm Annabelle, Robbie's daughter. You must be Mr

Edwards and Mr Harper. Robbie's expecting you, please come through."

They were taken along a thickly carpeted corridor where Annabelle knocked on the third door along.

"Come," intoned the voice within.

They entered a huge, high-ceilinged room, replete with fireplace, comfortable chairs, a mahogany table with a large vase of flowers upon it as well as a tray with a peculiar round bottle and glasses. Behind a sumptuous, inlaid desk sat a man that Roger could only think of as Dickensian with his side whiskers and steel rimmed glasses. It was difficult to say how old he was. He looked ancient but was probably only in his fifties. He stood up and greeted them.

"Thank you, Annabelle," he said and she left the room.

"Would you care for some Mateus?" asked Lowe going over to the tray with the bottle. "'I know it's on the early side but it is my practice to have a glass at eleven."

Roger looked at Edwards for his cue and was relieved to see his boss accept the offer. It would, after all, be rude to refuse their new client's largesse. It might embarrass Robson Lowe to drink alone at this time of the day though Roger doubted that. This is the life, thought Roger, as he sipped the pink, slightly bubbly liquid. He started to daydream then realised where he was. Robson Lowe was talking in tones that reminded him of the humourist Gerard Hoffnung and Roger remembered that he was supposed to be responsible for this man's account and therefore his public relations.

"So, I am going to be auctioning the Burrus collection, probably the largest stamp collection that has ever been assembled. Not only has it some of the very rarest stamps but also the finest philatelic specimens providing virtually a history of philately of some parts of the world."

"Where will the auction take place, sir?" asked Roger.

"The Dorchester Hotel. And please call me Robbie."

George Edwards then outlined the sort of service that the agency would provide in terms of publicising the auction.

"We'll obviously send press releases announcing the sale to all the dailies, BBC, ITN as well as the trade press. I imagine it will cause quite a stir especially with the possibility of a world record price being obtained."

"It's a certainty, not a possibility," said Lowe, sucking on his pipe. "I know of at least three top dealers, representing very rich collectors, who are after the Mauritius stamps."

Roger had done a bit of homework and knew that the Mauritius Post Office Penny Red and Two Penny Blue were some of the rarest stamps in the world.

Over the next two weeks Roger was busy drafting press releases which were approved first by George and then sent to Robson Lowe for any amendments. The subsequent mailings to the national press led to a number of phone calls from news editors asking when the 'big stamps' were to be auctioned. The answer was that potentially record price fetching stamps would be under the hammer throughout the day but the Mauritius stamp lots were likely to be sold about 2.30.

Now that he was a junior account executive, Roger had his own secretary or, rather, he had a share of a secretary. Carol was tall, and honey blond with large green eyes. She wore tight sweaters which showed off her ample bosom to advantage. Roger knew that Marian fancied him and he thought he might take advantage of that fact. His opportunity came when he had to work late the evening before the big auction. He asked Marian if she could stay a little late to help him put together some last-minute handouts. By 6.30 they were the only people left in the building and Roger found himself on the floor exploring the ample bosom he had long contemplated.

'Large tits, small nipples' he thought to himself as he nuzzled her. 'Very nice'. This became a routine activity and Marian was always obliging but Roger felt a bit of a heel because he had no intention of taking Marian out. He already had a girl friend with whom he was very content but Marian represented a nice little grope on the side.

Roger was at the Dorchester early next morning putting out the handouts and making himself acquainted with any press that had already arrived. Robson Lowe was looking resplendent in a garish check suit and floppy bow tie with a word for everybody. And he noted Annabelle looking stunning in a low-cut dress. There were banks of telephones available for dealers who represented remote buyers, some of them in New York as well as various parts of the Commonwealth. Most important of all were the stamps and covers which were under glass, and lock and key, and looked quite unimpressive thought Roger. Why would anyone want to pay thousands of pounds for these insignificant pieces of paper?

At 9.00am Robson Lowe took his place on the podium and called the room to order. He introduced the sale by talking about the history of Burrus's collection and indicating the range of items to be auctioned. He said that the sale would proceed as per catalogue which meant the order given in the catalogue. He asked bidders to make their bids clear and to announce themselves to his staff as necessary. It soon became evident that almost all bidders were known to the staff of Robson Lowe.

"Now to Lot 1, Cape of Good Hope triangular." boomed Lowe. By and large, the sales proceeded quickly without fuss. Roger had noted in his copy of the catalogue which were likely to produce a record price either for a particular country, or stamp, or most notably a world record price. There were a number of penny blacks in the sale but these were not expected to fetch record prices. By the time of the lunch break it was evident that the auction was going well and set to break all records for the sale of one collection.

"There's a buffet in the next room," Annabelle said to him in passing, "help yourself." He wished he could but settled for the buffet instead. Soon after the auction had restarted, the Mauritius stamps were in the frame. They did not disappoint. The Penny Red attracted a number of bids and the price zoomed up almost alarmingly. As Robbie had predicted, there were three principal bidders who seemed determined to acquire the envelope with the special little square of paper. Eventually one of them dropped out and it was down to a bidder in the room and one on the telephone. Roger sensed the tension as the price continued to rise. In the end the buyer in the room indicated that he was finished and the telephone triumphed, a bidder from New York, and a world record price was paid. Within five minutes that record had been broken when the same bidder went even higher for the Two Penny Blue.

To the extent that philatelists get excited, this could be said to be the phenomenon at large. The popular press certainly entered into the spirit of the occasion and Roger got requests for interviews with the buyer and with the auctioneer. The representative of the buyer in the room would only make a brief statement to the effect that he represented a collector in New York. The name was later revealed when Robson Lowe met the press. He insisted that he would only give interviews when the sale was over and that took another hour. A number of records were broken including the world record for an individual item and the highest total for one sale.

A familiar face came up to Roger and said that he would like to do a TV news report. He recognised a well-known ITN reporter and felt that he was entering the world of big time PR. The reporter checked his facts with Roger and then indicated where he wanted to film his report with Robson Lowe, still auctioning, in the background. His report was all about the Mauritius stamps which Roger knew would disappoint Robson Lowe since he was proud of having many other important specimens under the hammer. Nevertheless, a report on prime-time TV news was a feather in the cap for the agency and for Roger. He watched as the reporter, David something, rehearsed his piece, walking up and down memorising his words. Then suddenly the cameras were rolling and it was for real.

"Today, at The Dorchester Hotel in London, philatelic history was made when a Two Penny Mauritius Blue stamp sold for a world record price to a collector in New York. Robson Lowe, the

Pall Mall stamp traders, realised the largest ever amount for a single sale in philatelic specimens."

'Wow!' thought Roger. It gave him a buzz to think he was instrumental in creating some real news and for the first time in the job felt that he understood the creative possibilities and excitement of PR work.

With the success of the big Dorchester sale and resulting publicity which included all the dailies as well as the BBC and ITN, Roger was told he would now be in full charge of the Robson Lowe account. Unfortunately, subsequent sales did not match the scale and glamour of the world record event. Nevertheless, Roger diligently kept abreast of the Robson Lowe calendar and put out press releases to the news and trade press in advance of sales. He paid the odd visit to the Pall Mall premises and always got a nice smile from Annabelle, but seldom saw Robbie. Instead, it was his assistant David who saw him. David had none of the style of Robbie, and, more to the point, did not dispense Mateus rosé. Eventually, the visits became tedious as Roger listened to David bleating on about stamps in which he had not the slightest interest. He stopped taking notes, or even listening attentively. His press releases became pedestrian and he even missed the odd sale if he thought it was unlikely to attract any press interest.

He got away with this a couple of times but late one morning, George Edwards came into his room, red in the face.

"I've just had Robson Lowe on the phone. The balloon's gone up. We should have been at the big auction today. You'd better get down there, right away."

'Shit,' Roger said to himself, 'I've been found out.' Although the sale was one of the larger ones, it was still at the Pall Mall premises and he had failed to appreciate its significance. Annabelle was not at her usual place in Reception and when he entered the sale room he saw that she was administering to Robbie who did not look best pleased. The sale was, in fact, over and administrative details with some clients were being completed by David and other staff.

"So, Mr Harper, you've decided to honour us with your company," said Robbie in his Hoffnung voice.

"Yes, I do apologise, I'm afraid I made an error in my diary entry," wheedled Roger.

"Really," said Lowe, unimpressed. "Well, a good opportunity was missed. I suppose you know that we sold a Four Annas Inverted Head today and it realised a world record price."

He said this in a tone which conveyed deep scepticism at any notion that Roger had cognisance of the information.

'Oh no, not the Four Annas Inverted Head,' Roger's inner voice screamed sarcastically. Out loud he was more circumspect.

"Oh dear, in that case I'll put out a press release right away and get it round to the evening papers as well as the nationals and the news agencies."

"Well, you do whatever you think is best," said Lowe, "but I should point out that Annabelle has already spoken to a number of press people. She's been doing your job for you." With that, Lowe turned his back on him and went to speak to a client.

Roger looked desperately at Annabelle and she seemed to take pity on him. "You can't blame him for being upset," she said, "he feels let down."

"Yes, I know," said Roger, "I'm sorry."

"Well, stop apologising and get on with your job. Come to my desk and I'll give you the details of the major sales."

He went with her and took down the information she proffered. The smell of her perfume was alluring and he deliberately brushed her arm as he leaned across to pick up a catalogue.

"What are you doing?" she said.

"Nothing."

"Yes, you are, you're making a pass. I should warn you that I'm a happily married woman and, in any case, you're completely out of your depth, young man. Now, take yourself off, back to your grubby office and do what you are paid to do."

A week later, Roger was called into George Edwards's office.

"Shut the door, Roger. I've just had a call from Robson Lowe cancelling his account with us. I can't pretend it had nothing to do with your cock-up with the recent sale. But I blame myself, I should have realised that you are not ready yet to swim alone."

Roger returned to his desk, chastened but also relieved. He couldn't be satisfied by the sloppy practice that had caused his employer to lose confidence in him. This was an inauspicious start to his career as a PR account executive. But wasn't it also telling him that perhaps he was not cut out for this job? How long could he maintain enthusiasm for Two Penny Blue stamps, let alone cans of dog food? This seemed to be a signal for him to quit the world of spin and discover another way of life.

Rescued from the Watch Tower

Without trying she attracted attention. Pale, grave face, upturned nose, full lips, large blue-green eyes and, apart from the eyes, no make-up which was an attractive feature of that era, and straight, straw coloured, hair. She also had a good figure. When he tried to make conversation, she was difficult and generally seemed distracted. He found out almost nothing about her. Nevertheless, she did not leave him without hope. Although unsmiling, cold almost, there was something in her demeanour which suggested she was not totally dismissive of him. When he asked of others who she was, he was told that she had come with a group of girls from the Sutton area.

He got steadily drunk and made other attempts to engage her in conversation with no more success. Eventually he settled for another woman, a friendly redhead, and he was dancing with her when he saw the stranger putting on her coat, apparently leaving. He excused himself.

"Are you going?" She nodded at his statement of the obvious. "Can I give you a ring?"

"If you like. Joyce knows my number." It was Joyce's party.

"But what's your name?" he blurted out.

"Penny," she said and disappeared out of the room.

Next day he couldn't stop thinking about Penny. He got Joyce's number from a friend and rang her up.

"I'm not sure I should give you Penny's number. She's not your type. Besides, she's got problems."

He told Joyce that Penny had told him to get her number from Joyce. Reluctantly, Joyce gave him the number. After he put the phone down he stood looking at the number as if it contained the secret of the universe. Afraid of a rebuff, he refrained from making the call. In the early evening, he was having a drink with his best friend, Ian. Ian had been at the party too and given a lift home to a girl he met.

"Any luck?"

Ian shook his head. "Got a bit of a snog, but she wasn't having any more."

He discussed his dilemma over Penny with his friend.

"Well, you won't know if you don't give it a try," he said.

This amazing insight had also occurred to him and when he got home he rang the number. When an older female voice answered, he asked if Penny was in.

"Who's calling?"

"Roger," he said and wondered if that would mean anything to her.

A few moments later she was talking to him in a guarded but friendly way. He suggested they have a drink the following evening. She hesitated and said she was busy tomorrow but could make later in the week. They settled on Wednesday and he took her address. When he put the phone down he was shaking. His dream woman had actually agreed to have a drink with him.

The next forty-eight hours dragged unbearably. All he could think about at work was his date on Wednesday. He told no one about it but his colleagues must have sensed that something was on his mind as he was frequently day dreaming.

The drive over to Sutton was much further than he had realised but since he had given himself loads of time – rushing in from work, bolting down his evening meal, much to his mother's disgust, and quickly changing into his smartest unsmart clothes – he arrived only a few minutes late. Penny lived in a large detached house in a quiet, leafy suburban street. He was a little overawed. A woman answered the door.

"Hello, Mrs, er, I'm Roger, I've come to see Penny."

"Come in Roger. Penny won't be long. I'm Agatha James, Penny's mother."

She held out her hand and he shook it. He was taken into the lounge.

"This is my husband, Dennis, and this is Penny's sister, Ruth."

A man in his late forties barely looked up from his newspaper to nod at Roger. Ruth, a younger sister, and quite different from Penny, greeted him perfunctorily. She was seated at a table, possibly doing homework. He felt awkward – there was no sign of Penny. But then he hardly knew Penny anyway. What was he doing here? He sat down in the chair that was proffered and realised that he was being asked a question.

"What do you do Roger?" asked Mrs James.

"I work for a public relations agency in London."

"I'm not sure I know what public relations is," said Mrs James.

He looked at Mrs James. She was tall and slim with a thatch of auburn hair and with a slight smile playing round her lips. She seemed warm and friendly.

"Well, PR is very like advertising except that you seek to get publicity for your product or service in the media without paying for it. You might be surprised to know how much editorial content in newspapers and magazines is supplied by PR agents rather than written by the reporters themselves."

"Yeah, we're always getting PR bumf."

Roger realised that Mr James was talking.

"Bloody, self-serving twaddle, most of it."

Just then, much to Roger's relief, Penny chose that moment to enter the room. She looked gorgeous, dressed in a tight damson coloured sweater, to emphasise her splendid figure, and a short black skirt.

"Hi, Penny," he smiled.

"Hello," she responded.

Fifteen minutes later they were seated in the saloon bar of the White Hart in Sutton, Penny with a half of lager and lime and he the same without lime. He found her easy to talk to. She chatted a bit about her Mum and Dad. Dennis was a senior buyer for Selfridges, which explained why he was bombarded by PR material, while Agatha had once been a secretary but was now a housewife.

"What do you do?"

"I'm a model," she said. "Well, actually I'm at the Lucy Clayton Modelling School, training to be a model."

"Wow!" he said. "I thought you were a bit special. I've never met a model before."

"Well, I'm not a proper model yet, but that's my aim."

"I'm sure you'll have no problem," he said. "You look fantastic."

She smiled back at him and he blushed and felt light headed.

"Did you enjoy Joyce's party?" he asked.

"Not much."

"I didn't think so. You seemed preoccupied."

"Yeah, I've had a bit of a problem with my boyfriend."

This unexpected news hit him below the belt.

"Boyfriend?" he stammered.

"Yes, he's being difficult."

She told him about Owen – what sort of name was that? – who was a Jehovah's Witness and seemed to be doing his best to induct her into the sect. The way she talked about him indicated that she was somewhat in awe of him.

"Do you believe all that stuff?" he asked.

"Well, when I hear Owen and his Dad and some of the others talk, I find it very convincing. I think they are good people."

He felt out of his depth. He knew little about Jehovah's Witnesses except that they were a bit weird, not believing in Christmas and blood transfusions. He wondered how this lovely girl could be mixed up with this strange sect. Worse, she was going out with one of them. So much for his chances.

"Didn't Owen want to come to the party?"

"No, he doesn't really like parties unless they are ones run by the Witnesses."

"I bet they're a gas," he said.

"Well, they do know how to enjoy themselves," she said, "but I'm finding them a bit stifling."

Roger quickly realised that if he was not going to lose this wonderful girl he had to do something about her links with the JWs. And it was not purely selfish. He didn't think her life would in any way be enhanced by sacrificing it to this odd movement. He suddenly had an idea.

"Can I meet Owen?"

"Sure. We have a meeting on Friday at Owen's house."

Friday was his night out with the boys but this was more important.

"Well, if you think he wouldn't mind me coming."

"No, I'm sure. Anyone's welcome. Pick me up at 7.00 and we can go together."

Roger drove Penny home and was allowed a peck on her cheek as they said goodnight. On the drive home he considered the evening. It hadn't gone altogether badly though he had not been a hit with Mr James even if Mrs was friendly enough. Penny had also been an agreeable companion and he was conscious of how many envious male glances went in his direction while they were in the pub. But he had a rival. More than a rival. He sensed that Owen had a real hold over Penny. She was not only his girlfriend, she seemed in thrall to him. But Roger liked a challenge. Once he set his mind on something, particularly in affairs of the heart, he never took no for an answer. He would have to see what Owen was like and then plan his strategy accordingly.

The following Friday found Roger once more at the door of the James's house. On this occasion Penny was ready and so he was spared the ordeal of making small talk with the rest of the family. Penny was just as lovely as he had remembered but he found her distant when he tried to engage her in conversation. She seemed on edge and he assumed it was because she was going to be seeing Owen. Owen, whose second name was Stratton, lived in Purley. Roger had suggested that they have a drink en route but Penny vetoed this saying that it was important to be on time for the meeting.

The Strattons lived in a small terraced house. The man who came to the door greeted Penny with a kiss. She explained who her companion was and introduced him to Mr Stratton. He was a small, cheerful individual and welcomed them both into the front room.

"They think we're odd but we are quite normal. Just like other folk with our own strengths and weaknesses. I like this, for instance," he said with a twinkle in his eye, holding up a bottle of wine.

Roger accepted a glass and got into conversation with another man who said how pleased he was that Roger was joining the group. Roger tried to explain that he was only here as a guest but this was ignored. He tried to see what had happened to Penny. She had disappeared. Some while later, having listened to a tedious account of the forthcoming JW's big convention in Croydon's Fairfield Halls, he saw Penny come into the room with a young man he took to be Owen. Dressed in a sports jacket and tie and with horn-rimmed glasses and crinkly hair, he looked to be in his mid twenties. Penny came over to him.

"Owen, this is Roger. He was interested in coming to one of our meetings."

"Welcome," said Owen, putting out his hand. "I'm sure you will find our movement both uplifting and fulfilling."

He was relieved that Penny stayed with him while Owen went over to talk to some other people. Penny seemed a little more relaxed as if she had found her spiritual home. Mr Stratton called for everyone to go into the other room and take a seat in the circle. Drinks had to be abandoned and Roger found himself between Penny, who had Owen on her other side, and a large girl in check trousers. Mr Stratton remained seated but took charge of affairs. He asked everyone to hold hands while he recited an opening prayer. He then welcomed two newcomers, Stephen who had been introduced by John, and Roger who had been introduced by Penny. The tyros were asked to stand up whereupon they received a small round of applause. Penny looked up at Roger and beamed.

The rest of the evening was as bad as Roger had feared. Members of the group talked of their success, or lack of it, at recruiting new members in their house-to-house visits. Someone announced the volume of sales of The Watchtower and Mr Stratton drew attention to a particularly powerful article in the latest edition of the magazine. Plans for a bring and buy sale were outlined and then Owen was called upon to lead prayers. He spoke in an earnest, braying voice and Roger was aware that Penny was rapt during the homily that followed his prayers. As far as Roger was concerned it was all nonsense, and dangerous nonsense at that, and he was beginning to wish he was in The Harrow with the usual Friday night gang. A break was announced for refreshments. During the interval, Roger asked if they could go now.

"Of course not. We're going to talk about the convention after the break. Aren't you enjoying it?"

"Not particularly," said Roger.

"Well, don't let me keep you," said Penny. "You're welcome to go."

"But how will you get home?"

"Oh, someone will give me a lift. Don't worry."

Roger was in a quandary. He was reluctant to abandon this gorgeous girl yet it was clear that she was far more interested in Owen and his pathetic, troubling movement than she was in him. And could he stand another hour or so of this drivel? He looked at his watch. If he left now he could get to The Harrow in time for last orders and then join the others for their weekly game of poker.

By now Penny was talking to Owen and he went over to the pair.

"Well, I think I'll be off if you're sure you can get home."

"Don't worry about that old boy," said Owen. "Kevin will give her a lift."

Roger made his farewells and Penny went into the other room without a word. Mr Stratton took him to the door.

"Not for you, old chap?" he said cheerfully. "It's not everyone's cup of tea. Shame, though, that you didn't give it a bit longer."

Roger got out of the door, relieved to be away from their mad, cloying embrace. So that was it, then. The end of a very brief liaison with the most beautiful girl he'd ever set eyes on. Though Owen was not handsome in a conventional way, he clearly had something that Penny valued. There didn't seem any way in which Roger could replace him in her affections.

Over the next few weeks Roger found himself resuming his relationship with his old girlfriend, Helen. She was a delightful girl: pretty, good sense of humour and sharing his interests in books and music. Moreover, she lived just down the road. But he couldn't forget Penny. Images of her striking face and splendid body would haunt him. But she was unattainable so best forget her was his decision which was supported by his best mates. Then, about two months after his dreadful evening in Purley, he got a phone call.

"Is that Roger?"

"Yes."

"This is Agatha James, Penny's mother. Do you remember me?"

"Yes, of course."

"I'm sorry to ring you up out of the blue like this but I'm worried about Penny and I thought you might be able to help."

"Well, er, yes, if I can."

"It's this Jehovah's Witness movement that she has got embroiled in. I don't think she is happy in it but she cannot bring herself to leave it. I wondered if you would be prepared to discuss it with her. She told me that you were sceptical about it. Dennis and I are too but we are her parents and she won't listen to us. You might have better luck."

"I don't know. I suppose I might."

"We'd be very grateful, Roger. In the circumstances it would be good of you. Can I put Penny on the phone so that you can arrange to meet up?"

"OK."

"Hello Roger. I'm not sure if this is a good idea but Mummy seems to think it is."

"Well, let's give it a try," he said.

They arranged to meet in London. She told him the address of the Lucy Clayton School and he said he would collect her there after he had finished work and they would go and have a drink and perhaps a bite to eat.

What a turn up, thought Roger. Just as he was beginning to get over Penny, she reappears in his life again. He must have impressed Mrs James more than he realised. Or perhaps it was just that Penny had got into a certain amount of emotional turmoil and her parents were desperate to get her back on an even keel.

Next evening at 5.45 he was in the reception area of the Lucy Clayton Modelling School goggling as a series of mostly tall, good looking young women came down the stairs and past him into the street. Soon he spotted Penny who smiled shyly at him as she approached.

"Thanks, Roger." She took his hand. "It's good to see you."

Over a pizza in a modest Italian trattoria she told him about the mess she was in.

"It's swallowing me up. All the pamphlets they are giving me to read. At one moment I think it is brilliant and then I have doubts. And it is such a big commitment to give yourself totally to the movement."

"What about Owen?"

"Well, of course, he is very insistent that I enter fully into the church."

I bet he is, thought Roger.

"But, how do you feel about him?" he asked.

"I don't know. He's very persuasive and I think he's a good, clever person. But I'm not sure that I want to make this commitment."

"Well, you don't have to. Let's talk about the options."

They talked for over an hour about the tenets of the organisation and Roger put forward reasoned objections to the claims made by the Witnesses and the sort of life that Penny would end up having if she joined the church fully. Penny seemed to accept his criticisms but said that these objections were understood by the Witnesses and answered effectively in their pamphlets.

"I tell you what. Let me have a look at these pamphlets for a couple of days and then we can get together again and have a further talk."

They parted at Victoria Station and Roger felt ten feet tall as he kissed Penny goodbye and waved her off to the Sutton train.

Next evening he mentioned Penny's difficulties to his parents during dinner and his father suggested that he had a word with one of their neighbours, Norman Richardson, who was Editor of the Church Times. At first this seemed an odd suggestion but, on reflection, Roger realised that the established church was no friend of fringe sects, especially those originating in America, and so he took up his parents' recommendation. Without mentioning any names, he explained to Norman that a friend of his was getting sucked into a fringe religious movement against her will. He had exaggerated a little but Norman took the bait.

"We have some pamphlets of our own," he said, sucking on his pipe. "Look in tomorrow evening and I'll have some for you to give to your friend."

Norman was as good as his word and Roger spent the next evening reading the pamphlets. Since he was a member of the Humanist Association, he was not short of anti-religious propaganda, but he felt that this would be too drastic for Penny's situation. What Norman's material did was set out the ways in which the Jehovah's Witness position was at odds with conventional Christianity without any underlying foundation. Furthermore, it described the harm that parts of their dogma could do such as withholding blood to those who would die without a transfusion.

For the next three weeks Roger saw Penny regularly, sometimes after work in London and sometimes at her home in Sutton. They talked through her dilemma. Roger soon found that she preferred to discuss things with him rather than read the articles. At times Roger thought he was making progress only to discover that she was as committed as ever on their next meeting. Part of the problem was that she was still attending the meetings. At these she was under the less than benign influence of Owen and his chums. And here he was at a disadvantage because Owen was offering a way of life that was embedded in a network in which she had started to feel comfortable. Roger could offer no such support system. If it was going to be simply him against Owen and his sect he was not confident that he would succeed. He would have to find another way.

The good news was that he had been accepted by the James family. Even Dennis was beginning to be civil and Agatha was always pleased to see him. He also felt that Penny was starting to enjoy his company. She had even let him kiss her a few times but he had to admit that his kisses were not returned which meant that it was a little like kissing a piece of alabaster. Nevertheless, he felt his best option was to hope that Penny would fall in love with him and then he would have defeated Owen and the JWs. To this end he was hoping that his forthcoming 21st birthday party would represent a major break-through in his relations with Penny. His parents were making it into quite a big thing, hiring a suite in a hotel with a band and including a number of their friends as well his friends. Roger was inviting all the gang from the youth club including Helen, some old school mates, and some work friends. He asked Penny if she would come. She seemed uncertain. "You could come with Celia," he said. Celia was her best friend who Roger liked and had met a few times. Penny looked dubious.

*

Roger and Ian decided to get bespoke suits made for the forthcoming 21st party. They went for a number of fittings to a small tailor in Soho and were very proud of their dark grey, three-piece suits when they were finally collected. Proper RSVP invitations had been sent out by his parents and come the day he was still not sure if Penny would show up. Last time he had seen her she had refused to give him any assurance.

Roger hardly recognised some of his friends in their party best but he had to admit it was wonderful to see so many handsome young men and pretty girls in best bib and tucker. The four-piece dance band was perhaps a little square for his age group but they were accomplished musicians. The party got underway at 7.30 and by 9.00 there was still no sign of Penny. Roger had a few dances with Helen who looked very fetching in a black taffeta dress. For ages he had looked forward to showing off Penny as his stunning new girlfriend on this night when he was in the spotlight but it looked as though this dream was not to be. Food was now being served and he looked for somewhere to sit. Just then he noticed that Penny had walked in, wearing a shimmering blue dress. Needless to say, she outshone every other girl in the room. But she had come with someone; not Celia but Owen.

Roger felt himself getting hot. Was she deliberately humiliating him? He went over to greet them and Penny was frosty as was Owen. For God's sake, why had they bothered coming?

The party continued, more drinking, eating, dancing. He noticed that his parents' friends were having a particularly good time which was their wont and, moreover, the music was probably more to their taste. He asked Penny for a dance and she grudgingly agreed but it was a joyless experience. He did not know why she was in such a bad mood and now did not seem to be the time to ask. But there was something he did want to ask. He knew that at some point soon a birthday cake would be produced and he would be asked to cut it. He would like to have

Penny join him in this little ceremony. He asked her if she would do this for him.

"No way," she said.

He was crestfallen. He had pictured the moment as he anticipated the party and now it was all coming adrift. He felt obliged to have someone with him since the photographer, whom his parents had hired, was preparing to take a shot of him cutting the cake. He went over and asked Helen. Although he had ignored her much of the evening, like the decent sort she was she agreed to participate in the cake cutting. And when it arrived, on a special table, they stood together holding the knife over the cake, smiling falsely. In retrospect it had been a ridiculous idea – not the cake itself – that was a kind thought by his parents. No, the stupidity was to set the thing up as though they were a newly married couple.

After this he did not much enjoy the remainder of the party. Things reached their nadir at the end of the evening when everyone formed a circle and the band played Old Lang Syne and For He's A Jolly Good Fellow. It was evident that he was supposed to go in the middle of the circle but it was the last thing he wanted to do. His parents filled the embarrassing moment by entering the circle themselves. Roger felt there was some justice in this since they had generously financed the occasion but he still felt a fool.

After the debacle of the party, Roger decided that it was futile to have anything more to do with Penny. It was not just that she seemed unable to resolve her relationship with the Witnesses (and Owen) but the emotional strain was taking its toll on him. He decided to resume his relationship with Helen and enjoy the companionship of his male friends, friends who had never let him down. He resumed his regular Friday nights of beer followed by cards with Saturdays devoted to parties, if there was one, or the youth club with Helen, or the pictures with Helen. Sometimes he made up a foursome with Ian and his girlfriend, Julie. Although his feelings for Penny did not entirely disappear, he was beginning to get on an even keel again. He was almost happy. But then he ran into Penny again.

It was a weekend when Helen was away on a hockey tour and he went to a party in Hayes with some of the usual gang. Penny was there with her friend Celia but no Owen. Of course, they gravitated together and she smiled shyly at him.

"Where have you been, stranger?" she said.

"Oh, around, you know."

"I hoped you might call me."

"Well, after what happened at my 21st I decided that you didn't want any more to do with me."

She looked thoughtful and then touched his arm.

"I'm sorry about that. I was awful. I was having a bad time with Owen and I shouldn't have come to your party."

"How is Owen?" asked Roger, though since he had no interest in the crinkly-haired runt's welfare, he was at a loss to know why he was enquiring.

"I don't know. I haven't seen Owen for weeks."

"What? Aren't you attending the JW meetings."

"No. I've finished with them."

She looked triumphant and he felt like shouting out Hallelujah or something similar. All his old feeling for her flooded back, although he was not sure that it had ever really gone away. For the rest of the evening they were rarely apart, dancing, drinking, chatting, and later smooching. At midnight she said she should be going. He offered to run her home.

"That's kind, but you'll have to take Celia as well. She is staying the night."

"My pleasure," Roger replied, and meant it.

He was invited in for a nightcap and Celia soon tactfully went up to bed. For the first time Roger kissed Penny and felt she was returning his passion. God, this was amazing, how had it happened?

"My word, this is fantastic. I couldn't be happier."

"Me too," said Penny, her eyes shining.

"But I don't understand. What's happened?"

"Well, Owen was putting more and more pressure on me to

make a stronger commitment to the Witnesses. It got to the point where all my spare time was going to be taken up with them. I finally got round to reading the stuff that you gave me, partly because Mummy had read them and urged me to read them. She was getting more and more worried about the effect that they were having on me. When I realised what a total commitment – it seems to be all or nothing – it was going to be, I began to become seriously concerned. As I said earlier, these doubts were beginning to appear strongly just about the time of your party. Soon after that I had a terrible row with Owen who, I think, began to think the game might be up. He showed a side of himself that I found ugly and also dragged his father into it. The two of them together, arguing forcefully, almost made me falter but, thank goodness I had the strength."

"Thank goodness," murmured Roger, kissing her.

"But what about us? What if I hadn't run into you this evening?" said Roger.

"Oh, we would have met up eventually, I'm sure."

Then she said something that amazed him.

"I always knew that we were destined to be together ever since the first time I saw you. There was immediately something special between us. But at that time, it was impossible to have a relationship. I had to get my life sorted out. And, of course, you were the one to help me do that. You rescued me from the dreaded confines of the watch tower."

He smiled at her rather poetic turn of phrase. He wasn't sure he believed her but what did it matter. They were finally together and he could look forward to… to what? He didn't know precisely but right now she was with the person he most wanted to be with in all the world. He imagined things might not be straightforward but he guessed that life with Penny would not be dull.

Just Another Christmas

It was Christmas Day and I was finishing a lazy breakfast when the phone rang. Who's calling at this time I wondered. Probably one of my father's siblings. It was about the only time they ever rang. I picked up the phone and announced our number. There was a soft voice at the other end which I immediately recognised.

"I wanted to know how you were. I so enjoyed yesterday evening. It's all I can think about."

It was a colleague from work. We had enjoyed ourselves at the office party and then gone on to have a drink in Soho. She was married but unhappy and had poured out her frustrations and found a willing listener in me. She was a few years older than I; tall, blond and willowy with a dazzling smile and a quick wit. I was flattered that she wanted to confide in me but also worried that I might be straying into dangerous territory.

"Nice to hear from you," I said. "Have you got a busy day ahead?"

"No, I told you. He's on duty today. I'm on my own. Can I come round to see you?"

I couldn't believe my ears. Wanting to come round on Christmas Day. How was I going to handle this?

"Er, well, my parents are having a drinks party at midday. I'm not sure."

"Oh." She sounded disappointed. "I really need to see you."

"Um… Give me your number and let me think about it and I'll get back to you. It's rather a tricky day."

She rang off after getting me to promise that I would ring back.

"Who was that on the phone?" my mother asked.

"Oh, Jenny from work."

"What an earth did she want?"

"She wanted to come round," I blurted out.

"Wanted to come round? Here? Hasn't she got anything better to do on Christmas Day?"

"No, actually, she's on her own."

"All day?" asked my mother.

"Yes, I think so."

"In that case, why don't you ask her to our drinks party."

I weighed up the situation. My parents' friends were a pleasant, rather exuberant crowd but in the normal way I wouldn't let their presence put me off. The more sensitive problem was that I'd asked a number of my local friends along and I would be expected to play host to them. Among them was Anita who I'd had my eye on for a while and had been looking forward to seeing. On the other hand, Jenny seemed really keen and I found her alluring and exciting. It's Christmas Day, I said to myself, time to extend the hand of friendship. I fished in my pocket for the piece of paper on which I'd written Jenny's number. She said she would love to come to the party and took down my address and details of how to find my parents' house.

The party was in full swing and I was flushed after a few drinks. After exchanging the usual pleasantries and gossip with the gang, I was just starting to get into my stride with Anita when the door bell rang. I ignored it and continued my banter with the dark eyed Anita. I was suddenly aware that my father was beside me.

"Your friend has arrived," he said, indicating the woman just taking off her coat. It was, of course, Jenny.

"Oh, thanks. Excuse me Anita."

I went over to Jenny and she put her arms round me and gave me a smacking kiss.

"Happy Christmas," she breathed. I inhaled her exotic scent and took her hand. I took her over to introduce her to my friends.

"This is Jenny. We work together. This is Rob, Eddie, Helen, John. I went round the group. When I got to Anita she gave me a strange look and virtually ignored Jenny. OK, I thought, I've blown that one. Jenny needs me at this point.

Jenny was a great success at the party, especially with my parents' generation. I could see some of the men eyeing her lasciviously. Eventually people started drifting off and my gang of friends said they were going on to the Queen's Head and would see me there if I could make it. I noticed Anita slinking off, refusing to make eye contact with me. I looked round for Jenny and then heard her in the kitchen chatting away with my mother as though they had known one another for years. She had the rubber gloves on and was washing up.

"Jenny has been an enormous help," said my mother. "She can come again any time," she continued, laughing.

"Um," I said.

"But she has to get back now, her husband is due home at 5.00. Take the car and give her a lift."

Nowadays this would be a ridiculous suggestion since I was way over the alcohol limit but then it mattered rather less. I was surprised that Jenny had been so frank with my mother about her marital status but then reflected that this was probably a sensible strategy.

"Is that OK with you?" I asked Jenny.

"Yes, that would be lovely."

She seemed happy as we drove to Croydon and said how much she had enjoyed meeting my parents and my friends and my parents' friends as well. How welcome everyone had made her. Including Anita? I said to myself. When we arrived at her terraced house, she apologised for not inviting me in explaining that Terry, her husband, would be home soon and expecting a meal. She needed to get on with that.

"I can't wait for Wednesday," she said.

Wednesday? Oh yes, that was when we went back to work.

"Mmm. Look forward to seeing you again, then."

She embraced me warmly and then jumped out of the car and ran in to the house, turning briefly to wave.

A week later and I was back at work and back living in my London flat. Jenny had been friendly but discrete while we were at work together, but one afternoon she asked if I could have a drink with her after work. In The Shaftesbury she said that things had come to a head at home. There was no future for her and Terry. They were arguing all the time. She had to get away. She asked if she could come and stay with me until she sorted herself out. This woman doesn't pull her punches, I thought. Always direct. I considered her request. It wasn't only up to me. I had three other flat mates but there was a downstairs spare room.

"I'll ask them this evening. When do you want to move in?"

"Tomorrow," she said.

Why should I have thought otherwise.

She did move in and we had an amazing few weeks together. At first we pretended that nothing had changed and we would leave work separately but she soon dispensed with that artifice and the office came to know that Jenny was now living with me. Her experience, particularly in matters romantic, benefited me considerably, and I looked forward to our nights together. But it didn't last. Her husband met her from work one evening and convinced her that they should have another try at making their marriage work. This did not altogether displease me. Although my flatmates were understanding, having Jenny around distracted me and meant I spent less time with my friends. It was also another mouth to feed though she contributed generously to the housekeeping.

We both knew we were living a sort of dream. In particular, I was heading off to University in Scotland in a few weeks and I became ever more excited about this opportunity and the future that beckoned. At my farewell party at the office, she was a little tearful, and said she wished I wasn't going.

"But, you're back with Terry now. You're making a go of it, aren't you?"

She looked rueful. "I don't know. I don't think he's right for me."

It turned out that she was right. By the time I was next back in London, some months later, she had left Terry again and moved in with another colleague from the office. I later learned that she was a serial offender, but a very seductive one.

The Joint is Jumping

I looked round the table and, as I surveyed my companions, asked myself what the hell I was doing here. There was Grover, a red haired, spotty youth with a strong Black Country accent. I have nothing against red heads, indeed, I think red haired women are extremely attractive, but there is something about young male red heads which screams anger, rawness and dismay as though life has let them down in some way. Then there was Tom Carter-Dixon, a large, cheery soul, a smile almost always on his lips, apparently reading history. I say apparently because I never saw Tom engaged in any study. Indeed, the only reading material I ever saw him with was The Sporting Life. What Tom didn't know about horse racing wasn't worth knowing. Finally, there was Arthur Wimple, a diminutive, fresh faced lad doing economics. I don't mean to be patronising but Wimple looked as though he should still be at school. He probably felt the same way because he was nearly always to be seen carrying a school satchel.

The four of us were seated round a table in Mrs Morrison's dining room, having our evening supper. This consisted of mugs of cocoa and some buttered oatcakes. It was 8.30 in the evening and the expectation seemed to be that we would go to bed after our supper. Bed at 9.00! What was this place, a borstal? What it was, in fact, was digs for my first term at University in the small town of Carnoustie in the county of Angus. Carnoustie was famous for its golf course – which had hosted a number of Open Championships – and little else. In fairness, you could call Carnoustie a dump. Nothing happened there except every ten years when it hosted the Open Golf and everyone became excited at the prospect of Arnold Palmer, Jack Nicklaus and Tom Watson showing their faces.

It seemed like some sort of conspiracy that had landed me in a remote Scottish backwater with three losers as my companions. Grover, his first name was Kevin but everyone called him Grover, just as everyone referred to Wimple as Wimple, was complaining that the cocoa was cold.

'Jesus,' I thought, 'is that the best you can find to moan about?'

"Still, jolly good evening meal, wasn't it?" said Tom.

I couldn't believe my ears. Carter-Dixon had obviously gone to a third-rate public school where he was grateful for anything that resembled food. If he could not just stomach, but regard as 'jolly good', the revolting fatty mutton stew with dumplings and greens we had been served at 5.30, then he could eat anything.

As we finished our sumptuous supper, I asked if anyone fancied going to the pub.

"What pub?" said Grover.

"I don't know," I said, "but I assume a swinging town like this has a pub."

"I think Mrs Morrison expects us to go to bed," said Wimple.

"Well she's got another think coming. As far as I know we're not in a monastery. We have some freedom of action."

I felt a little better at airing my grievances.

"She locks the door at nine o' clock," said Wimple.

Grover nodded. I remembered that they'd already been here a couple of days. I had only arrived quite late the previous night.

"What about a game of cards," said Tom.

Being a gambler, I suspected that Tom was not a good person with whom to play cards, but the lack of enthusiasm for the pub made it the only acceptable suggestion.

"Yes, OK," I said. "What games do you play Grover?"

"Three card brag," responded the young man from Wolverhampton.

"What about you Wimple?"

"Um, well, I don't play cards unless you count clock patience."

Tom looked at him kindly. He was obviously going to be putty in his hands.

"Don't worry Arthur, I'll teach you pontoon. It's the easiest game in the world."

So we played pontoon, with Tom, obviously, as the first banker. Wimple was nervous about playing for money but Carter-Dixon pointed out that there was no point in playing pontoon if money wasn't involved. It was as pointless as fish without chips. Grover said he didn't have any money but that didn't put Tom off.

"That's all right old chap. I'll stand you a stake and you can pay me back tomorrow."

After ten minutes everyone was down except the bank.

"Don't worry, the luck will soon change," said Tom.

At that moment Mrs Morrison came into the room and looked askance.

"Goodness gracious me. Are you boys gambling? Gambling in my house. I can't believe my eyes. This is a Christian house, not a den of iniquity. Gambling is the devil's work and you young men should be ashamed of yourselves."

"I wasn't aware that a game of cards with a few pennies involved was against the law, Mrs Morrison," I said.

"Don't try to be funny with me, young man. While you are in my house you will observe my rules."

She brushed imaginary crumbs off her pinny and took away the empty dishes tossing her head. As she left the room she said:

"I'm locking up now. I think it's bedtime, don't you?"

I made sure she was out of earshot before saying:

"I think we should have a group prayer before retiring, don't you lads?"

I suppose I shouldn't have been surprised when Wimple said:

"Yes, jolly good idea."

A Pressing Engagement

Most remember John's 21st birthday party for the events preceding it when he had a malfunction with his new suit trousers. But I remember it for a scandalous incident at the party itself when I was at the centre of a husband and wife row. I had forgotten about the whole thing until very recently when I encountered a little old lady at a function at my late father's golf club.

"You remember Alice?" said my mother.

There was dim recognition and I mumbled some pleasantries to this chatty, trim, white haired woman. Then, later, as I sat down at the lunch table, surrounded by people even older than I, it all came flooding back.

John worked at Meakers, a men's outfitters, in Bromley on Saturdays and had spied a suit that he thought would set off his handsome figure perfectly for his special party. He had the day off because it was his birthday but nevertheless went into the shop in the morning to buy the suit complete with his staff discount.

A normal person would have been more than happy to be putting on a smart new suit for their party especially when they were the main attraction. John was not normal and decided that the new trousers did not look new and smart enough. In short, they needed a press. The ironing board was put up, a clean tea towel was dampened and the boy who had just achieved his majority began to iron. In the middle of the proceedings the front door bell rang and, as no-one else seemed interested, John was obliged to get the door.

History doesn't relate who the caller was, perhaps a travelling salesman, an evangelist, someone bringing food or flowers for the evening party. Whoever it was should not be held responsible for what happened next but John probably saw things differently. The first thing he must have noticed was a smell of burning. Then, quickly, he saw the iron sitting squarely in the middle of his left trouser leg. He breathed a sigh of relief – it was only the tea towel that was burning. But he was mistaken; the iron had burned right through the tea towel and left a very neat hole, precisely the shape of an iron, in the new trousers. John let out a loud expletive and was close to throwing the iron across the room. The commotion brought my mother from the kitchen.

"Oh dear! Perhaps I can mend it," she said plaintively.

"Don't be bloody ridiculous. They're ruined."

I came in from the garden and tried to keep a smile off my face as I saw what had transpired.

"It's not funny, Harper. I've got nothing to wear now."

I thought of offering him my second best suit but quickly decided against it knowing the ridicule it would elicit. There was absolutely nothing in my wardrobe that would earn anything but scorn. He looked at me.

"Don't even think about offering any of your rags."

My mother surveyed the sorry mess. It was clear that she was still looking at the possibility of salvaging something.

"Yes, you could cut the trousers in two, remove the affected part and then stitch them up again. I'd have one leg a little shorter than the other but I'm sure no-one would notice," said John sarcastically. "No, I'll just have to go to Meakers, speak to old Craddock, and see if he will let me have replacement trousers only."

"That's assuming they have any in the right size," I offered helpfully.

"Oh, thanks Harper. You really are a comfort in difficult times."

John had a habit of calling me by my surname, echoes of school, when he was annoyed. Next thing we heard him roar off in the Morris Minor and hoped that he made it to Bromley and back without any further mishap.

Meanwhile, I was dreaming about the evening. The weather was set fair for the party which was taking place in the large garden of a neighbour. I was home for the vacation from university in Scotland and I was currently unattached. I anticipated that there would be a number of girls there similarly unattached and I was looking forward to playing the field. But there was one person I was particularly keen to see.

Over the summer we'd got to know an older crowd who hung out in the local pub. They were only a few years older but they seemed sophisticated to us. They probably just tolerated us but we had been invited to a couple of their parties. Rather to our surprise the women, most of whom were married, were particularly friendly and I had struck up a good relationship with Alice. A pretty strawberry blonde with a flashing smile, she was married to Rod who was small and unprepossessing and did something in market gardening. Arrogantly, I decided that Rod was not good enough for Alice and she seemed to agree. We tended to end up together chatting at parties or in the pub. Sometimes I managed to hold her during a dance and even sneak a kiss. Rod looked a bit irritated but never said anything.

John returned from Bromley, triumphantly holding up a bag in which was a new pair of trousers. My mother told him that they didn't need pressing. He looked unconvinced but time was against the man who took at least three hours to get ready. And he'd not had his bath or washed his hair yet.

The party is a terrific success. My brother's friends are mostly my friends as well and it is wonderful to see so many familiar faces all enjoying themselves in the warm July evening. The party is centred on the large lawn of the tennis court which has a marquee at one end with a small bandstand beside it. There are quite a number of my parents' friends present and a relaxed feeling is in the air. The drink is flowing and we bop around to a local group called The Hittites who are friends of friends. They actually appeared on Top of the Pops once and had a record in the top twenty. Personally I'm glad when they take a break and we can have the tape that we've made which includes some smoochy stuff.

I've already had a dance with Alice and I can see she is up for a bit of fun. When a slow number starts up I look for her. She readily joins me on the 'floor' and I hug her to me eagerly. We dance for a while, steadily getting more intimate.

"I wouldn't mind a breather," I say. "Shall we step outside?"

We go hand in hand to another, darker part of the garden, by the vegetable plot. By now we are in one another's arms, kissing passionately. Do I stop to consider what I am doing with another man's wife? The answer, unsurprisingly, is that I do not. Alice is gorgeous to kiss and embrace; I am a bit drunk and so is she; we're having a marvellous time.

Suddenly, there is a shout.

"What do you think you are doing?"

It's Rod, sounding very angry.

"Come here woman." He drags Alice away from my clutches.

"You whore!" he bellows, and slaps her across the face.

Alice utters a low cry and holds her face, head down. I realise that people are starting to gather and I recognise some disapproving voices. Rod takes Alice away and an old friend of my mother comes over to me.

"Come on, you. Get back to the party and let's forget about this rumpus."

I feel very bad at what has happened to Alice and a burning hatred of Rod. Why doesn't he pick on someone his own size? But, come to think of it, there are not many his size. I suppose I'm a little too drunk to be disaffected for long and quite soon I'm dancing with a girl called Julia.

During the next few days I was desperate to see Alice. I knew where she lived and I was very tempted to call on her during the day when I knew Rod would be at work. I knew it was a stupid idea but eventually I succumbed. Once I had knocked at the door, I realised what a crazy thing I was doing. What if Rod answered the door – what was I going to say? Apologise, I supposed. It was a relief when Alice opened the door. She looked surprised and smiled nervously.

"Oh, Beast, it's you. Come in but you can't stay."

We went inside. I made to hold her hand but she resisted.

"Look, I'm very fond of you. I might even be more than fond but there's no future in our relationship, is there?"

I looked at her freckled face, large eyes, auburn bob and raspberry mouth. I felt huge desire but also knew that she was right. I was at the start of a university degree in Scotland and given that I had already made a number of sacrifices to fulfil my dream of higher education, the last thing I needed were complications like this.

"I'm sorry Alice. I felt terrible when Rod hit you and called you that name."

"Don't worry. He's not very articulate. He knew something was going on but allowed it to continue too long. He needs me. I couldn't leave him."

We part sadly. I saw her a few times in the pub in the weeks that followed but we only exchanged pleasantries. We realised we were being watched. Then I returned to Scotland and by the time I was back the following Christmas, I was in a new relationship and life for Alice, as far as I could tell, had returned to its familiar routine.

And what of John? I lost count of the number of times the story of the disastrous ironing of the new trousers was told. He enjoyed his party immensely but it always became remembered because of what happened to half his suit. My part in the assault on Alice had been totally forgotten until I saw her at the golf club nearly fifty years later. Before I left the lunch I went over to say goodbye. As I approached her table I could see that she was in animated conversation. When I leaned over and started to speak she got up and faced me. I started to say how smitten I had been with her all those years ago. She placed her hand on my jacket lapel and stroked it.

"I was in love with you."

She went on to say that Rod had died about seven years ago but that she'd married again to a keen golfer, hence her presence at the golf club. We chatted on about people we'd known mutually in those long ago times. But what I really wanted was a chance to be alone with her. To complete the scene that started in a garden on a warm July evening half a century ago? No – hardly a realistic option. But, having awoken a period in my life that had been buried, I wished to know what she thought had happened and how much damage I had wrought. Now, I suppose, I'll never know.

Romance in Ruislip

What was I doing in Ruislip? I pondered this question as I walked down the High Street on the look-out for Downing Road. For some reason, this small town in extinct Middlesex on the west edge of London had always seemed a bit of a joke like East Cheam or Neasden. Anyway, here I was walking down an undistinguished road beginning to think I'd made a dreadful mistake; that, at the very least I was on a fool's errand and possibly something much worse.

It had all started some weeks ago when my cousin's girlfriend had introduced me to a friend of hers at a party in Kensington. Laura was a young opera singer which made her exotic. She was also attractive in a classically English way: tall, honey blond long hair, clear complexion with a delightful figure. I was particularly drawn to the full breasts but there was much else to admire as well.

Inevitably we talked about music and I learned that she had recently graduated from the Royal College of Music and was now a trainee in English National Opera. As a music lover myself, but not in any sense a musician, it was gratifying to converse with someone who was completely steeped in the subject. My knowledge of opera was sparse but she seemed happy to humour me and advised me to see the great 'set-piece' operas with large casts like Aida before they became too expensive to put on. When

I enquired about Elizabeth's personal circumstances she said that she was married. That took the wind out of my sails and I began to lose interest. However, I heard her saying that the marriage was a failure and that she and her husband were having a trial separation. 'Better,' I thought. 'But what possessed a man to leave a woman like this?'

By the end of the evening, the budding opera singer and I were firm friends and I was keen to take things further. She then announced that she would have to leave as Brian, her husband, was picking her up. More cold water thrown over me. What was going on? She seemed so warm and receptive while we were dancing. As she departed she told me to give her a ring; she had written her number in lipstick on a paper napkin. I clutched the precious piece of paper as though it was a large cheque and put it in my inside pocket.

Subsequently, my cousin's girlfriend, Jill, told me a little more about Laura's circumstances. She had married her childhood sweetheart at a tender age and only discovered when it was too late that he was extremely dull and insanely jealous. He couldn't stand the fact that her career inevitably put her into intimate contact with other artists. He became so possessive that her social life became non-existent. When he finally agreed to a trial separation, it was only on the condition that he saw her regularly to keep tabs on her wellbeing. In other words, he was a control freak. He'd got to hear of the party in Chelsea and insisted that he would pick her up and take her home as she would have missed the last train to Ruislip.

"She's given me her telephone number," I told Jill.

"Yes, she likes you. I know she'd love to see you again."

"But what about Brian? I don't fancy running into the jealous husband."

"He doesn't live with her at the moment and anyway, she is often at home during the day and you're free at the moment."

That was true, I was on vacation from university and had a few weeks in the capital before returning north.

A couple of days later I took out the napkin with the scarlet number and dialled it. Imagine my horror when a man's voice answered. I mumbled wrong number and put the phone down.

Well, that's the end of that. A pity because I was really attracted to her. But it was not the end. A few days later Jill rang to ask if I could join them to make up a foursome for dinner at a restaurant in Ealing. Having nothing better to do, I accepted.

I arrived a little late at the venue and the other three were already there. I wondered what my 'date' would be like. I was taken aback to see Laura giving me a dazzling smile and looking sensational in a black dress.

"What a nice surprise," I said uncertainly.

"Well, I hope so. I told Jill not to tell you as I feared you might not come if you knew it was me."

She had discovered that I had rung and been answered by Brian.

"He'd popped in to get some books and happened to be near the phone when it rang. He had no business answering it. I wondered if it might be you and when I talked to Jill she said it was probably you."

We soon resumed where we left off after the party and had a gorgeous evening rounded off by a passionate kiss.

"When are you coming to see me?" she asked.

"Next week?" I suggested.

"Wednesday afternoon would be good. Say 2.30." She had written her address on a piece of paper but not with lipstick.

Thus I found myself looking for 35 Downing Road, Ruislip the following Wednesday afternoon having got a tube from Gloucester Road where I was temporarily lodging with friends. Number 35 was located, a modest 1920s semi, and I walked up the short garden path and rang the bell. What if Brian answered, I asked myself. Have to make some excuse, I suppose. But it was the fragrant Laura who opened the door and admitted me. We hardly had time to exchange pleasantries before we were in a powerful embrace and in no time in the bedroom where she got undressed without any embarrassment. I did the same and we were soon between the sheets. The lovely figure was as good as I hoped it would be and our love making was ardent.

"Would you like a cup of tea?"

I laughed at the banal question after such a glorious experience. She laughed back and got out of bed and I marvelled at the delightful curves. After tea we indulged in some more love-making. She then became sad and I asked her why.

"I won't see you again, will I? You'll go back to Scotland and all the girlfriends you have there and forget about me."

"You can be certain I'll not forget you. But you're right, I am going back to St Andrews next week. I wish we could have more time together. I love being with you."

I'd completely forgotten about her circumstances and her jealous husband. Could I be cited for adultery?

"You need to get out of this relationship, Laura. He's ruining your life. You've got so much to give and you would have no difficulty finding a wonderful man, I'm sure. You must meet some interesting people in your profession."

She looked a little doubtful.

"Brian is very persistent but I know you're right. I just need to be strong and get a divorce."

We parted with a sweet kiss and I said that I would be in touch when I was next in London and I would hope to hear good news from Jill. I also gave her my address.

She did write me one letter but I never saw her again and I don't know what happened to her. I half expected to see her one day on an opera stage but that never materialised either. But I have never been able to hear or see the name Ruislip without an image of a beautiful English rose coming to mind. My fervent wish is that she got rid of Brian and fulfilled herself both artistically and romantically. She deserved it.

The Rent Collector

Long ago, way before Margaret Thatcher decided that it would be a good idea to sell them off, there were many quite pleasant large local authority estates with semi-detached houses having two, three or four bedrooms and small gardens. They were far removed from the sink estates of today and, by and large, the tenants took a pride in their community and avoided litter and graffiti. The local authority also took its responsibilities seriously and kept the streets clean and tidy, mowed grassy areas and maintained the houses properly. Part of the contract was the regular payment of rent.

This was also long before many council house dwellers had a bank account, let alone a system of standing orders or direct debit. The rent was paid weekly, in cash, either at the local authority rent office or collected at the house by the rent collector. Almost all tenants preferred to use the service of the rent collector. Into this delightful world stepped Roger Harper, an undergraduate at an ancient Scottish university, but residing in the vacations in North West Kent. An enquiry at the local labour exchange resulted in an offer of temporary rent collector in one of the local authority's largest estates. This seemed acceptable to Roger and, when he heard what they were paying, he almost bit the hand off the labour exchange functionary.

He was required to bring no special tools or uniform to the job, merely to appear in jacket and tie at the collector's office by 8.30 am the following Monday.

The rent collectors' office was little more than a large prefab, consisting of three rooms. The largest was where the collectors had their desks. Half a dozen men were at these desks, busying themselves, drinking tea, and preparing for the day ahead. On announcing himself, one of the men said:

"Oh, you're the temp are you? A bit young. You need to report to Mr Charles." He was directed to the other room which was opposite a small kitchen area. He knocked on the door and went in to see a grey-haired man with a tired smile.

"You must be Roger. Lesley Charles." He put out his hand. "Welcome to the mad house. Have you ever done anything like this before?"

"No, 'fraid not." he said.

"Not to worry, it won't present any problems to a smart lad like you." He suddenly looked up. "You can do arithmetic I presume?" Roger nodded. "There are accounts to complete at the end of the week."

"Fine, OK," Roger replied not having a real clue what he was talking about.

"I'm going to put you with Terry to learn the ropes. Stick with him this week and you'll learn all there is to learn."

Mr Charles took him back into the main office over to a thickset man with a ruddy complexion, probably in his late forties.

"Terry, this is Roger. I mentioned him to you at the end of last week. I'm putting him with you this week. Show him the ropes will you. And introduce him to the other chaps." With that he disappeared back to his office.

"Hello, my old china," said Terry, shaking hands. "All the boys are going out now so you can meet them this afternoon, when we get back. Come with me."

Terry hoisted a leather satchel over his shoulder with a greasy looking ledger poking out of it. They went out of the back door into a small car park.

"Are we driving?" Roger asked.

"Unless you wanna take the bus," Terry grinned.

They drove in an old Morris Oxford about a mile to the eastern edge of the estate. Before they got out of the car, Terry gave him some instruction.

"There's fwee books you gotta wemember." Terry had difficulty pronouncing his Rs. Rather cruel of his parents to call him Terry, thought Roger.

"The big book, the ledger. We call it the bible." He held up the heavy tome. "And the wepairs book", he produced a much smaller notebook, "where you wite down any wepairs that a tenant wequests. But what is the third book, I hear you asking."

"Oh, yeah, what's the third book?"

"The tenant's went book, of course," said Terry as though speaking to a child. "You 'ave to make sure you enter the date and amount paid and initial it. You've also got to enter the same details in the bible. OK, my old china?"

"Yes, fine," said Roger.

"No, not fine," said Terry. "You've forgotten wather an important fing."

Roger looked at him.

"The bleedin' money, my old china!" Terry laughed as though he had just heard one of Tommy Cooper's funniest jokes. "Make sure you get the wight money and give 'em the wight change if needed."

Roger joined in the laughter as they got out of the car and proceeded to the first house in the road. Terry was a cheerful, if not particularly stimulating, companion, whistling as he went from house to house.

"Morning missus," he would shout as the door was opened, almost invariably by a woman. He rarely had to say what he was there for as his clientele recognised him and knew that Monday, for them, was rent day. He watched Terry take the money, count it, put it in his satchel, with a special compartment for paper money, give change if required, and write down the details in the ledger. Then he would update the tenant's rent book.

"Evweefing all wight, missus?"

Roger took this to mean were there any problems to report concerning the fabric of the property in which case Terry would have to make a note in his repairs booklet.

"Yes, they've mended the gate," said the woman.

"Wighty ho. Bye missus," and Terry whistled down the path to his next tenant.

This procedure continued for the next twenty houses or so, about half way along the road.

"Fancy a cuppa? We'll be OK at this one." Terry patted the side of his nose with his index finger. He rang the bell. A large woman appeared at the door.

"Ello Marge. This is Wodger."

"Come in, then." She bustled into the back to her kitchen. Terry took off his satchel and sat down heavily at a small table.

"Take the weight of your feet, Wodge," he said.

A mug of strong, milky, sweet tea was put in front of him. Apart from being strong, milky, and sweet, it was fine.

"Ave a custard cweam," said Terry, proffering a plate of biscuits.

They must have been there about twenty minutes as he listened to Marge tell Terry about her ne're-do-well son, Roy, as well as gossip about the neighbours. He was suddenly jerked awake from his reverie about the redhead he had met at a party at the weekend.

"Come on, Wodge. Can't sit about here all day. Fanks Marge, don't wowee about Woy. E'll be all wight."

A little later they arrived at a house where they went to the back door. It was open and they walked in.

"Hello Walter. It's only me, Tewee." They went into the front room where a gas fire was on despite it being a warm July day. A bed, which half filled the room, contained an emaciated elderly figure that Roger presumed was Walter. He said something in a quiet voice which was lost on Roger. The old man appeared to have no teeth and this did not aid comprehension.

"Where's Maisie?" asked Terry.

Walter pointed to the ceiling. At that moment, a woman appeared, also elderly but in far better shape than Walter.

"Hello, Terry. Hello young man. I've got the rent in the kitchen."

They went with Maisie to the kitchen and Terry did the necessary admin.

"How is he?" Terry jerked his head in the direction of the front room.

"Won't be long now. The doctor said he should be in hospital but he refuses and I don't blame him. I can look after him and he's happier in his own home."

Roger was struck by her quiet dignity and total lack of self-pity.

"We'll just say goodbye to him then," said Terry.

They all went back into the hot room and Roger was aware of a sickly smell. Terry went over to the bed and took the old man's hand and squeezed it.

"Bye Walter, mate. Mind how you go. See you next week."

They let themselves out of the back door. "Gwand ole feller. You'd never think he was once a stwapping bloke, a fireman, stwong as an ox."

They continued in silence and collected more rent. They started a new street. In the second house, Terry knocked on the door but received no reply. He knocked again.

"Come on Tess, I know you're in there."

Terry went to the back door and knocked again. Eventually, there was the sound of someone coming to the door. A pinched woman, probably younger than she looked, with badly dyed hair and in a dressing gown, looked out angrily.

"What do you want?"

"What do you think?" said Terry mildly.

"I've paid the rent. I went to the housing office."

"Well, it's not in the book," said Terry consulting the bible. "If you'd paid, it would be down here. According to my wecords you owe two weeks."

"Well, I've paid and I ain't got no money in the house, so there."

Terry sighed. "OK, Tess, I'm not gonna argue with you. But I have to tell you that you'll get a notice to quit if you continue to fall behind with your payments. If you don't settle the awears by the end of this week, there's gonna be pwoblems."

Terry made an entry in his book and we left the property. Roger saw that the garden was badly neglected which stood out since tenants generally took care of their little gardens.

The morning continued like this with another stop, this time for sweet, weak, milky coffee which Roger found almost as revolting as the earlier tea. Terry lapped it up.

After collecting another road, Terry said, "Well, that's it for today. Let's get back to the car. It's not far away."

As they strolled along, Terry kept his hand on the satchel which was now quite bulky. A stocky man approached them with a dog. Roger wondered if he was suspicious.

"Hi Terry, how yer doin?"

"Oh, up and down Wedge, like Tower Bwidge." Terry guffawed.

"That's my cousin," said Terry proudly. "He's a gardener. Looks after some of the big gardens in Morewood Park."

Terry drove back to the office and parked the Oxford. When they got into the big office, all the desks seemed to be occupied. Everybody was chomping on their packed lunch. Roger hadn't brought anything.

"You got any lunch, Wodge?" said Terry.

Roger shook his head. "Is there a sandwich bar anywhere nearby?"

"Yeah, on the other side of the main woad. Only five minutes away, but mind how you go. The buggers don't stop for anybody."

When he got back, Roger found that they had made space for him and he actually had his own desk. Terry introduced him.

"This is Wodger." He then went round the room. "This is Smudger." A balding man with glasses nodded. "This is Nobby." A short, fair haired man grinned. "Len". A huge older man grunted at him. "And last, but not least, The Pwof." A medium height figure in a blazer, nodded. "Hello Roger, welcome aboard."

"If you'd like a drink, help yourself in the kitchen," said the man called Smudger. "There are some spare mugs in the cupboard but you may prefer to bring your own mug tomorrow. And membership of the tea/coffee club is two bob a week."

There was a certain amount of good-natured banter between the men over lunch, mostly concerning what they had done over the weekend. Their talk of DIY activities and gardening was of supreme indifference to Roger and he only perked up when Nobby reported seeing a football match at The Valley, Charlton Athletic's ground. Roger had been to The Valley occasionally with his father. When they started talking about their cars, and the various maintenance jobs they'd been doing on them, Roger switched off completely. He vowed to bring a book the next day for the lunch break.

Terry took Roger out for an hour and a half in the afternoon to complete another couple of streets. Back at the office, Roger watched as Terry counted his money, wrote down a figure on a slip of paper and put the lot in a canvas bag. This was tied at the top and then Terry got up and took the bag to Mr Charles's office.

"Come with me, Wodge. You need to see this."

Mr Charles took the sealed bag and placed it in a cupboard in the wall, which Roger realized was a safe. Then he stamped a page in Terry's ledger to confirm that the money had been received.

"Everything OK, Roger? Has Terry showed you the ropes?" asked Mr Charles.

"Yes, fine thank you." He felt he had been properly exposed to the 'wopes' by Terry.

Terry beamed. "I'll take 'im out again tomowow, Les. He's fine."

They returned to the large room where everyone was beginning to pack up. Roger looked at his watch. It was only a quarter past four, fifteen minutes to go.

"It's all wight, Wodge, you can go, now. See you tomowow."

"Yeah, right, thanks Terry. See you tomorrow."

The next day was almost a replica of what had gone before. Again, Terry found places where he could cadge a cup of tea and again he found himself in a house with old people that had a nauseating smell that he could scarcely stomach. And again he learned that Terry was "up and down like Tower Bridge", one of his catch phrases.

At lunch time he now had his own packed lunch and had remembered to bring a mug. He also read a book to while away the time before he went out again. This appeared to amuse the other collectors.

"What's the book, Roger?" asked Smudger.

"Lolita, by the Russian writer Nabokov."

"What you reading that for? That's a mucky book."

"Oh, have you read it?" he asked Smudger.

"No, course not," Smudger replied.

"Well, you ought to, it's a tremendous book."

Smudger shook his head and The Prof laughed. Before he went out in the afternoon, Mr Charles took Roger to one side.

"I want you to go out with Len tomorrow. It will give you a chance to see another part of the estate, on the other side of the railway line."

Len was a more bluff character than Terry. He looked massive behind the wheel of his little Ford Popular as he drove them to the far side of the estate. It seemed that everyone apart from Nobby had a car which seemed almost a requirement of the job. He wondered how he would manage when he was on his own. He had heard it mentioned that Len had been off sick for some time and asked him how he was. Len looked surprised.

"How did you know?" he asked.

"Well, I just heard the guys in the office saying you had been off for a while."

Len said nothing and they proceeded to a part of the estate with which he was unacquainted. He noted that Len was not as familiar with the clients as Terry but he was brisk and efficient. After they had been collecting for the best part of an hour and a half, they arrived at a row of shops. Len went into a little café and Roger followed him.

"I think it's time for some refreshment. What will you have, Roger?"

They enjoyed a decent cup of coffee and a flapjack. Len relaxed a little.

"Yes, I have been off for a while but I haven't been ill. Well, not in the usual sense of the word."

Roger looked at him expectantly.

"I got duffed up on the job. Just near here, actually."

"You were attacked?"

"Yep. It happens sometimes."

"Oh dear. I'm sorry."

Len laughed with little mirth. "Yeah, well the job does carry some risks but they don't tell you that when they interview you."

Roger must have looked worried because Len sought to reassure him.

"It's all right, son. These instances are pretty rare. More likely to happen nearer in to London. Downham estate has a pretty bad record. The worse places are blocks of flats. There are some on this round. I'll show you in a minute. The thing to remember is it ain't your money and if the bastards jump you, just give it to them and you won't get hurt. My problem was that I tried to fight back. That's a bad idea."

Roger digested this along with his flapjack. He tried to pay for his coffee and cake but Len wouldn't let him. They walked to the end of the parade of shops where there was an entrance and stairs to a block of flats, some of which were above the shops.

"The robbers prefer to be in the shadows rather than broad daylight, so watch it in the flats. Try to go in when other people are around."

"Christ," thought Roger, "I need danger money for this job."

Nothing untoward happened and Roger found himself warming to the big man of few words.

"How did you get on with Terry?" he asked as they drove back to the office.

"Oh, fine," said Roger.

"Yeah, he's all right. A bit of a bullshitter, but quite harmless."

When he arrived on Thursday morning, everyone was at their desk with large sheaves of paper in front of them. He was told to sit next to Terry. The last two days of the week were spent doing the accounts and updating repair records. A record of every transaction was listed on the sheets, that is, the name and address of each tenant on the estate, compiled street by street, or more strictly, round by round. The amount paid by each tenant had also to be entered on the sheet, remembering that these were still the days of pounds, shillings and pence. A rent might be £3 – 18s – 4d, and rents varied according to the size of the property and its amenities, and the total of rents had to be summed for each page and entered in the appropriate slot. Totals were carried over so that running totals and eventually a grand total were computed. Not that any computers were involved in those days of pencils and rubbers. Things were only *inked in* when everything had been double checked.

Book-keeping of this nature held no fears for Roger but it was tedious sitting next to Terry as he laboriously entered the information required. Lunch was a more relaxed affair on Thursdays and Fridays and Terry was talking about an incident on his round on the previous day when Roger had been with Len.

"Bleeding hot yesterday, wasn't it? This woman comes to the door with a wubber apwon coverwing her fwont. When she turned back to the kitchen to get the went, do you know what? She was bollock naked!"

"That must have been interesting," the Prof observed dryly. "A case for medical science."

"Cor blimey, gave me quite a turn," said Terry ignoring the Prof.

Roger looked across at Len who gave him a wink.

The following week Roger was entrusted with Terry's round as the latter was on holiday. Smudger gave him a lift to the start of the round and told him he would pick him up at the same spot at 12.15. Because Roger did not avail himself of Terry's tea stops, there was no difficulty in meeting Smudger's timetable. He did go inside and see Walter and nearly wretched at the stench in the old man's temporary bedroom. Although he did not enjoy the experience, he appreciated that Terry was more than the man that collected the rent; he was something of a social worker as well.

All was going well until he did his totting up of the money at the end of the day. He couldn't get the figure to match the total in the ledger.

"Something up, Rodge?" asked Nobby.

"Yeah, I seem to have too much money."

"You wouldn't be three pounds fifteen shillings over by any chance would you?" said Nobby.

"Yes, how did you know?"

Everybody in the room was cackling.

"Because, that's your float, my old son. You haven't taken it off."

The reaction from the old hands indicated that this wasn't the first time this mistake had been made and Roger joined in the laughter at his own expense. When it came to the accounting at the end of the week he didn't have a problem but it didn't stop Smudger and Mr Charles keeping a close eye on him.

Terry was off for two weeks and Roger filled in for him again the following week. Again it went smoothly. He almost found himself having a row with a tenant who harangued him because her gate had fallen off its hinge and she had reported it three weeks ago and no one had been to repair it. He said he would put in another docket but it did not stop the abuse. He was about to say:

"Would you like me to go to Stapleys (the large ironmongers in Orpington) and get a new hinge and put it on for you?" but thought better of it. Sarcasm would not go down well with this lady.

On Thursday he dealt with all the accounting and surprised himself by completing it by 4.00 on the Thursday, a day early.

"Finished!" he shouted triumphantly.

The rest of the room looked up.

"Yeah, I've completed the sheets," he grinned.

There was silence in the room.

"No, Roger. You haven't finished," said Smudger.

"Yes, I have." He held up the last sheet to show them.

"Listen to me, Roger. I said you haven't finished and that's that. The accounts take two days to complete and so you can't have finished them in one day. It's not possible. So you better go through it all again tomorrow."

Roger sensed the hostility in the room and so he didn't dispute Smudger's logic. It was apparent that a form of Parkinson's law was in operation here and the men were determined to ensure that if accounts were assigned two days, then the procedure would take two days. They clearly enjoyed their sedentary two days in the office. It was safe, warm, and away from the elements and danger. They certainly weren't going to have some clever Dick from university telling them what the appropriate time was for the work.

After work, while he was waiting at the bus stop a car stopped. When the window was wound down he realised it was The Prof offering him a lift. He got in.

"I can take you to Green Street Green if that's any help."

"Thanks, that would be good."

He asked the older man why he was called The Prof.

"Well, it's ridiculous, I know, but it's because I am perceived to use long words and I speak something a little closer to Received Pronunciation than the other chaps."

"Did you have a life before rent collecting?" Roger asked.

"Oh yes. I was a history teacher in a secondary modern school. It got me down I'm afraid. Don't misunderstand me, teaching is a noble profession but when you come up against stubborn resistance to being exposed to knowledge you begin to wonder why you are there."

"But does this job satisfy your own intellectual needs?" Roger asked.

The Prof laughed. "I had a bit of a break-down in my old job. I needed to move away from anything challenging. Rent collecting fits the bill fine, at present. But I am always on the lookout for something that befits my *intellectual* status, as you put it. I'm friendly with someone in the education department of the local authority and he is looking out for a suitable post." He smiled. "But you are right, Roger. The likes of rent collecting is not a suitable long term activity for the likes of you and me. Incidentally, don't worry about what happened today. They get scared stiff when they think someone is rocking the boat. We know, and I suspect they do too, that you don't need two days to do the housekeeping but they would fight tooth and nail at any suggestion that it could be reduced."

Roger was now into his final week of this temporary work. He was covering for Nobby and Terry gave him a lift to the start of the round. Driving rain was coming in from the west and Roger began to see some of the downsides of the job. He was fighting a losing battle as he tried to keep himself, his satchel and the ledger dry. He got back to the office, saturated and bedraggled, to find Mr Charles, who he now had to call Les, looking concerned.

"Did the police find you?" he asked.

Roger looked at him, fearing some tragedy was about to unfold.

"No, why?"

"The police have been touring the estate with loud hailers, calling out your name."

Infuriatingly, the man was not telling him why the police were looking for him.

"Les, what do they want?"

Les must have seen the worry in his face.

"Sorry. You should have been in court this morning to answer a charge of leaving the scene of an accident without reporting it."

"Oh that. I wrote pleading guilty to the charge and so I didn't think I would have to appear."

"They told me that this was the second time you had failed to make an appearance. I think you may be in trouble. They left this letter for you."

The incident happened during the Easter vacation when he was again down from Scotland. He had contacted his old girlfriend Penny to see if she would like to meet up for a drink. The last time he had seen her at New Year, they had one of their innumerable arguments. They seemed constantly unable to be together without finding issues to bicker about. After some days of this they agreed that they weren't suited and would finish the relationship. But as soon as they did this, they would miss one another and find an excuse to resume the affair. But with Roger away in Scotland, the prolonged break gave them an opportunity to discover if they really couldn't do without one another.

Penny agreed to come for a drink and they had a pleasant time in a pub near Purley. As he was exiting from his parking place, Roger felt a slight bump and realised that he had hit the car in front.

"Shit. I've caught that car. I'd better get out and see what the damage is."

He went to the front of his car and found no damage. He looked at the front of the car he had touched and again an inspection revealed no damage. Although it was dark the street lighting was efficient and so he was pretty confident he could drive off safe in the knowledge that nothing untoward had happened. A month later a letter from Surrey police was forwarded to him in Dundee charging him with the offence of leaving the scene of an accident without reporting it to the police. Moreover, he was ordered to appear in Wallington Magistrates Court on May 10th. The thought of going back home, not to mention the expense, to face a charge which, technically, he was guilty of, did not appeal to him. He wrote a letter to the Magistrate's Clerk pleading guilty and forgot all about it.

Another letter was sent to him which he never received. This repeated the order to appear in court to face the charge. When he did not appear for a second time, the magistrate issued orders for the police to arrest this dangerous criminal and bring him to the court forthwith. Roger was probably taking shelter in a café from the rain since he never heard the police sirens and loudspeakers going. He decided that the farce had gone on long enough and rang the number on the letter the police had left with Les. It connected him with the Clerk of Court. He explained what had happened and why he did not think he was guilty of the crime since he had stopped and examined the vehicle that he had collided with. But technically he supposed he was guilty of an offence and therefore had pleaded guilty. Much to his surprise the Clerk said:

"Mr Harper, I think you should defend yourself against this charge since you have a reasonable defence to offer."

"But I reside in Dundee for much of the year and I can't afford to attend court in Surrey in term time."

"Well, you're not in a position to tell the court when it should sit. However, I will schedule a new hearing at a time when you are resident in the south, that is, during your Christmas vacation. In the mean time I will arrange for the police to visit you and take a full statement."

Roger finished his final week at the rent collecting office having now become an infamous celebrity. Everybody seemed to know that police cars – it had now become more than one car – had been touring the estate looking for this fugitive from the law.

"You can't hide forever, you know," said Len. "The police always get their man."

"Where you gonna wun to, Scotland?" asked Terry. "I'll keep mum if you make it worth my while."

At the end of the week, they went to the pub for lunch, and drank a toast to his future. They were sure he was going to become a famous shrink. He was touched when he learned that they had clubbed together to buy what for him was the perfect leaving present, a book token.

"I promise not to buy another Nabokov," he said.

Some weeks later, back in Dundee, he got a letter with a police insignia on the envelope. It informed him that the police would be visiting him in two weeks' time in Dundee to take a statement about the incident that had occurred earlier in the year. He presumed that he would get a visit from a local constable and was astonished when two uniformed police turned up at his house in Dundee having travelled all the way from Croydon. He learned that they had come up the previous day and had a night in a hotel in Edinburgh. They would have another night there on the return journey making a total absence of three days. Why two men had come was unclear and the overall expense involved, including travel, hotel, and sustenance did not bear thinking about. This didn't take into account the two missing court appearances and the cost of sending a police car to seek and arrest him. Nevertheless, he reflected, there was something to be said for British justice.

He next received a phone call from the Clerk of Court reiterating that he had a reasonable defence against the charge he faced. When he asked the Clerk about the cost of engaging a defence counsel, the Clerk advised him against that.

"You could end up paying a lot of money. No, this is only a magistrate's court. Defend yourself. Have you got any witnesses?"

When he was back in the south and the date of the hearing was looming, Roger realised that he had not done anything about getting a witness. Of course, there was only one possible witness and that was Penny. He hadn't seen or heard from Penny in months. Eventually, he rang her up and explained what he wanted of her. She was gracious and agreed to meet him for a drink at the same pub.

As soon as he saw her again he was immediately smitten but knew that he must try to keep this 'professional'. They went through the incident and Penny's recollection was exactly as he had outlined in his statement. She reminded him that she had got out of the car and looked at the effects of the impact with him and they had both concluded that, since there was no damage, there was no need to leave a name and address. Penny, who was now an aspiring actress, began to look forward to an appearance in court.

Roger's father came with him on the day of the court appearance. They picked up Penny, who was 'resting' and therefore did not need to take time off work, and they arrived in court in good time – for a change. The clerk to the magistrates explained what would happen. The police would first make the case for the prosecution and call any witnesses they had. Roger would have the opportunity to question the police and witnesses. He would then present his defence and call any witnesses on his behalf. Roger was told to sit at a table in front of the magistrates' bench.

When the police made their case, it became clear that they had only become aware of the incident because someone walking through the adjacent church yard had seen the entire event. Behaving like an amateur sleuth, this person had taken out his diary and written down a description of the car and the registration number. He had then torn out a page of his diary and written down the same number and brief details of what had happened together with his own name, address and telephone number, and placed it under the windscreen wiper of the victim's car.

Very public spirited, thought Roger. The police then went through the litany of Roger's failure to appear at earlier hearings, the wild goose chase round the St Paul's Estate, and the visit to Dundee. Roger's statement was then read out by one of the policemen he had seen in Scotland. He was an amiable soul and Roger felt like nodding and smiling to him but thought better of it.

The police witness was now called. Stanley Flood was a nervous, middle aged man in a grey suit who was asked by the magistrate to say what he had seen on the night of March 28th in the road outside The Jolly Wagoners public house. In a halting way he recounted the event as he had seen it and was thanked by the magistrate. The chair of the magistrates asked if Roger had any questions of the witness. Roger stood up.

"Mr Flood, did you see me get out of the car after the collision?"

"Yes."

"And did you see me examine the effects of the collision on my own car and the car that I had hit."

Flood replied affirmatively again.

"And did you see my passenger also get out of the car and inspect the two cars?"

"Yes" said Mr Flood once more.

"When you got to the scene, did you see any damage to the car that I had touched?"

"Well, I'm not sure."

"Please answer the question directly Mr Flood," said the chair of the magistrates.

"No, I didn't see any damage."

"Thank you," said Roger. "No further questions." He was beginning to enjoy the role of Perry Mason and was running the risk of irritating the magistrates.

Roger was now asked to present his own version of events. He said that he did not dispute the statement that had been read out by the police. He did not deny that a slight collision had occurred on the night in question but he did deny that he had left the scene of an accident without taking appropriate action. He asked for Miss Penny James to be called as a witness.

Penny went into the witness box looking stunning in a blue dress and navy jacket. Like the young actress she was hoping to be, she looked poised and yet convincing. The chair of the magistrate tried, quite unnecessarily, to put her at ease.

Roger asked her if she had got out of the car following the bump to ascertain any damage for herself. She assented to this and Roger asked if she had seen any damage.

"Yes. One of the headlights on your car was broken."

"And was there any damage on the other car?"

"None that I could see."

It became clear that the chairman of the magistrates did not want Penny to leave the witness box and he asked for some clarification which seemed quite irrelevant. Eventually she was told to stand down.

Roger summed up his defence.

"I don't deny that I collided with a stationary blue Vauxhall Victor on the evening and place in question. However, as Mr Flood and Miss James both attest, I didn't leave the scene of the accident without checking to see what damage had been caused. And, furthermore, a careful inspection revealed that the only damage sustained was to my own car. The two witnesses, Miss James and the witness for the prosecution, Mr Flood, have corroborated this. For this reason I thought it unnecessary to leave a note with my name and address on the windscreen of the Vauxhall. I also thought it would be a waste of police time to call in to a police station to report an accident where there had been no victim other than myself and that very minor."

Roger finished by saying, "I regret that rather a lot of time and trouble has been caused to the police and others by this rather trivial incident. Although technically I am the cause of this excessive attention, my original intention and action was precisely to avoid such a brouhaha."

As he sat down to what, in his head, was ecstatic applause, he thought he had gone a little over the top with 'brouhaha'.

The magistrates now conferred for a few minutes while Roger smiled across at Penny who was sitting with his father. The chair of the magistrates called for quiet.

"We dismiss the case against Roger Harper of failing to stop and report an accident. We note that the complainant, Bruce Canning, owner of a Vauxhall Victor, registration BLT 809, has made a claim against Mr Harper's insurance company of £178. In the circumstances this seems unduly excessive and we instruct Mr Canning and his Eagle Star insurance to reconsider this claim."

Over a cup of coffee in an adjacent cafe, Roger basked in his triumph with his father and friend.

"It was Penny that did it," said his father. "She had that magistrate eating out of her hand." Penny beamed.

"Yes, she was great but I thought my arguments were rather telling," said Roger.

Just then Mr Flood came into the cafe. He looked uncertain when he saw Roger and his party but came over to them.

"Look, I'm awfully sorry. I didn't mean to get anybody into trouble. I was just trying to do my duty as a citizen."

"That's OK, old boy, don't give it another thought," said Roger.

Penny leaned across, put her hand on his sleeve and in her most disarming voice said:

"Please don't worry Mr Flood. We know that you didn't mean any harm."

Later, they took Penny back to her parents' house. Roger got out of his father's car to take her to the front door.

"Look, Penny, thanks a million. You were wonderful today; I so appreciate it. Perhaps we can get together soon?"

She looked at him coolly. "I don't know, Roger. Perhaps."

It's More Than Black and White

"It's a beautiful country spoilt by the regime that runs it."

This was the verdict of Frank, the man who was giving me a lift from Jan Smuts Airport, Johannesburg, to Durban. Since the journey took about six hours there was plenty of time to interrogate Frank about the place. Ever since I had learnt that my application to a charitable organisation to spend the summer vacation in South Africa had been successful, I began to question the wisdom of this decision. Why would a woolly liberal like me want to visit a country notorious for its illiberal stance on human rights?

"How do you see it panning out?" I asked Frank.

"What do you mean?"

"Well, the regime you mentioned is very much a minority, isn't it? I think I read that nonwhites outnumber them by twelve to one. How long can they oppress the majority?"

"That's a difficult question. The state machinery is so powerful that opposition is not tolerated. You probably know that all the important guys are on Robben Island or under house arrest."

"So you're pessimistic?"

"Right now, it's hard to see this thing ending without bloodshed. When you reach the point where you think you've nothing to lose, you put your neck on the line."

"But isn't South Africa practically a pariah state? Once UN sanctions start to bite won't they change their tune?"

Frank shook his head and was silent for a while. I looked out of the window. By now it was completely dark.

"Look at these poor buggers." Frank pointed out some figures huddling by the side of the road that were caught by the headlights. "Under the blanket we call it. That means they live with little more than what they stand up in trying to survive. They'd be better off in a township but there aren't any round here."

It was one in the morning by the time we reached my destination, a pleasant house on the coast north of Durban. My brother was a lodger with a colleague in his company but this arrangement had to come to an end with my arrival since there wasn't room for two lodgers. We had a few days to find alternative accommodation which didn't prove easy. Eventually, since accommodation for two was only needed for three months, we decided to move into a small residential hotel which was mainly populated by students. We could rent a double room at a price we could afford, as long as I could pick up some work. Meanwhile, we enjoyed the last couple of days at the posh house. My brother came down to breakfast on the second morning to find me making toast and tea and boiling an egg.

"What are you doing?"

"What does it look like?"

"Why isn't Chemist doing that?" Chemist was the name of the black servant.

"I told him that I could do it," I said "so that he could get on with something else."

"You mustn't do that," said my brother. "Fixing breakfast is his job."

It hadn't taken me long to be sensitive to the way that my brother's colleague and my brother himself spoke to the black Africans. It was a curt, unfriendly tone. On the few occasions that I found myself alone with Chemist or one of the gardeners,

I would try to engage them in conversation and generally behave in a congenial fashion. After all I was interested in them and their viewpoints. My brother had noticed this.

"It's a waste of time. They don't want you to treat them on equal terms. I tried it when I arrived, being friendly and trying to chat. They were completely resistant to it, really uncomfortable. And I got a bollocking from Bob. He didn't want me making life difficult with the servants." Bob was the owner of the house.

"There are white people here who do have a more egalitarian relationship with their servants but they tend to be shunned by other whites. If you are indiscrete with the blacks you can get into real trouble."

My brother's words came as a shock to the woolly liberal. Despite knowing that I'd entered a very different society, when the realities of daily life revealed themselves so crudely the effect was depressing. I had expected to be disturbed by the general conditions of the black populations but I hadn't been prepared for the way in which it would impinge on the behaviour of the white minority. In curtailing the Blacks' freedoms, you were also inhibiting the affluent and powerful Whites.

The Merlin Hotel was a weird place. It was run by a pair of skinflints called Adrian and Pamela. They affected old world charm but it was of an extremely faded sort and when they observed that you were unconvinced by it, they tended to drop pretences. Our room, on the first floor of the annex, was basic but adequate with hard beds, thin mattresses and scratchy blankets. The bathroom, shared with four other residents, was no more than satisfactory. Getting bed linen and towels changed almost always meant a battle with Pamela. If you tried to by-pass Pamela and talk to Adrian, it got you nowhere.

"Sorry, old boy. Not my pigeon, that's Pam's department."

But compared to the board, this was a minor problem. They insisted that residents took their meals as part of the package even though it soon became evident that it would have been better to have eaten elsewhere. But we, like nearly all the other inmates, couldn't afford to pay for meals and then not eat them. So, watery soup, small portions of gristly meat, overcooked vegetables and sparse salads became staple parts of our diet. Both my brother and I were lucky in that he got decent lunches in his company canteen and I was fed at the hotel where I subsequently worked. Most of our student fellow inmates were not so fortunate.

The saving grace of The Merlin was the people we lived with, some of whom became good friends. Most of them were students and this was congenial for me since that was also my status. Conversation was lively and on our limited budgets we managed to have a reasonable social life. But there was a serious issue which became apparent during one of our conversations over a few late-night beers in one of the rooms.

"But who is it?" said Karin, a second year history student.

"I've narrowed it down to three," said Gerry, also a history student.

"What are you talking about?" I said.

"The informer," said Gerry.

Robin, a gay performing arts student, was sceptical.

"I really don't know what your evidence is for this informer idea."

"Look man," said Gerry, "this place is just the sort of target for special branch informers. We know there are some activists here and The Merlin has a record for this sort of thing."

"What do you mean?" I said.

"Last year there was a police raid on this place and two students were removed in the middle of the night."

"What happened to them?" my brother asked.

"Good question," said Gerry. "One of them got badly beaten and from what I've heard he is still in a bad way – lost all his confidence. No one seems to know what has happened to the other guy."

Robin sashayed to the other side of the room to get another beer. He was always breaking into dance steps.

"Well, even if there've been problems in the past, that doesn't mean there is anyone suspicious at the moment."

"Robin," said another student called Vanessa, "get real. This country is crawling with informers and they put them in places where they know they can do some damage such as in universities and university residences. You're just too caught up in your music and dance to notice such things."

Robin gave her a high kick by way of a response. Vanessa, Karin and Gerry then went through the people that could possibly be informing, including Adrian and Pamela. When everyone had gone, my brother and I reflected on what we'd heard. This was a new world to me and to my brother who, though he had been in the country for six months, had not mixed in these circles before. It seemed incredible that what was virtually a hostel for students and young people should be regarded as a place where special branch kept an active watch for subversives. But once such a seed had been sown, it was impossible to uproot. From then on we began to look on our fellow residents in a new light though we had no reason to think that any of our immediate friends was suspicious.

Though life was otherwise good in Durban, I was running out of funds and desperately in need of work. The charitable organisation under whose auspices I had travelled were supposed to help with finding work but that was conditional on staying in the Transvaal. What I quickly learned was that all the sorts of jobs typically open to students at home were not available here. All manual jobs were done by cheap black labour and the only jobs that appeared in the paper were for taxi drivers to work at night which I didn't fancy. One day as I passed the race track, which was in the middle of town, a group of horses rounded a corner and I pondered putting my remaining money on a horse. At this moment, a voice hailed me. It was a friend of my family who lived out here. I had seen them once or twice since my arrival but when I realised that we had little in common and their politics were repugnant, I made little effort to keep in touch. Reg was sitting in a bar.

"How you doing, Roger? Have a beer."

I accepted his invitation. He enquired if I had had any joy in getting a job and I confessed that nothing had turned up. He reminded me that he had pointed out that it would be difficult for a visitor to get temporary work which was very helpful. But then he made a more useful suggestion. He offered work at the hotel which he managed for his wife's brother-in-law, the wealthy owner of a chain of hotels in South Africa. He said he had been discussing it with his wife Maggie and they thought they could offer me some work as a receptionist. He suggested I call by at the hotel at ten o clock the following morning.

I turned up at the appointed hour looking as smart as I could. Maggie and Reg gave me a perfunctory interview in their small office and then looked at one another.

"Yes, I think we can turn you into a sort of receptionist," said Reg, "but you'll have to smarten up. Fortunately, we provide a jacket and tie."

Ignoring his condescending manner, I thanked them. I was really very grateful. Even though it was shift work, either 6am – 2pm or 2pm to 10pm, it was straightforward work in pleasant surroundings and would provide enough money to live on.

Apart from the slightly antisocial hours it was a cushy job. I was hardly anything more than the assistant receptionist and most of the time I had the manager, Maggie, or Christine the proper receptionist with me. I was pretty much a spare part. Adjacent to the desk was the switchboard, manned by one of two Indians, John, the older, or Kumar, the younger. Durban had a very large Indian population and it was here that Ghandi lived for twenty years before the First World War. Relations between the Indians and the Zulus, the local African people, were generally strained and occasionally boiled over. This was said to be due to the commercial exploitation of the black Africans by the Indians who dominated the retail outlets. There had been more than one bloody riot when Zulus marched into Durban ransacking shops in the Indian quarter, pangas at the ready, and massacring any Indian who was unfortunate enough to resist.

John was in his forties, quiet, respectful but happy to talk to me unlike my other experience with non-whites. Sometimes in the evenings we were the only people on reception and if it was quiet we would chat. I learned that he felt very fortunate to have the job of chief switchboard operator at the Criterion Hotel since it provided for his wife and two children. In contrast to John, Kumar was a bubbly youngster, always smiling and playing jokes though careful not to antagonise Maggie or Reg. He knew that he could get away with being cheeky with me and even Christine but it was more than his job was worth to upset the bosses.

My relationship with the bosses was cordial and clearly, like John, I felt fortunate to get a job, particularly a temporary job. It was apparent that they had really created a position for me – reception would not suffer when I moved on – and I had reason to be grateful that my mother had an old and close school friend in this part of South Africa. I soon realised, however, that my liberal views with respect to the country and its politics were not shared by Reg and Maggie.

During my first week in Durban I had contacted them to pass on my mother's greetings and they had invited me round for dinner. My brother was also invited but he declined saying he had a prior engagement. Their smart flat was a contrast to the shabby rooms of The Merlin and I was made very welcome. But only as long as I did not stray into local politics. When asked the standard, charged question: 'So, what do you think of our magnificent country?' I made appropriate noises about the physical beauty of the place and the wonderful climate. I also commented on my fascination with the different cultures, saying how fortunate to have the indigenous African and Indian peoples alongside the Dutch and British. It did not seem to have occurred to them that this might be interesting.

"They're a shiftless bunch," said Reg. "Without us they would still be living in the dark ages."

Remembering the 'blanket people' that Frank had pointed out on the way south from Jo'burg, I reflected that 'with us' they were pretty much in the dark ages.

"Maybe," I said, "but I still think you have a wonderfully colourful community here."

No pun was intended but Reg sniggered. In the conversation over dinner, I listened as these comfortable, middle-class whites complained about the constant battle they had to get their 'native' staff in the hotel to do a decent day's work. When they emigrated from England in the late 1950s Reg had had a fairly lowly job as a blue collar GPO engineer or something like that. Thanks to his brother-in-law's successful hotel business, he and Maggie had done well in Durban. Neither of them seemed to realise, however, that they enjoyed a lifestyle in South Africa, including servants, way above anything they could have experienced in Essex, thanks to the exploitation of the non-white population. One of the depressing things about those who had lived in modest circumstances in Britain was that they enjoyed the feeling of superiority they had over the indigenous population. They might have been relatively poor in the old country but that was soon forgotten with no feelings of empathy with the deprived in their new country.

I was reminded of this the next day in the hotel. An African bellboy appeared in the lobby and seemed to upset Maggie who was behind reception with me.

"You're late, Joseph."

"Sorry Madam," he responded softly.

"I don't want sorry. Why are you late?"

He was silent and stared at the floor.

"I'm waiting Joseph," Maggie persisted.

"My father died Madam. I had to go to the undertakers this morning."

"Oh, well I'm sorry to hear that. Couldn't your mother have gone to the undertakers?"

"No Madam, she is not well and she has three children to look after."

"OK Joseph. But smarten yourself up. Why haven't you shaved?"

Again, the young man looked uncomfortable. "It's our custom Madam. We do not shave for ten days after the death of the father."

"All right, run along, but do your buttons up," Maggie said irritably.

One evening I was working the late shift and finished at 10.00pm.

"Goodnight, John," I said to the telephone operator who was shutting down his board.

"'G'night Moses," I said to the night porter as I left through the side door.

I walked to the bus stop which was only about a hundred yards away. Within ten minutes a single decker bus appeared and I got on and sat about halfway back. Suddenly I spotted John getting on the bus and coming towards me. This was a surprise as I'd not seen him join the queue.

"Hi John," I said, moving over so that he could sit next to me.

John ignored me and continued past me to the back of the bus. I was shocked and hurt. Only half an hour ago we'd been laughing and joking about a client who had come to reception to complain about the softness of his mattress. I tried to explain that I was not in any position to do anything about it at 9.30 at night since the chamber maids were all off duty.

"Can't you do something, man," he said.

"Sorry sir, I do not have access to spare beds or mattresses. But I will make a note of your complaint and make sure that it is handled first thing in the morning."

Mr Katzenellenbogen shook his head and went away muttering.

"I wouldn't say no to one of those beds," said John ruefully. "'What's the man complaining for?"

"Clients think that is their right," I said. "'When you are paying for accommodation, especially in a four-star hotel, part of the enjoyment for many people is keeping the staff up to scratch by a steady stream of complaints. I think it makes them feel important. In fact I think this approach is endemic in South Africa where one group, the whites, behaves towards the other group, the non-whites, in a superior, condescending not to say domineering manner."

I realised that I'd gone off on a bit of a rant and I looked at John to see if I had upset him. On the contrary, he was stifling a chuckle as he busied himself on his switchboard. The late shifts allowed this sort of banter as the managers were rarely around and we could therefore relax a bit. It was therefore particularly upsetting to be ignored by John as he passed me on the bus. I told my brother the story when I got back to The Merlin.

"If it was a single decker bus then he would have to sit at the back with the other non-whites. Normally the blacks have their own buses but on some routes there is sharing where the blacks either have to go upstairs or at the back of the bus."

"Christ, what a country," I said.

"Yep," said my brother, "let's go and have a drink."

At the end of the week our practice was to find a nice bar and enjoy the fruits of our labour. Sometimes we got invited to a party. Having got pretty legless one Friday, we found ourselves in a dive with what seemed to be mostly women. My brother got upset when a couple of women refused to dance with him. They preferred to dance with one another which seemed to particularly irritate him. Meanwhile I was entrapped with an older woman. My brother came over and said:

"What are you doing with this old slag, Roger?" I tried to brush him off but he was pulling me away. A bouncer was looking at us darkly and I realised it was time to go.

My brother, who was completely paralytic, somehow got into his red Mini and drove us away at high speed. It is not clear how we got back to The Merlin without incident. I got out but my brother had fallen asleep at the wheel. I left him and bumped into a couple of girls we knew in the hotel.

"Where's Andy?"

''In his car, asleep."

The girls went down to the car and tried to get him out but also without success. Next morning, he was not in the other bed in the room. I got dressed and went outside and noticed for the first time that he had not actually made the car park last night but had run into a hedge that bordered the parking area. The back end of the car was sticking out like a wounded animal. Andy was still fast asleep but by now the sun was well up and it was starting to get hot. I got the driver's door open and shook him.

"What the hell…"

"Come on mate. Get out of there and come up and have a shower." He complied like a chastened dog.

We were due at a wedding at 1.00pm. It was a Tamil wedding to which I had been invited by Kumar, the assistant telephone operator at the Criterion Hotel. I was invited to bring my brother and accordingly we presented ourselves at the venue soon after 1.00pm. There seemed to be hundreds of people there but few, if any, other whites. I had been told that it was considered an accolade to have white people at an Indian wedding. We were made very welcome but felt strange. It was not clear whether the wedding ceremony had taken place or not. People were milling about all over what seemed to be a park. Dozens of outdoor tables were covered in mysterious food and we were encouraged to help ourselves and then sit on benches provided. It was all a bit hopeless. We didn't understand a word of what was going on even though the guests constantly smiled at us. The food didn't agree with our churning stomachs, still abused from the previous night, and our heads throbbed in the burning heat.

"When is it decent to leave?" I asked my brother.

"God knows," he said, "but I've had enough. Come on, let's get out of here."

I found Kumar and made our excuses. He looked amazed. "Mr Roger, the wedding has only just begun. We will be going on for many hours well into the night."

"Sorry," I said, "my brother is not very well and I must take him home."

Whether or not Kumar believed this story I didn't really care. We made our way out past the colourful saris and the smart dark suits.

"That'll teach them to invite white men," said my brother ungraciously.

In a town centre bar one evening with some girls from The Merlin we got chatting with a chap who turned out to be from a visiting Royal Navy submarine. We got on well and by the end of the evening had arranged to meet up again the following day, Saturday. However, he was duty officer aboard HMS Ambush for that day and so invited us to be his guests aboard ship.

"Bring the girls," was the last thing he said.

Next afternoon, about five o' clock we were down in the docks looking for Ambush. It was not too difficult as it was the only Royal Navy sub in port. Because of the closure of the Suez Canal due to the Israeli – Arab Six Days War, all vessels had to round the Cape of Good Hope to get from the East to Europe and the Americas.

A sailor met us at the gangplank and asked us to wait while he found our friend Jamie. This time Jamie was in uniform and impressed the girls with his dashing looks.

"Good to see you," he said, "come aboard."

He showed us to the wardroom and got us some drinks. After we'd had a couple of naval stiff ones Jamie offered to show us round the ship. This was an eye-opener to one who had not seen close up the compressed circumstances in which forty odd men lived for weeks on end. We returned to the wardroom and continued drinking. All was going well though I realised that we were starting to make quite a lot of noise. At some point there was a bit of a kerfuffle and I realised that another officer had entered the mess. He seemed to be annoyed with Jamie about something and was told to 'fuck off' by Jamie.

"Who was that?" I said.

"The first mate," said Jamie. "I'm in trouble."

And he was. Jamie was confined to the ship for the next two days and only allowed off on the last evening in port when we were able to get together for a final drink in a Durban bar. We expressed commiserations about his punishment and hoped we weren't to blame.

"No, of course not. My fault. I usually get on OK with the first mate but he only told me to keep the noise down and I went too far. Doesn't do to tell your superior officer to eff off."

That was the last we saw of Jamie and I often wondered how his naval career progressed from there. My impression was that he was not cut out for a life of taking and giving orders but I will never know.

I sometimes worked at weekends which meant that I got a day off during the week. I'd expressed an interest in visiting Zululand and Reg, the manager, offered to lend me his car so that I could see it properly. This was a generous offer even though I had to endure Reg's insufferably smug manner as he handed me the keys to the car.

"You know how to drive one of these?" He pointed proudly to his Singer Gazelle.

"Sure," I said. My own car was a Morris Minor but I had sometimes driven my Dad's Vauxhall Victor and so the Singer held no terrors.

I set off north to Zululand with only a superficial map to guide me. I was excited because the Zulus intrigued me. The previous weekend there had been a gathering of Zulu dancers in Durban taking part in a sort of competition. The teams or 'impis' of warriors were a formidable sight as they advanced in formation wearing grass skirts, holding shields and spears and stamping the ground so that it literally shook. The leader of each impi blew on a referee's whistle which signalled switches in their advance. It didn't take much imagination to realise what a terrifying enemy they must have been in the field especially as Zulu bravery was legendary.

Gradually I got into the Zulu homelands where the populations still lived in grass mud huts and the women walked around bare breasted. It was surprising to see this old tribal life style only thirty miles away from the sophisticated twentieth century city of Durban. In the heat of the afternoon I arrived in Groutville where, a few days earlier, the funeral of Albert Luthuli, President of the African National Congress, had taken place. Luthuli was a world-famous politician having won the Nobel Peace Prize in 1961. He had been a banned person for much of his life and was under house arrest when visited by Senator Robert Kennedy in the previous year, 1966. Luthuli had been killed by a train while crossing a bridge, probably an accident though some claimed his death was suspicious.

It may have been the middle of the Zululand winter but it was hot as I got out of the car and approached the church where Luthuli was buried. I went into the church which was empty. There were notices printed on white cards. One said 'Whites Only' and another 'Slegs Blankes', the same notice in Afrikaans. It was horrifying to think that even at this distinguished man's funeral, the brutal rule of apartheid held sway. On the floor, near the altar, were a number of spent flash bulbs presumably left by press photographers. I went outside and found the fresh grave covered with flowers that were already dusty. He had only been buried a few days ago, at a funeral attended by 10,000, yet already he seemed forgotten. I was quite alone as I gazed at the messages on some of the wreaths.

I got back in the car and started to head back to Durban. But I wasn't sure of the route and mostly drove on dirt tracks hoping that I was heading in the right direction. I noticed that I was getting low on petrol. I hadn't seen a single petrol station while in the tribal lands. I hardly saw another car. I wondered about asking a local for directions to a petrol station. But suddenly the locals didn't look friendly and I wasn't sure if they spoke English. My imagination started to work overtime and it occurred to me that there was absolutely no reason for the natives to be friendly. Wouldn't they be just as happy to dispose of a hated white if it could be done without anyone knowing? Fortunately, this notion wasn't put to the test since, just when I was beginning to despair of getting petrol and the gauge was nearing empty, I came across a single pump. I pulled in and was relieved to find that it worked and so I was rescued.

Life continued at The Merlin, the appalling meals and the Spartan rooms. But we had ways of amusing ourselves. We played cards, listened to music and continued to speculate about who the informers might be. Robin, the aspiring dancer, would play Stravinsky's Pulcinella endlessly and often demonstrate some of his steps. Vanessa, an arts student with a penchant for heavy make-up, was always on the look-out for new experiences. One evening she announced that she had been told that if you smoked banana skins you would have a mystical experience not unlike that provided by mescaline. We were dubious about this even if we'd known how to smoke a banana skin. Nothing daunted, Vanessa sent her friend Karin to acquire a banana. It was duly skinned and Gerry produced a pipe into which the banana was stuffed. Of course, it was far too damp to light.

"I'll go down to the kitchen and dry it in the oven," she said. We ignored her and returned to our beer and cards. Twenty minutes later she was back with a warm, dryer banana skin which she returned to Gerry's pipe. Determination was finally rewarded and the banana skin started to smoulder while Vanessa sucked vigorously on the pipe.

"Wow!" she said. Her eyes started to disappear under her lids and she weaved around. "'This is amazing," she cried.

Robin grabbed the pipe and inhaled deeply then coughed horribly. No one else enjoyed the experience that Vanessa claimed to have and most felt a little sick.

"I'm sorry for you guys," said Vanessa. "That was way out."

Even Karin doubted her claim but we had to give Vanessa her due for fulfilling her dream.

One night, about half an hour after going to bed, we heard shouting outside. My brother put his head out of the door and said that there were some people marching about down below. Perhaps we'd been obsessing about the informers and the dangers of a raid but we became convinced that we were experiencing a raid. It seemed like soldiers were going up and down stairs, along landings knocking at doors. We decided that our best option was to lie low and hope they would go away. Eventually the noise subsided and we finally got to sleep. In the morning no one seemed to know what had happened but there was general nervousness in the residence.

I told myself that I should visit the Psychology Department in the University of Natal on one of my days off. The opportunity arrived when Karin, who was a studious type, suggested that I go up with her and have a look at the University. The campus had a wonderful situation on a hill with a good view of the city and the Indian Ocean beyond. I was surprised to see a number of black and Asian students on the campus.

"Yes, there are some but they have their own college," said Karin.

Naturally I thought. But it did occur to me that the regime was asking for trouble in providing tertiary education for its enemies.

I went to the Psychology Department and presented myself at reception as a visiting student from the University of St Andrews. I mentioned an academic at St Andrews who had asked me to pass on greetings to Professor Fraser. I was told to take a seat and after a few minutes a tall man with grey hair and a slight limp came into reception.

"You must be our visitor from Scotland?"

He invited me to his office and I said that Ian Johnstone had asked me to look in and say hello.

"Ian, my word, it must be ten years since I saw him. I guess it was a conference in London."

"Are you still in the same line of research, Professor?"

"Yes, still investigating visual perception and understanding of illusions in the native population."

He rabbited on for some time about his research and I dropped in some 'how interestings' and 'reallys' to show how fascinated I was. I tried to steer the conversation in the direction of the political situation and how it affected university life and freedom of speech but he seemed reluctant to take the bait. Instead he made an enquiry of me.

"And what are you doing, Roger?"

"Oh well, I'm only second year and so I am still undecided about my research project which will be in the fourth year."

I sensed that Fraser had lost interest in me, if he had ever had any, and he intimated that the audience was at an end by proffering me a selection of papers.

"Oh, thanks very much Professor. That is very kind."

"Not at all. Please give my regards to Ian."

I left the Psychology Department and wandered back to the Student's Union where I had arranged to meet Karin. She was with a knot of students and they were talking about the political situation. Among the group, to my surprise, were a couple of African young men, one of them quite vociferous.

On the bus back to The Merlin, I mentioned my surprise at seeing her with black students.

'Oh, yeah, they're very keen to discuss political matters.'

'But, isn't that dangerous?'

Karin looked at me quizzically. "Of course, it's dangerous. But you can't pretend we don't live in a shit country. If we do nothing we are just condoning this foul policy. Those two black guys, Thomas and Franklin, have just joined the South African Union of Students. But once they start to make trouble, which they will, the authorities will step in and they will be banned. In fact, already, there is talk of black students being prohibited from joining the Union."

Karin was slight and generally quiet in contrast to her noisy friend Vanessa but I could see that she was the deeper character. Her commitment and bravery were impressive and I realised that I'd underestimated the resistance that was coming from some white South Africans.

My time in Durban was coming to an end. Before getting the flight back from Johannesburg I wanted to try to see a little more of the country. An opportunity presented itself when Bruce, the son of Reg and Maggie, suggested I go with him to visit Eastern Transvaal and the famous Kruger Game Park. Although Bruce would not have been my ideal travelling companion, I realised that this was too good to pass up. The last few days went by quickly. There were goodbyes to be made to the friends I'd made at the Criterion Hotel. I promised Christine that I would visit her parents in Northumberland, a promise I failed to keep, and I undertook to pass on Reg and Maggie's love to my parents.

"You make sure they come and visit us, do you hear? You've seen this wonderful country and so you can tell them they've got to come."

The last night at The Merlin was memorable. Adrian even put a complimentary bottle of wine on the table, even if it was barely drinkable. Later in the pub, a vast quantity of beer was consumed and there was a lot of laughter, hugs and later tears. Everybody promised to keep in touch with everybody else, details were exchanged and Vanessa, Karin, Gerry and Robin solemnly vowed to meet in London in the next couple of years. It was tough to leave my brother but he seemed to have plenty of friends and his job was working out well. But he assured me that he would be returning home after his two-year stint was up.

Bruce collected me at 8.30 next morning and we drove north to Transvaal. As well as being hung over, I was still full of the convivial spirit that I'd enjoyed the previous evening but sorry to be leaving such good people. Bruce's prattle was irritating and he must have noticed I was preoccupied but I didn't care. We drove through some spectacular country including the Drakensberg Mountains and also Ladysmith, scene of the famous siege during the Boer War. We were staying with some friends of Bruce's family en route to Kruger in a satellite town of Johannesburg called Benoni.

On arrival Clive and Jean made us very welcome with tea and biscuits. We were then shown our room and told that dinner would be in an hour. During supper the talk was initially platitudes about what we might see in the Kruger Game Park. But after a few beers we moved on to a more unbuttoned discussion about life in South Africa. I didn't know if these people had been warned by Reg and Maggie, or indeed Bruce, about my political stance but it was as if they felt it necessary to defend the status quo. Clive kept referring to the 'Blecks' as ungrateful, lazy, thieving, bastards.

"Look at my boy, Wireless. He gets perfectly good native food, bought by us, but I still found him stealing some of our potatoes."

"What did you do?" asked Bruce.

"Gave him a bloody good whipping, of course."

Bruce laughed.

"I dare say our liberal friend Roger thinks we should be kinder towards the natives," Clive continued. I didn't rise to the bait.

"No, I'm sure you do. But you bleeding heart liberals don't understand these people. They don't thank you for trying to civilise them. They prefer their own primitive ways. They'd rather live in a mud hut than in decent conditions."

"Well, I'll have to take your word for that since I've not had much of an opportunity to discuss the situation with the black Africans."

"If they're honest, they won't tell you anything different, man."

I'd been in the country long enough to know that it was pointless trying to have a reasoned discussion with these people and after the meal I excused myself, saying I was very tired after the journey from Durban and also that we were leaving early the following day.

"Funny man, that Clive," said Bruce on the road the next morning. "He kills me."

For a moment I thought Bruce was criticising a man whom I'd found a sickening racist. But it soon became apparent that Bruce genuinely found him amusing and agreeable company. I wondered how I was going to get through the next few days without having an unholy row. Fortunately, the country offered enough fascination for us to avoid tendentious topics of conversation and instead focus on the wildlife.

We were in the Park for three days, staying in wooden huts contained within encampments encircled by stockades. In those days, it may be different now, we were able to drive in the park, which is vast (nearly 20,000 square kilometres), on our own with the proviso that we didn't leave our car. At night we were entertained by tales from the warden and also able to see some wildlife at the local waterhole which we overlooked from the veranda. During the night we heard noises and scratching on the walls of the hut. This may have been innocent but neither Bruce nor I felt inclined to investigate.

An early start was recommended so that we could watch the big cats hunting. After about twenty minutes we came across a pride of lions that looked as though they were seeking breakfast. Even at 6.30 it was already warm and we had our windows down. Suddenly we seemed to be surrounded by lions that were determinedly moving in one direction following a herd of antelope. I leaned out of the car with my cheap camera to take some snaps. This was amazing. I then became aware that something was brushing against my arm, something furry. It was the back of a female lion who had passed right next to the car as though we were not there, so great was her concentration as she hunted for her meal. I was grateful that the beast was not desperate enough to exchange a human limb for antelope. After that I kept my window up. This proved to be a wise move since once the lions had completed their kill and settled down to enjoy it, a troop of baboons surrounded the car and jumped all over it. They glared at us through the windscreen and bared their teeth, all the time making screeching noises. They seemed frustrated that they couldn't get inside the car.

The day continued in this way and my irritation with Bruce lessened as I appreciated the time he had made available to me to see Africa's astonishing array of wildlife in its natural habitat. We saw pretty much everything including elephants, hippos, rhinos, crocodiles, zebras, warthogs, monkeys, jackals, hyenas, and gazelles of all sorts. In the evening, we ticked off all the species we'd seen. Just about everything we decided.

"But we haven't seen giraffes!" Bruce exclaimed.

He was right and I hoped this would be remedied in the one morning we had left. We were due to leave the park at lunchtime. Next day we continued to see everything except giraffes. It seemed unreasonable for me to be disappointed simply because I'd missed out on one species, however exotic. By 11.00 we had still not seen one and we realised that we only had an hour left. Then, round the next corner, was a herd of giraffe moving in that stately way they have. We were mesmerised. For the next hour we saw virtually nothing else but giraffe so that we almost began to get bored with them.

It was a long drive to Johannesburg mostly on dirt roads which threw up a cloud of red dust, much of which seemed to get inside as well as cover the outside of the car. We stopped off in Pretoria for a couple of hours which had the clean look of an administrative capital – white buildings and well mown lawns. It seemed to suit the Afrikaans mentality which was much in evidence in this part of the country. We then drove on to Jo'berg and checked in to a small hotel in the city centre. At reception we made enquiries about visiting a gold mine. Jo'berg, of course, is on the Rand, the location of the major gold mining region of South Africa. We booked for a visit at 11.00 the next day.

A small coach picked us up from the hotel and took us to one of the biggest gold mines. We joined a party of about a dozen and were assigned a guide who explained the depth we were going to go in the lift, the production process and the amount of pure gold produced per annum. It was hot in the area where extraction was taking place and the miners, who were all black but with some white managers, worked stripped to the waist. After observing the raw mining, we were taken to a plant where the ore was washed and underwent a process by which pure gold was produced. It seemed an uneconomic business since more than three tons of ore were needed to produce a single ounce of gold. I mentioned this fact to a tall blonde girl who was in the party.

"Yeah, but do you know how much they pay the miners?"

Subsequently we were taken to the lodgings of the miners. Presumably the company, Anglo American, were proud of their facilities but they looked mean to me. When I later learned that the men only saw their families once a month, it seemed even meaner. Before we left this area a group of the miners performed the gumboot dance for us. Wellington boots were worn in the mines because of the wet conditions. I felt uncomfortable watching the display and when my blonde friend said they do this because they are not permitted to have drums or other musical instruments, I was even less happy.

The final part of the tour took place in a hall, almost like a library, with a balcony all the way round on which were exhibits in cabinets illustrating the gold mining process and many examples of what the finished product could become, from gold bars, the famous Kruger rands, to ornaments and jewellery. While we wandered about we were served wine or soft drinks and canapés. I noticed that the blonde girl and her friend were enthusiastically attacking the wine and I needed no encouragement. I got chatting to the two girls and motioned for Bruce to join us. He seemed reluctant. The girls were also students on a visit from Holland. I asked them if they preferred to speak English or Afrikaans while in South Africa. Ulrike, the blonde, laughed.

"English. We find the Afrikaans quite difficult to understand though we can read it well enough. And anyway, we want to improve our English. Of course, if we are with people who prefer to speak Afrikaans, we speak Dutch."

By the time the visit came to an end, the Dutch girls and I were pleasantly inebriated but Bruce had stuck to orange juice. The girls came on the coach with us but left the bus at a different hotel. Before we parted they invited us to a party and suggested we meet at their hotel in the bar at 8.30.

Bruce wasn't keen to meet up with the girls again despite my urging. This put me in difficulty because it was my last night with Bruce and I felt bad about leaving him. But he wouldn't be budged and told me to go ahead and enjoy myself. He would see me at breakfast in the morning. Enjoy myself I did. Ulrike and Kitty were terrific fun and the party, which was in a house only a few streets away from their hotel, was a lively affair. I spent much of the evening wrapped around Ulrike either dancing or on a sofa and it was hard to leave her at the entrance to the hotel. But we both knew there was no future in our brief relationship and, as I sat in the taxi on the way back to my hotel, I was grateful that my stay in South Africa had ended on such a happy note.

After breakfast next day I made my farewells to Bruce. He wasn't the sharpest knife in the drawer but I couldn't fault his kindness. He talked of taking me to the airport but I said it was out of his way and there was a regular bus service. I had plenty of time as my flight wasn't leaving until the evening. I stored my bags in the hotel lobby and went for a wander in the city centre. It was lively and colourful and not yet the dangerous city that it was to become. After lunch, I took the bus to the airport and met up with some of the guys I recognised in the check-in queue. People were exchanging stories of their time in the country. Almost all had remained in the Johannesburg or Pretoria area. They had interesting stories to tell but I was more than content with how my visit had panned out. I had packed a lot into three months and also felt that when discussions about apartheid came up in the future, there was a chance that I would know what I was talking about.

Seven days in Russia

After nearly ten days in Denmark, Sweden and Finland, either under canvas or on ferries, or simply driving, the real adventure was beginning. We were driving from Helsinki to Leningrad not knowing what to expect. There was an air of anticipation since Russia, in 1968, was a mysterious place. Very much in the heart of the cold war, it was an era when tourists were regarded with suspicion by the authorities and with curiosity by the citizens. The only way to see Russia was to go with the Intourist organisation, Russia's official body for managing visits from outsiders. This meant being closely attended at all times by one or more provided guides. It was unsurprising that Intourist was a branch of the KGB.

We discovered that there was a way to avoid Intourist and that was to camp. There was a camp site north of Leningrad to which, as students, we had been given permission to use for one week only. But first we had to get there. We arrived at the control of the Russia-Finland border in the early afternoon of a glorious August day. Our papers were quickly checked and we were waved through.

"That was easy," I said to my friend James who was driving the Triumph Herald.

"I'm not so sure. I think we still have to pass through the Russian check-point."

Checkpoint, I thought, that makes it sound like a Le Carre novel but I couldn't deny a tremor of excitement as we drove along a forest road. Suddenly, two men in uniform appeared at the side of the road. We slowed up but they waved us on. Such figures were then to be seen at intervals along the road, usually saluting us as we went by. After more than five minutes we came to a barrier with a low building. A number of officials were gathered at this location but no other cars from either direction. We had to get out various documents which I kept in a plastic briefcase. Passports, visas, camping carnet, currency receipt (we were restricted to 50 roubles each), car insurance documents and logbook. I handed this lot over and put another irrelevant sheet back in the briefcase. A thin, dark man in a red peaked cap took the documents and then motioned towards the paper I had put back in the briefcase.

"This?" I said, holding up the paper. "No, you don't want that. That's..."

Before I could say more, he shouted something and grabbed the paper from my hand. He took all the documents into the sentry box and then called over a colleague. I could see that they were uninterested in the conventional documents and only interested in the diagram contained on the additional piece of paper they had taken from me. Clearly this was regarded with suspicion, perhaps a diagram containing the location of foreign agents or secret installations.

The men then went into the low building and a few minutes later a motor-cyclist with side-car appeared from the Russian side of the border. The two officials came out from the building and I saw them hand over our document and say something to the rider who then shot off back in the direction from which he'd come, with our paper stuffed in his coat.

James and I had no Russian and these men appeared to have no English and so it was impossible to explain to them. The situation was farcical, two men at the border control, one motor cyclist and whatever persons might now be involved, all earnestly examining the instructions for erecting a hired tent. It was like life imitating art, reminiscent of Graham Greene's 'Our Man in Havana' where the Russian agent is fooled into thinking that a diagram of a vacuum cleaner is something far more sinister. Although we knew the situation to be ludicrous, since we had now been at the control point for nearly half an hour, it seemed that our Soviet friends did not appreciate the joke.

Eventually the motor cyclist hove into view and the offending document was returned to the border guard and words exchanged. He then came over and gave us all our papers and saluted and waved us on. As soon as we were out of sight we exploded with laughter. However, we calmed down when we realised we had now to locate our campsite with the aid of rudimentary directions. Given that all signs were in the Cyrillic alphabet, and our instructions were not, this complicated matters. The other slight worry was that thanks to the actions of the border guards, we were beginning to approach the curfew hour. One of the conditions of staying in a campsite as opposed to an Intourist establishment was that we had to remain in the campsite during the hours of darkness. In the event we found it without too much trouble. It resembled an army camp with lots of huts of various sizes as well as areas pitched with uniform grey-green tents. After producing our documents once again – the tent erection diagram securely hidden away – we were relieved of our passports and camping carnets and told where to pitch our tent.

There was enough light to put up our tent and do a little unpacking. We then familiarised ourselves with the washing and cooking facilities which seemed quite adequate. While eating our modest meal in the dining area we became aware of English voices and got chatting with a middle-aged Kiwi couple and then some older Americans. Clearly, camping was not confined to students. These people gave us some advice about what to see in Leningrad. The American couple, called Walter and May and dressed identically in denim dungarees, had been travelling for three weeks over a large part of the Soviet Union and seemed to be fulfilling a life-long dream. They belonged to an organisation called Friends of the Soviet Union and Walter was a retired trades union official and clearly sympathetic to the ideals of communism. At an adjacent table was a man with a child, a boy who looked about eight or nine. They whispered to one another as they ate but made no attempt to join our group.

Next day found us in the city of Leningrad, roughly forty minutes drive to the south. The scale of the place was astounding with such marvels as the Winter Palace and the Hermitage hard to absorb. Even though I knew Western Europe well, this felt quite different. The feeling of alienation was exacerbated by the various street signs, which were incomprehensible, by the scarcity of private cars, and by the absence of shops. After wandering around the enormoue Winter Palace square we drifted down to Nevsky Prospect where Dostoevsky's hero in *Crime and Punishment*, Raskolnikov, haunted the city suffering from terrible guilt. Nevsky Prospect was easily the busiest thoroughfare and we found somewhere to have lunch. The price of the meal – soup and a roll and a beer – scared us since we realised that our roubles would not go far. We had been given an exchange rate of two roubles to the pound which we discovered was derisory. We noticed on a stall, for instance, that eggs were a rouble each. £6 for a dozen eggs seemed highly unlikely. It was apparent that the exchange rate was completely arbitrary, since the Soviets preferred westerners to spend dollars or sterling rather than change any money into the home currency. We later discovered that Intourist holidaymakers were directed into special shops and restaurants that only dealt in 'hard' currencies. Our budget meant that we could not afford such luxury.

After a brief look at The Museum of Atheism, ironically housed in a former church, we walked back down Nevsky Prospect until stopped by two young men, similar in age to ourselves.

"Hello," the taller one said, "where are you from?" We told him.

"'London, my, how I would love to go to London,'" he said in good English with a slight American accent. "Are you students?"

When we nodded he indicated that he and his friend were also students, and that he was doing English. He suggested that we went to a café for a coffee. James and I looked at each and after a moment's hesitation said, "OK." The café was down a side street and packed with students.

"I'm Valentin and this is my friend Yvgeny."

We shook hands. Yvgeny was shorter and stockier than his companion and, though he smiled a lot, he said little. Suddenly, Valentin pointed to James's jeans and said,

"Do you want to sell those?"

James laughed. "Not likely, I've worn these round half of Scandanavia and mean to return in them."

He didn't seem very interested in my shorts but said he liked my top.

'So you would like to buy some western clothes would you?' I said.

"Yes, maybe," said Valentin and Yvgeny nodded.

We spent another half an hour chatting about life for students in our respective countries and it became clear that the two things they craved were western clothes and western popular music. Yvgeny said that they had to go and went to the bar to pay the bill. While they were away, I suggested to James that we might be able to supplement our meagre number of roubles if we did some illicit business on the black market. This, of course, was explicitly forbidden in the literature we had been given with our visas but, at the moment, that didn't seem important. When the Russians returned to our table I asked them if they would like to see some clothes we had that they may wish to buy. Valentin nodded enthusiastically. When he learned that we had a car they both became even more excited.

"You come to Leningrad tomorrow, with the clothes?"

"Yes, we have some shirts and sweaters that you will like."

"Good," said Valentin. "Let's meet in the square on Nevsky

Prospect at two o' clock. But leave the clothes in the car. We need to go somewhere else to do business."

We looked through our motley collection of clothes, deciding what we could afford to dispense with. We both had a shirt and a sweater that we could do without. At the last minute I threw in another sweater, knitted by a girlfriend. Hardly stylish but they might fall for it. We met up as arranged and Valentin said that we should go to his parents' flat. We drove for some fifteen minutes into a depressing suburb consisting of high-rise blocks. A crowd of children gathered round the car when we got out. Clearly any car around here was an event and a British car was unheard of. James was worried that the car might be damaged but Valentin assured him that it would not be touched. We entered an apartment block and rode to the 12th floor. We were both a bit nervous since we knew we were flouting the terms of our visa in even being here, let alone engaging in black market trading.

The flat was sparsely furnished but the room we were taken into was dominated by a heavy sideboard with an ornate canopy. I wondered how they had got it into the 12th floor flat. A pretty, blonde girl came in and Valentin introduced her as his girlfriend, Natasha.

"Hello," she said. "'Would you like some tea?"

We accepted this offer and opened the bag with our clothes. Yvgeny immediately grabbed James's blue shirt and held it against himself.

"How much?" he asked.

This is something we'd not considered. We'd failed to value the items and really had no idea what to ask.

"What will you offer me?" said James.

'Twenty roubles," Yvgeny replied.

'Thirty," said James.

"Ooof!" said Yvgeny, giving a wave of his arm and putting the shirt down.

Valentin looked through the rest of our meagre wardrobe and took a liking to one of my sweaters.

"Very good," I said. "Marks and Spencer."

Natasha brought in some black tea and some little cakes. After going through the stuff and discussing it among themselves they made an offer for everything except my knitted sweater. This didn't surprise me. Apart from anything else, one arm was longer than the other and the turtle-neck design was unflattering. But I decided to go for the hard sell.

"This," I said, "is very special. It is hand-made. English, hand knitted. Excellent quality." They looked sceptical. "And very warm. Good for your cold winters."

Eventually they agreed to take the knitted sweater along with the other clothes and we settled for 110 roubles for the lot. Valentin wanted to play us some music and we listened to a Russian rock band for a while. Having completed our deal, we were anxious to get clear of the scene of the crime and we indicated that we had to leave. Valentin asked if we would like to visit Novgorod, the medieval walled town about fifty miles from Leningrad. We looked at one another, doubtfully.

"It is wonderful," said Valentin, "it has a Kremlin." For some reason this was the clincher and we agreed to meet them again on the Friday, our last full day.

"We all go in the English car!" Yvgeny shouted.

We left Valentin and Natasha at the flat and Yvgeny guided us back to the River Neva where we dropped him off. Once back at the campsite we counted our money and realised we had untold riches for the few days that remained.

In the evening, Walter and May, the New Zealand couple, and a Scottish husband and wife joined us. We chatted about our experiences of Russia, particularly the closed nature of the society. We didn't mention our trading experience but said that we had been befriended by some local students. Walter and May defended the Soviet system, saying that the lack of freedom was the price that had to be paid in order to raise a country from serfdom to something approaching parity with the West. We went on discussing and arguing, consuming quantities of earthy Russian wine, when I was suddenly conscious that someone else had spoken. It happened when Hamish, the Scotsman, said,

"But would you really want to live in a country that you could never leave?"

"You can leave. I have spent time outside my country."

The figure who spoke was the man sitting at an adjacent table. It was the man who had been there the previous night with the young boy.

We had discovered a real Russian in our midst and we fell upon him as though he was a rare jewel. He accepted a glass of wine and for the next hour we had a dialogue, mostly us asking him questions, which he patiently answered. He was a research chemist and had spent some time in Germany and Britain attending conferences and visiting various chemical plants. When asked about the absence of basic human rights he put up his hands.

"Is difficult now but it will change. There will be more freedom when the economy is better."

We asked him how it was that he was staying in the foreign visitors' part of the campsite. It seemed that he was a trusted member of the society with special privileges; allowed to travel abroad and use facilities intended for tourists and VIPs. When he made his excuses and left us, we all agreed that he had been charming. In the warm glow of the inferior wine, we warmed to our Soviet hosts. Before going to bed we had a wander round the camp site and reached the perimeter which had a high fence. Beyond the fence we could see a railway line. It was a moonlit night and we watched as a goods train chugged past. It was very long and the train seemed to be carrying scores of vehicles. And then we recognised the vehicles as tanks.

"I wonder where they're going?" James muttered.

Next day I had a hangover. We went to the Hermitage and during our visit encountered a large party of Australian visitors, all young women. They were loud and friendly and it turned out they were staying at the same campsite. We couldn't believe our luck especially when they invited us to join them for a drink in the evening. When we left the amazing museum, I noticed a coach waiting outside with the Australian flag in the window. The driver was seated at the front and gave us a friendly wave. I sauntered over and asked him why he was not in the Hermitage with the party.

"I've seen it mate," he said.

Given that someone has calculated that it would take a year to see all the exhibits in this massive treasure house of the arts, even if you stood for only five seconds in front of each item, his reply amused us.

My delicate state almost made me throw up as we waited to board the hydrofoil that would take us to the Summer Palace. The cruise up the river was therapeutic and we marvelled again at the scale of the buildings and the ingenuity that had gone into the gardens, especially the 'secret' fountains.

After supper, back at the camp site, we searched for and found the Australian party and they made us very welcome. Each of them seemed to have a bottle of vodka and it was distributed generously so that we ended up carousing. Somehow we got back to our tent; next morning we surfaced with another thick head.

It was Friday, our last full day. We'd arranged to meet the Russian students in the usual spot in Nevsky Prospect. Valentin, Yvgeny and Natasha were there, Natasha in a mini skirt. I noted that, sensitively, neither of the men was wearing any of our clothes. I suggested to Valentin that he took the front seat so as to direct James but he said that they would go in the back. They provided directions from the rear of the car and all proceeded well. We arrived at a large square and what appeared to be a check-point. I asked our guides which exit we should take. There was no reply and when I looked round I saw that they were all crouched on the floor.

"Straight on," muttered Valentin.

The guard at the checkpoint slowed us but then waved us through. Once we were clear the Russians got up from the floor and laughed uproariously. James and I were a bit nervous. We didn't realise that local citizens were not allowed to travel without permits.

Novgorod was indeed special and we wandered round the old walled town with various sights being pointed out by our companions. It was stiflingly hot and soon we suggested that lunch would be a good idea. Since we were leaving Russia the next day and were still swimming in roubles, we asked our guides to find a really good restaurant and told them that it was our treat. They took us to a restaurant with a shaded courtyard and let them order anything they wanted including the best wine. What appeared on the table was little better than any other food we'd eaten in the country but the surroundings, at least, were charming. Yvgeny said that we must try the local delicacy which turned out to be a honey liqueur a bit like mead. The bill, when it came, still made only a small dent in our pile of foreign currency.

After lunch we wandered outside the Kremlin and lay in the sun beside the River Volkhov. The effects of the lunch and the heat made us drowsy and we dozed. When we woke it was quite late and we had still to drive back to Leningrad and then get back to the campsite before nightfall. We traipsed back to the car and set off on the return journey. The Russians were in a good mood and Yvgeny made an enquiry.

"This car, what is it called?"

"Triumph Herald," James replied.

"Triumph Herald! Triumph Herald!" Yvgeny shouted. "English car. Best car in the world!"

After this clowning the Russians soon fell quiet and we realised that they were asleep in the back. Fortunately, the signs to Leningrad were clear enough and we proceeded serenely with, as usual, regular sentries on the roadside, saluting as we passed. But as we entered the outskirts of the city we woke Valentin. It was getting dark, not because it was yet particularly late but because of a build-up of threatening clouds. As we entered the city the first flashes of lightening were visible on the skyline. Within minutes there was thunder and then torrential rain. The roads were soon like shallow rivers and with the generally poor street lights it was difficult to see where we were going. Suddenly there was a loud bang.

"Christ!" shouted James, "what are you doing?"

I had hit a traffic island that I totally failed to see. The car seemed to be OK but I pulled into the roadside. James poked his head out of the window to see if he could spot any damage but it was now almost dark. All he got for his trouble was a soaking. We were beginning to realise that we might not be able to get back to our camp site before the curfew. We also didn't want to dump our friends in this appalling weather. Valentin suggested that we drive to his parents' flat. James took over the controls and we slowly made it to the tower blocks. We ran from the car to the block and rode up to the apartment. Once again there was no sign of Valentin's parents in the flat. We had some tea and some of the same little cakes. Valentin wanted to exchange addresses with us. He asked if we could send him tapes of western music. He promised cassettes of Russian classical music which he said was both excellent in quality and very cheap.

The storm had not abated and we stood on the little balcony watching the flashes of lightning over the city and listening to the boom of thunder.

"You cannot go back to your camp tonight," said Valentin. "It is too dangerous. You must stay with us."

"That's kind of you," said James, "but we have to be out of your country by midday tomorrow and we are supposed to be in the camp site tonight. And we have to do all our packing and take down our tent and get our passports back."

"You go out in this weather? It is dark now. Leningrad is not good to travel at night." This was a rare contribution from Yvgeny.

It occurred to me that the Russians were feeling guilty for

taking us to Novgorod and then returning too late. But they were not to predict the weather. I talked to James.

"I think he's right. It would be a murderous journey and we might even find that the camp site is locked. I think we would be better setting off first thing tomorrow in daylight. As long as we are there by eight or even nine we would have enough time."

After talking it over a bit further we decided to accept the hospitality that had been offered.

"Good," said Valentin. He talked to Natasha and then said. "But you cannot stay here. Because there is no space and also it is long from here to the camp. So you can stay with Natasha at her house. But before you go we will have something to eat."

Some soup, bread and cold meat were produced though we were not very hungry. We were thinking of the number of misdemeanours we'd committed on Soviet soil on our short visit: black market trading, staying out beyond curfew, taking residents without a permit to an outside city, residing with the indigenous population and staying at an address unknown to the authorities. We just hoped that we didn't supplement that list by failing to exit the country before our visas ran out.

After the refreshments we said our goodbyes to Valentin who was not coming with us. We were to go with Natasha and Yvgeny. I felt I had got to know Valentin well in just a short time. He was quite emotional in his farewell.

"Please write to me, you have my address," he said as he gave me an embrace.

"Of course I will," I said.

We set off in the direction of the city following Natasha's directions. Her English was patchy but between them she and Yvgeny managed. I realised that they were used to travelling either by Underground or bus and so must not have taken much notice of directions. We parked the car and she took us into a building. Although it was not eleven o' clock, the house was in complete darkness. Natasha led us through a couple of rooms and then pointed out a bathroom. "You sleep here," she said, pointing to the floor in a room where other people seemed already to be asleep. "I get blanket." She came back with what seemed like a towel and a coarse blanket. She laid the towel on the floor – our mattress – and put the blanket on top.

"Sorry not comfortable." At this point she gave us each a kiss and Yvgeny shook hands with us.

It would be an exaggeration to say we passed a good night. Sleeping on a towel on a stone floor, and sharing that towel and the itchy covering with another adult, would not even pass for a one star facility. On top of that we had the accompaniment of loud snoring throughout the night. Exactly where this came from was not apparent but we were conscious of both other adults and children in the room.

It was one of those long nights not helped by the worry about our predicament and whether we were going to depart this country safely. It was a relief when we were given a shake by Natasha. It was 6.30. We got dressed and used the bathroom and then retraced our steps from the night before. We were amazed to see that there was a double bunk bed in our small room with an old man in the top bunk and two children in the bottom bed. We then passed through another room where an adult couple slept and beyond that we could see a further annex with beds. We remembered Valentin saying there was not space in his parents' flat. Natasha's kindness in the midst of what we would call poverty was humbling.

We declined a cup of tea and said we would get off. Natasha took us out to the car on what was a bright, fresh morning. She told us how to get to the road that led out to the north side of the city and embraced us.

"Goodbye English," she said.

James started the car and then let out an oath. We were almost out of petrol. This meant that we now had to find a petrol station, not easy at the best of times and especially this early in the morning. We were starting to despair of finding anywhere open when we encountered a garage at the start of the northern exit from the city. We pulled up beside a pump and James got out his wallet. You didn't pay for petrol, you used coupons provided with the visa. We had specified and paid for an amount, doubtless at an extortionate price, and we were required to present the coupons at filling stations.

"Christ, I can't find the coupons. Have you got them?"

"No. Are you sure we have some left?"

"Yeah, we had enough to get us out of Russia. Shit!"

We went through our wallets, pockets and the glove compartment but found nothing. We tried to offer the attendant some roubles but he waved us away. Having got so far, it was frustrating to be thwarted by the absence of a little piece of paper. A Russian lorry driver came over and said something we did not understand. We pointed to the pump and said "no coupon" and held out some roubles. He seemed to understand and gave us a coupon for 20 litres and took some roubles from us. Saved! Then James looked concerned.

"Oh, no. This coupon is for 88 octane fuel. This car won't run on that."

When the attendant came over, James held out the coupon but pointed to the 97 octane pump. The attendant shook his head and went to the other pump. James refused to have this put into the car. I pleaded with him saying that I very much doubted that it would do any damage to the car. In fact I had no confidence in my prognostication but in our current situation felt we had little option. Eventually James agreed to give it a try and we had 20 litres of low grade fuel put in. The car gave a little cough when James turned the ignition but it caught and we drove off.

Back at the camp site we cruised past the office straight to our tent, hoping we had not been spotted. We were relieved to find that the tent had survived the rain storm and though the canvas was wet, everything inside was dry. We packed everything including the few knick-knacks we'd bought in Novgorod. We then went to the superintendent's office to get our passports and carnets. The superintendent looked at us searchingly and I thought he was going to refer to our absence the previous night. But he said nothing and returned our papers wishing us a good journey.

While checking the papers I came across the currency document. We were supposed to keep a record of money spent with receipts and present it to the officers at the border on leaving. We had vaguely been keeping receipts but when I totted them up I found that we had only spent about half our allowance. This was because we'd been gaily using the ill-gotten black market gains. Having survived the various vicissitudes, surely this would not now scupper us. We counted out the amount we were officially supposed to have left and then hid the remainder inside a sleeping bag.

Apart from the odd miss, the car performed fine and we made the border with about ten minutes remaining on our visa. The formalities did not take as long as on our incoming crossing a week earlier but there was a period of alarm when I handed over the remaining currency along with our receipts. The large, heavy-jowled officer looked at us with a hint of a smile and then spoke to a fellow policeman. He came back looking at the evidence and then looked at us.

"English students, very poor. Heh, heh."

"Yes," I nodded, realising that we had lived for a week in Leningrad on £25.

Eventually, he gave us a receipt for the money which was left over. Apparently, we could cash this in if we were to return within 3 years. We were pleased to leave this money with him knowing how worthless it, and that hidden in the sleeping bag, was in the west.

That night, camped beside a Finnish lake, on a night so calm and clear that you could see reflections of the stars in the water, we quietly thought about the seven days in Russia. We had met an English couple while we were washing up and chatted about our exploits. It was then that we learned that Soviet tanks had entered Prague three days earlier to put down, with considerable savagery, the uprising led by Alexander Dubcek. That came as a shock and we realised that we were fortunate not to be caught in one of our many 'crimes' at a time when security forces might be trigger happy. In years to come we would remember where we were when the Prague Spring happened but we would remember it not for the ruthlessness of the Soviet regime but for the humanity of its citizens, whether the earnest chemist, the kind lorry driver or the people most like us, the friendly students of Leningrad.

The Beautiful People

When you arrive at university it is not long before you become aware that there is a group that attracts the gaze of others. What is it that they share? Good looks, money, intelligence, class and the relaxed bearing of those who know they are special. For want of a better term, I shall call them the beautiful people. They went to all the parties and had names like Quentin and Jemima. Between lectures they would congregate in the Union for coffee and everyone would be aware of them holding court, often with hangers-on at the edges hoping for some recognition or at least a bit of gossip to pass on. Others kept their distance, either seething with envy because they were excluded or resentment because of the unfairness of things.

I was not one of the beautiful people but I became a sort of honorary member for a period. In my second year I was appointed editor of the University student newspaper which meant I had to run a fairly large organisation that produced a decent weekly paper that had a broad readership. Through the newspaper I met some of the more interesting characters in the university since a number of them wrote regularly for the paper. Others, because of their position – such as president of the union – were regularly interviewed and if I felt like conducting the interview, I could do so. Politics played a big part in student life and the leaders of the student Labour, Conservative and Liberal clubs also featured regularly. The arts were taken seriously and I had a clutch of reviewers for concerts, theatre, cinema and exhibitions. And there were weekly sports reports.

The beautiful people presumably read the student paper, if only because their names frequently appeared in it. Much of it was tittle-tattle that filled the Diary column but some of my contributors were themselves part of the inner circle. Perhaps the most challenging part of being a newspaper editor, even at the student level, was writing the weekly editorial. In theory, it was a wonderful platform. You had fifteen double column inches to expound on any subject you wished. But it was not something that came easily to me. I had to rouse myself into hopefully some genuine indignation at an injustice I perceived or a cause that I ardently supported.

I admired the facility of one of the paper's principal contributors, George Robertson, who could turn out five hundred words on something that was concerning him at the drop of a hat. George later went on to become Defence Secretary in Tony Blair's government and subsequently Secretary General of Nato.

I was never a celebrity but my name was known in the university because it appeared every week in the paper and I formed a circle of friends and acquaintances that worked on the paper and it was a congenial group. I was having coffee one morning in the Union, chatting with a group when I looked at my watch and noticed I had a tutorial in five minutes and got up to go. Everyone cheerily waved me off and when I looked back I realised that I had been sitting with the beautiful people.

There was member of the group to whom I was strongly attracted. She was called Little Jo to contrast her with her friend and flatmate, Big Jo. Little Jo was pretty, lively, outrageous and when she wanted to be, delightful company. But she was totally unpredictable. The faculty ball was upcoming in May – the end of the university year. I wanted Little Jo to come with me to the faculty ball. When I suggested the idea she said: "That might be nice" but would not commit. When I found that the other girls in her flat were going, I confided in Big Jo. She promised to help and the next time I found myself with Little Jo she said conspiratorially: "I hear we are going to the ball together. You're going to be my prince charming."

I've failed to mention another significant thing about Little Jo – she liked to drink. On the night of the ball I arranged to pick her up at the flat. Since all her flat were going – they comprised a significant number of the beautiful people – all the male partners were invited to drinks beforehand. I found Little Jo well-oiled by the time I arrived. They had concocted a very powerful cocktail and I found myself beginning to reel after a couple of them.

Their flat was very close to the ball venue and we walked in a crocodile that weaved its drunken way to the party. It was always a bit of a shock to see scruffy students in dinner suits and ball gowns but it made for a spectacular sight. A table had been commandeered and I was pleased to sit down since my head was still spinning. I asked Jo what she would like to drink.

"Get a bottle," she commanded.

The bottle made a hole in my modest resources and I was a little dismayed to discover there were already bottles on the table when I returned, part of the meal we'd paid for. Jo wellied into the wine and I followed suit. We pecked at the food but carried on drinking. As the coffee was served, the President of the Faculty Society got up to propose a toast. He was a mature student called Montague and I knew that Jo didn't like him.

"Sit down you old fart," she shouted. We both giggled. After the toast, Montague got to his feet again to give a speech reviewing his year in office. He droned on and was frequently subjected to jeers and remarks from Jo. It caused quite a lot of amusement and after a while I found myself joining in. At one point Montague was saying: "It gives me great pleasure..." and I shouted out: "Which is more than can be said for your speech..."

Jo erupted in peals of laughter and a few others joined in. But there was also a faction which thought this barracking quite undignified and we were told to shut up. Mercifully Montague completed his speech and a jazz combo struck up. It was also announced that there would be dancing in the basement. Little Jo and I never made the basement. When we tried to get up we almost fell over. Jo announced she was going to the loo. A while later, Big Jo came over to me and said, "Little Jo wants to go home. She's by the Ladies." I struggled to my feet and went to find her.

Somehow we managed to walk the short distance to her flat. Once inside I made us both a cup of black coffee. The coffee perked her up a bit but I knew that the end to our evening that I had imagined was out of the question. She settled in my arms for a while and I inhaled her perfume, Estee Lauder Youth Dew, a fragrance I've never forgotten.

"You're nice, you know," she said. "Thanks for taking me to the ball. Sorry I got pissed, I always do." She smiled in her impish way.

"It was a good evening," I said and I meant it.

We did have one or two other dates after that but it never went anywhere. Little Jo seemed to find men an occasional convenience rather than a necessity. But I never forgot the time I got a little close to the beautiful people and whenever I catch a trace of that distinctive aroma it all comes flooding back.

The Talking Doll

"Tom, are you free for lunch? I want to work out the practicalities of our new research method with you." The speaker was, Dr Gregson, a slight, dark-haired woman in her early forties who was head of a research project in Edinburgh funded by a national research council that was investigating the thinking and language skills of three and four-year-old children. Tom Pearson, the new research associate, affirmed his availability for lunch and Dr Gregson said she would meet him at the staff club after she had dictated some letters to her secretary.

As he walked across Nicholson Square towards the club, Tom reflected on the remarkable couple of weeks he had already had in Edinburgh. Because he had started in the vacation when many people, including the children in the research nursery, were away, he'd been left mostly to his own devices, to read reports and background papers so as to be fully acquainted with the project's goals and initial outcomes. At the time the Edinburgh festival was in full swing and he revelled in the opportunity to immerse himself in culture.

One day Dr Gregson came into his room and said she would like some help with an exhibition. Doesn't she mean conference, thought Tom? Academics don't do exhibitions. But he was wrong; Deirdre Gregson was a keen artist and had been persuaded to mount an exhibition of her work in the final week of the festival.

Her style was abstract, influenced by Ben Nicholson. Precise, geometric reliefs in black, red and white with the occasional metal strip. He helped Deirdre to hang the exhibits in two rooms of a building on Chambers Street. When they were all in their place, Deirdre said that all that remained to be done was to price the exhibits. Tom couldn't believe that he, a complete novice, was expected to help her put a sum on all these works. The criterion they employed was one of labour supported by aesthetics. Deirdre estimated the amount of time she had spent on each work and Tom aided Deirdre in their estimation of the work's appeal. Eventually they were all priced. When they sold out within two days of the exhibition's opening, he realised that they had undervalued the paintings but Deirdre didn't seem unduly worried. On the contrary, she was gratified at the reaction of the public.

At the staff club, Tom found Dr Gregson sipping a glass of wine in conversation with Emeritus Professor Miles Robertson who had recently joined the University from Oxford. He was introduced to the eminent psycholinguist and muttered some pleasantries about wine, which was the subject under discussion. At one point, the old man sneezed and Tom was astonished to see that the handkerchief he withdrew from his pocket had three or four knots in it. So it wasn't a myth after all.

After lunch, and excused from the professor's company, Deirdre and Tom got down to serious discussion about her new idea in research methodology.

"The way we can completely gain the children's confidence and get them to demonstrate their degree of knowledge in a particular domain is to allow them to be teachers. My idea is to present them with a doll that is learning to talk and to ask them to assist in this process."

"You mean we say that they are good talkers and so will be able to help the doll become a better talker," said Tom.

"Exactly. But, of course, the doll will not be saying just any old thing, he will be making statements about situations that will give us insights about the way the children are thinking."

"Like sentences containing 'more' and 'less', and 'all' and 'some'," said Tom.

"Yes, all those logical terms that are so important in the instructions for Piaget's tasks and whose meaning for the child Piaget took for granted."

Tom knew that Dr Gregson's work was based on a re-examination of the famous Swiss psychologist's theory of cognitive development. She was a great admirer of Jean Piaget and was one of the few British psychologists who had actually worked with him and his team in Geneva but this did not prevent her being critical of some of his assumptions.

"If we can get the children to make a judgement of the doll's statement, essentially saying if it is true or false, then we can infer from that what the child believes to be true or false, uncontaminated by any adult influence."

Tom was enthused by her idea and was given a time scale of three weeks to get the talking doll laboratory up and running. Deirdre had set her heart on a panda as the talking doll and Tom was dispatched to Jenners to buy a soft toy preferably one that was as big as a four-year-old child. One of the advantages of a panda was that it had a large head. This was unceremoniously slit open by the technician that was assisting them on the acoustic side. He inserted a small speaker into the toy's cranium with its front behind the panda's mouth. A concealed lead issued from the rear of the toy's neck to be connected to the source of the panda's voice. This would require the construction of a sound proof cubicle, an expensive item in the late 1960s.

Tom's room was effectively to become the talking doll lab and a team moved in to construct the sound proof cubicle, a heavy large metallic box with a door and a one-way window so that the doll's 'voice' could view the scene without being seen. Test trials worked well, even adults soon feeling that it was natural to talk to the doll. A strange phenomenon, thought Tom, but when a creature starts to talk to you even when it is a large, black and white soft toy in the shape of a bear, it was impossible not to reply.

A decision that still had to be made was who would provide the voice of the doll. Tom couldn't do it because he was needed to bring the children from the research nursery to his room and to 'manage the experiment'. Deirdre knew an engaging third year student, Mark Georgeone, who she thought would fit the bill. This young man from Fife, with Italian forebears, was the perfect choice. He had the gift of the gab, a good sense of humour and was unflappable which was essential since you never knew what a four-year-old might say to you.

The technique proved a triumph. An element of nonverbal technology was introduced to the procedure in the form of a bell and buzzer device. The children were trained to press the bell to indicate a judgement of 'yes', or 'true', and the buzzer for 'no', or 'false'. The children liked this action element to their task and it helped to eliminate ambiguity. It was explained that the panda, named Chi Chi, liked to hear the bell or buzzer since it helped him to understand better and talk better.

All the children adored coming to see Chi Chi with the exception of Callum, the largest boy in the nursery, who was scared stiff of the panda. This was Tom's fault. He'd forgotten that Callum had been away when the introductory trials had taken place during which the children had been taken in groups of three to meet Chi Chi. On that first occasion the doll did not talk. They simply met him and were told that he was shy but was learning to talk. They were asked if they would come and see him again and, as good talkers, would help him with his language. They were all enthusiastic about this idea. Callum, however, had been absent during the introductory sessions, and his first experience with Chi Chi was on his own when the doll was to make his initial vocalisations. Tom introduced Callum to Chi Chi.

"Chi-Chi this is Callum. Say hello to Callum."

"Hello, Callum," boomed Mark.

On hearing the panda talk at him, Callum jumped up and rushed out of the room. Here was an unfortunate case of classical conditioning and it took some patient remediation for Callum to agree to take part in further sessions.

The experimental trials were successful and the research couldn't have been going better when Mark dropped his bombshell. It was just before the Easter break.

"I'm afraid I'm going to have to stop all this even though I'm in love with Fiona McDonald." Fiona was a demure, four-year-old blonde.

It transpired that Mark was getting close to his exams and even though the money was good and he enjoyed the work, he felt he no longer had the time.

"Oh, Mark, you're going to be a hard act to follow," said Tom.

"Aye, well, I've a mate called Dougie who might be interested. Should I ask him to come and see you?"

"Yes, of course," Tom replied.

Dougie was a psychology student who kept goal for Berwick Rangers, a Scottish second division football team, in his spare time. A tall, muscular youth, he couldn't help filling any room he happened to occupy. He seemed an odd choice for the voice of the talking doll.

"What do you know about this work?" Tom asked.

"I'm to talk to the wee bairns. Mark's told me about it."

"Do you think you're up to the job, Dougie? It's important that you can think on your feet, not be phased by the things the children say, and stay in character."

Dougie seemed hesitant. "I don't know. But Mark says I can do it."

This seemed a slightly dubious recommendation but with the next set of trials due to start on Monday Tom felt he had little alternative. He told the big man to come in on Monday at nine.

Dougie arrived punctually sporting a black eye.

"Are you OK?" Tom asked.

"Aye, just a kick in the match on Saturday." Tom thought it best not to ask the score.

"You've met Toby?"

"Aye," said Dougie.

Toby, a three-foot-high red dachshund, had been substituted for Chi Chi in order to accommodate the new voice. Tom explained that four-year-old Elspeth was going to be the first child to meet Toby and that Dougie should say a few things about himself and generally establish a good relationship with Elspeth.

Dougie went into the booth for a sound and video check. Tom fetched Elspeth from the nursery at the end of the corridor. As she entered the room Tom was telling her that she was the first child to meet the new talking animal. Elspeth sat down with Tom beside her and he suggested that she say hello to the dog. Dougie responded in a deep voice that Tom had not heard before.

"Hello, my name's Toby. What's your name?"

"Elspeth."

"Hello, Elspeth. What have you been doing this morning?"

"I've been playing in the Wendy House with Jean and Maggie. What have you been doing?"

"Oh, I've been in the park for a walk," said Toby.

"Yes, I saw you," said Elspeth.

"Did you?"

"Yes," replied Elspeth. "I was having a picnic and you were playing with some children."

The conversation was taking a dangerous turn. Toby was not supposed to have a life outside the research laboratory. If the fantasy got out of hand, and Toby was deemed to be living a life somewhere in the neighbourhood, control – a critical component of research – might be difficult with respect to Toby's identity.

Tom need not have worried; Dougie rose to the occasion.

"No, that wasn't me Elspeth. The only children I see are here. Can you help me to talk better?"

At this point Dougie went into the pre-arranged script designed to elicit responses from the child. He did it to perfection and Tom realised that the big goalkeeper defied the stereotype of the tongue-tied footballer. At the end of the session Tom told him how pleased he was with the way it had gone and asked him to become a regular part of the team.

"On one condition," he said.

"What's that?" Tom asked, believing him a little presumptuous to be making conditions when this was a well-paid job for a student.

"That none of this gets back to the football team. Ma life will nae be worth living if the folk at Berwick find out I'm talking to wee lassies dressed as a red dog."

Game for Lunch

We passed the lodge cottage at the entrance and drove up the long drive to Bankside Hall. It seemed to go on for ever, rolling parkland with majestic trees. It was like entering a National Trust property. When we eventually reached it, the grey stone, Georgian building, with its two wings and numerous outbuildings, looked imposing. I was nervous and felt that I was under inspection to see whether I was suitable for the young women sitting beside me who was the niece of the owner of the house.

We were welcomed by my girlfriend's mother, the sister of the owner. Both women were small and dark but while one, Grace's mother, was quiet but friendly the other sister, known as Aunt Bee, was energetic with a beady eye. She used this to size me up and I wasn't convinced that I fitted the bill.

It was a bright day but with a cold easterly wind. We were told that we would have a walk in the grounds before lunch. I'd brought walking shoes, as instructed, and the party that set out consisted of Aunt Bee, Grace's mother, Henry, Bee's stepson, and the two of us. If I thought the approach to the house had been extensive, I now discovered that it was nothing compared to what was on the far side of the Hall. Most immediately there were vast lawns, flower beds, ponds, a vegetable garden and a number of glass houses. We headed up the long meadow towards a wood. In the distance, on the edge of the wood, was a large sculpture mounted on a high plinth. When we got closer, it materialised as a horse. Grace told me it was a statue of Hector, Aunt Bee's favourite horse, that had died two years earlier.

Everyone made respectful noises about the sculpture and what an amazing likeness the artist had achieved. I offered plaudits as well which was a mistake.

"Do you ride?" asked Aunt Bee.

"I'm afraid not," I replied.

"Oh," sniffed Aunt Bee. A black mark.

As we continued our walk through the woods, the women formed into a little gossiping bunch and I fell into step with the other man, Henry. He was tall and beginning to stoop even though he was only in his early forties. He asked me if I liked trees. I suppose I had never really thought about it. I certainly had nothing against them and I guessed that a world without them would be a dull place. I didn't voice this banal notion which was as well since I discovered that Henry had a passion for trees and his father before him. Indeed, the copse in which we were walking had been planted by the family and as we walked Henry pointed out the names and provenance of different trees.

Henry had obviously been to an expensive public school and spoke with an accent that you could cut with a knife, each word enunciated with great, but effortless, care. It was difficult not to feel slovenly in his company. We got through the woods to see fields waving with ears of wheat as far as the eye could see.

"Is this all their land?" I asked Grace.

"Yes, and a lot more besides. But Henry mostly leaves the handling of it to his farm manager. He runs the auction business."

"He seems to know a lot about trees."

"Mm, it's one of his hobbies. He's recently started a conifer plantation. I think he's after the Christmas tree market."

Money on the scale that this family must have was another world to me. We returned to the house via a lane which passed yet another pond and eventually came through some stone barns in which were housed a great many bullocks. Grace asked Henry when they would be going to market.

"They will have two months grazing outdoors and then they'll be off (pronounced 'orff')," he said.

Poor buggers, I thought. We entered one of the wings of the Hall when we got back, and changed our shoes and removed our outdoor coats in what was called the Tack Room, a large area full of boots, galoshes, walking sticks, hats and a variety of outdoor garments. But curiously, no saddles.

"The gents is there, if you need it." Henry waved an arm in the direction of a door off the Tack Room. I took advantage of the offer and was surprised to see a number of cartoons of dogs on hind legs engaged in various toiletry activities.

Subsequently we decanted to what was known as the Smoking Room and there I met two other members of the household. Kate was Henry's sister and a similar height but broader. She was about twice the size of her stepmother and any possibility that Bee was her biological mother would have been dismissed just seeing the two of them together. Kate was hearty and welcoming and, I understood, a local councillor. I didn't need to ask which party she represented.

The other person was an older version of Henry, being more stooped but with the bearing of a military man. Uncle Cecil gave me a brief smile on being introduced but I scarcely heard him say a word during my entire visit. He sat in 'his' chair by the log fire and accepted a gin and tonic when it was brought to him and otherwise busied himself with the East Anglian Times.

Henry addressed me in his meticulous voice.

"What will you have to drink? I have some very agreeable local ale."

He'd obviously decided I was a beer man. I thought I should humour him and said I would try the recommended ale. This was served in a pewter tankard and was revolting. I regretted not joining the rest of the company in their aperitifs. Most were drinking G&T but Grace's mother was sipping at a sherry. Her name was Cynthia but I was invited to call her Cyn, pronounced 'sin', by which name she was generally known. A more inappropriate name, for a woman whom I felt had never committed any sort of sin, it was hard to imagine.

The Smoking Room was so-called because it allowed the men to smoke their pipes or cigars. I suppose it had a fug much of the time, provided by the smoke from the log fire as much as tobacco. Grace wanted to show me something.

"Can I show him the secret door, Aunt Bee?" she asked her aunt.

"You may."

Grace walked over to a large bookcase which covered most of one side of the room and must have pressed something whereupon part of the bookcase swung back and revealed that it was a door. It opened into a passage which I later discovered led to the east wing. I presumed that this was once servants' quarters and it allowed the owners to enter this area at their leisure though I suspected the entrance was one way, which indeed it was. I don't know if this consideration ever entered Grace's head but I did learn that the 'secret door' was an amusing diversion in the childhood of Grace and her siblings when they visited Bankside Hall during their summer holidays especially as they were often quartered in the east wing.

Just then a gong sounded.

"Luncheon is served," intoned Henry.

I was hungry, the walk had put an edge on my appetite, but I refrained from leading the charge to wherever the grub was and instead held back, as a gentleman should, while Uncle Cecil and the ladies shuffled out of the Smoking Room and across the hall into the dining room.

The dining room had beautiful panelling and a fine view over the southern aspect of the house which was protected by a ha-ha. However, a small deer was grazing outside on the lawn which suggested that the ha-ha was not earning its keep.

"Damn nuisance these muntjacs," growled Henry, and Aunt

Bee and her husband nodded and muttered in assent. It seemed that these miniature wild deer, which were introduced from Asia in the 1920s, had increased their population rapidly in recent years and were considered a pest by many farmers.

I was seated between Aunt Bee and Grace and was feeling nervous as the soup arrived at the table. I felt my behaviour, especially my table manners, would be under close scrutiny. I was unnerved by Aunt Bee's first question which I had assumed would be something like 'would you pass the butter'.

"Do you say controversy or controversy?"

"Controversy," I answered with only a momentary hesitation.

"Good," she responded.

Perhaps that had erased the earlier black mark. Henry asked if I would take wine. I refrained from saying 'Does the Pope have a balcony?' but remembered that one of us would have to drive. Grace encouraged me to drink and so I assumed she would drive.

"Thank you," I said.

"I think this offering from the New World might amuse you," said Henry.

Evidently my enthusiasm for wine had preceded me and I realised that they might be putting me to some sort of test. I tasted it and recognised a Coonawarra cabernet, an excellent claret lookalike, and pronounced my pleasure at the flavour and length. Henry looked a little disappointed, perhaps that I had correctly identified the bottle or that I countenanced wine from the colonies over the real thing from Bordeaux. Fortunately, those who knew anything about wine, which excluded Cyn, agreed with my verdict.

I managed to eat the celery soup in what I thought was the prescribed manner, that is, tilting the bowl away from me as the quantity reduced, and all seemed to be going well. A couple more gulps of wine and I was starting to feel almost at home. I should have realised that this was when danger was likely to strike.

"Do they have a maid?" I whispered to Grace when a woman in a black skirt and white blouse took away the soup bowls.

"No, they used to but now they only get someone in when they have visitors."

Kate had served the soup from a large toureen but the next course came in on a plate and consisted of a small roasted corpse. I looked at it with fascination and concern. It had bits sticking out of it like stubby legs and a small head with a long beak. I assumed it was game of some sort.

"Are these the ones you shot in Wales?" Aunt Bee looked at Henry.

"Yes," said Henry. "They don't need to hang long."

"Difficult blighters to bring down," said Uncle Cecil.

"You're damned right, Father. They never fly in a straight line."

Aunt Bee fixed her beady eye on me. "Have you eaten woodcock before?"

"No, never."

"Well, you are in for a treat. They are considered the king of the game birds."

I helped myself to the vegetables which were on the table and then contemplated this unusual offering. I noticed that the others were hacking into the beast and cutting off pieces. I tried to do the same but found that the quantity of what I considered meat, was distinctly lacking. Whenever you cut into the blighter, to use Uncle Cecil's term, you encountered bone. In fact the woodcock seemed to consist almost entirely of bone. After ten minutes of chopping about, my plate was littered with bits of bone and gristle and I had barely tasted flesh. Kate seemed to notice my predicament.

"Pick it up," she said.

I noticed that others were indeed picking up pieces of bone and chewing on them. This was not something I indulged in usually, not being a fervent carnivore. However, it seemed the appropriate course to adopt and I followed suit. This resulted in my hands and face getting covered in grease and I made a mess of my napkin as I tried to clean myself up.

"So, what do you think of woodcock?" asked Aunt Bee.

"Interesting," I said lamely.

"Is that all? I don't think you appreciate the king of game birds."

I didn't think there was any suitable rejoinder to that and so I let it go as another black mark. I was able to do justice to the jam roly poly and custard and accepted some port when it was served with cheese. I feared that I would be left with Henry and his father, having assumed the ladies would leave us, but this convention was ignored since the men were not allowed to smoke in the dining room and it was clear that Henry and Cecil were impatient for their pipes.

Coffee was served in the smoking room and afterwards Grace said, "Come on, let's go and help with the washing up."

We went into the kitchen where Kate and the maid were busy.

"Don't worry you two. I'll be along shortly."

We ignored her protestations and did some drying up. I asked Kate if council work took up a lot of her time.

"Well, yes, but I spend more time fund raising for the party. There seems to be some function or other almost every week. And I'm quite involved with our local agent and the MP. He takes a special interest in the police federation."

She mentioned a name I recognised. It struck me that she had more contact with the real world, however coloured it was by her shire background, than the remainder of the household. As we wandered back to the smoking room, Grace pointed out a painting.

"This is a picture of a famous first world war battle, where Uncle Cecil's regiment was surrounded. He survived and won the military cross."

"He doesn't seem to do much these days."

"No, I think he's stopped going into the firm. But Mummy tells me that he is still Master of the Hunt though I think he steps down from that this year."

When we got back to the smoking room, Aunt Bee patted

the adjacent seat and told me to sit next to her. What now, I wondered.

"I hear you work with children. Tell me about your work."

I tried to explain the research I was engaged in that examined the thinking and speaking skills of young children in a specially set up research nursery. She looked sceptical and went off on a tangent.

"Present day parenting leaves a lot to be desired. If children don't have clear boundaries and firm discipline they will run wild."

Since I was not a parent myself, I was reluctant to get drawn into a dialogue about child rearing even though I was familiar with the research and theory and her view seemed out of date. I contented myself with:

"Yes, I think clear boundaries are important as are affection, stimulation and security."

She grunted and asked Cyn if she wanted any more coffee.

Later, as we drove away, I asked Grace how she thought I'd done.

"Very well. They liked you."

"Really. I thought they regarded me as a dangerous, socialist revolutionary out to destroy their world."

"No. They're stuck in their ways. A bit of a time-warp in a way but even if they don't share your views they respect your right to have a different opinion and they like a good argument."

Right, I thought. Should there be another time at Bankside Hall I will look forward to engaging in real debate.

The Big Day

The big day dawned, Easter Monday, bright and breezy, enough to make the bridesmaids and other women hold on to their hats. Still a little fragile from my stag night two days ago, not to mention my dinner for the ushers the night before, I was nevertheless fully prepared for what was to come.

Since the best man was my brother, I spent more time getting him ready for the occasion than he directed towards me. He drove me to the church in his orange Ford Capri where we were greeted by ushers in morning dress, more than were actually needed. The bride was late, as is the custom, but since she only had to walk from two doors away, there was not much excuse.

The corpulent ageing minister, a friend of the family, carried off proceedings in a slightly bumbling way but without a blemish which surprised me because he could never seem to remember my name whenever I encountered him. The choir sang beautifully which was not a surprise since my brand new wife had been a member of it since she was a young teenager and they pulled out all the stops for one of their own.

We walked down the aisle to the traditional sound of Mendelssohn to be greeted by the photographer who soon got Aunt Laura and others of that ilk in the right place though he could not get her to release her newspaper and umbrella. In those days, mercifully, the photographer was not the autocrat that rules the roost in contemporary weddings, causing guests to hang around for ages.

It was all over without fuss and we scrambled gratefully into the limousine which was to take us to the University Staff Club, the location for the reception. We enjoyed the seclusion of the ride into the city centre and prepared ourselves for the next phase of the big day.

Sparkling wine, Veuve de Vernay, as I recall, was dispensed to the guests on arrival and the speeches were delivered quite early on before we descended on the buffet. My job seemed to be to thank everyone under the sun and I had been given a long list of 'thank yous' the day before. I was aware of my new sister-in-law looking at me and pointing at the minister. It seems that I had omitted him from those to whom we owed gratitude. Quite why, I was unsure, since he was being paid for his trouble.

One of my new brothers-in-law acted in place of his late father. He was a polished public speaker since he had been on the stage and worked for the BBC. I felt sorry for my brother who had to follow him, especially when he started with the same visual joke, the one where you announce you are only going to say a few words and your sheet of paper concertinas down into something resembling a toilet roll. But he got through it and we gratefully got stuck into the food.

After the meal my wife and I circulated separately, thanking the various guests for making long journeys, for their generous gifts, and their valued company. All went well until I reached Morag, my boss at the research centre where I worked.

She seemed preoccupied and I sat down next to her.

"Thanks for coming Morag. Are you OK?"

"No, not really."

I looked at her questioningly.

"It's Jonathan. He's asked me to marry him."

"Well, that's wonderful news, isn't it?"

As I said this I realised that she was far from elated. Jonathan was a distinguished young research scientist who Morag had been seeing for some time. They seemed well suited.

"Well, yes, but I can't marry him. I'm twelve years older than him."

"But that doesn't matter does it if you both want it?"

"Well, he says it doesn't matter but I'm not so sure. I am no longer in a position to have children. He says he doesn't want children but he could change his mind. I don't think I should tie him down."

Poor Morag, she looked close to tears. I took her hand.

"Look, if anyone knows his own mind, it's Jon. You can see that he is devoted to you and it's what he wants. If you feel the same about him, I wouldn't hesitate."

She looked at me gratefully.

"Do you think so? Oh, I don't know. It's such a mess."

At this point I was aware of my wife staring at me, clearly wondering why I was spending so much time with my boss, and perhaps wondering why I was holding her hand. She passed by and in a stage whisper said:

"You need to keep circulating."

I felt I couldn't leave Morag like this and continued to counsel her. Eventually I released her hand.

"Look, you've got nothing to lose. Happiness has come to you a little later than it does for many but you should grasp it. Jonathan loves you – make him a happy man."

Goodness, I thought, a new career is opening up for you as an agony uncle. Morag smiled weakly.

"Thank you. You've helped a lot. I shall think about what you said."

All this time she never referred to my own situation, the first day of my married life. My wedding day! She was completely absorbed in her own dilemma. But that was all right. She was a good boss, a good colleague and a good person. It amused me, nonetheless, that she should regard me, an old married man of nearly three hours, as equipped to give her advice.

Fast forward fifty years and not only are my wife and I still happily married but also Morag and Jon. She is over ninety now and famous, with her portrait in the Scottish National Gallery. She remains as sharply perceptive and inquisitive as ever. And Jonathan continues to go into his lab every day and has earned a world-wide reputation in the area of renewable energy. She never refers to our conversation on my wedding day and nor do I but I cannot imagine that she has forgotten it. I am simply glad that I gave her what turned out to be good advice and that she has had a fulfilled life with her partner.

PART TWO

MEMOIR (1942-1972)

Chapter 1
Beginnings

I was born at a quarter to midnight on October, 31st, 1942 in a hospital in Clapham, south west London. It was a Saturday and marked by a major bombing of Canterbury by the Luftwaffe. By all accounts it was not an easy birth and there were worries about my mother's well-being but she pulled through. I was therefore a Halloween baby, an accident of birth I've never particularly enjoyed. I don't remember my birthday being celebrated by any special Halloween events until I was at boarding school at age eight when activities like ducking apples and eating sticky buns attached to a string were the subject of shrill shrieking. The business of kids dressing up as witches and wizards and knocking on doors for the appalling 'trick or treat' was a much later phenomenon, one of the less endearing imports from the USA. I had particular cause to regret this one year when we were living in Princes Road and a load of yobs chucked eggs at the house. Ever tried removing dried raw egg from brickwork?

My other defining characteristic (no, not being a Scorpio – I've no time for astrology) is that I was a wartime baby. And it's hard to escape from the influence of that catastrophic event on one's early life. You could say I had a good war. Being blown 50 yards by a German rocket in my second year and having not even a scratch to show for it suggested that luck, if not God, was on my side. For more than fifty years this incident was buried as a vague image in my mind. Many times, when the subject of early memories was raised, I said that my earliest memory was unclear but that it consisted of me drying up cutlery and then rushing into the garden. This unremarkable little story was always greeted by looks of incomprehension by those best equipped to know and eventually I stopped enquiring about it though it always nagged at the back of my mind.

Psychologists will tell you that earliest memories are difficult phenomena to access because they are frequently contaminated with confounding influences like photographs and family reminiscence. For example, my parents would often tell to anyone who was prepared to listen that at the age of two I would answer the telephone in best King's English by giving my name, age, address and telephone number. But I don't actually have a memory of that. My other earliest memory was sitting on a hard chair in the sitting room watching while a stranger kept placing a metal needle in my knee. I subsequently discovered that this was a doctor who was stitching a wound. And I still have the scar to this day! The injury was sustained while I was clambering around a bomb site with my friend Richard and was caused by falling on a broken iron bath. I sometimes think that I can also conjure up an image of me slipping on the bomb site but I don't remember Richard or any other activities we must have got up to at that time. The only reliable recall is of me being somewhat unhappy, I think I was crying.

What these two incidents have in common, of course, is that they both come under the heading of traumatic experiences, a feature of many early memories. But what of 'cutlery and garden', as I will denote the other 'memory'? This was only finally resolved at my sixtieth birthday party in front of a room full of people at a celebration at the local golf club. Rashly I'd asked a friend to say a few words at the event by way of giving people an excuse to raise a glass to me at my great age. What I hadn't anticipated was that said friend promptly recruited three other persons, including my mother and brother, to join him in what turned out to be a

60-minute extravaganza using power point and video projection in a darkened room. Leaving aside the embarrassment and unwelcome attention, it meant that the jazz band which I'd hired at considerable expense was sitting drinking at the bar, also at my expense, instead of doing what they were paid for.

As I indicated, my mother had a role in this production. The story of the precocious child answering the telephone with "This is Tulse Hill 3824 and my name is Peter Lloyd and I am two years old and I live at 3 Rudloe Road" was trotted out for the umpteenth time and I was beginning to nod off when I suddenly realised that my mother was telling about the time I was blown out of the house when a bomb fell at the end of the street. At the time I was 'helping' in the kitchen while she was doing the washing up. I am insufficiently knowledgeable about munitions to know whether I was blown or sucked out of the house but dimly recall that a vacuum can follow a bomb blast and that this may have been enough to lift me off my feet, shoot me down the hall, through the front door (which presumably was blown off by the blast), and into the road outside. "Amazingly," my mother told the spellbound gathering in the golf club, "when we got to him he was sitting up and completely unharmed." Perhaps I was reciting my name and address to any curious observers but history doesn't tell us this. When later I mentioned to my mother that for years I'd been asking her about the early memory I had of rushing outside into the garden while carrying cutlery, she denied all knowledge of my ever having said such a thing. This is why I feel quite confident in saying that 'cutlery and garden' is a genuine memory.

I've done a modicum of research to try to date the event. My best guess is that I was the victim of a V2 rocket on January 26th, 1945, which landed at 10.45 on the west side of Rodenhurst Road, off Poynders Road (now part of the South Circular), which was at the end of our street. It demolished or damaged a lot of property but the official record says that there were no casualties. I clearly didn't count. I would have been two years and nearly three months which would qualify as a rather early earliest memory.

My Parents

My father, John Noel Lloyd, was born on December 25th in 1912 in Ainsdale, a village south of Southport on the Lancashire coast about twenty miles north of Liverpool. The eldest of eight in a working-class family, he found the demands of being expected to help in the raising of his brothers and sisters a suffocating experience. In a house as crowded as his, the idea of any real autonomy let alone privacy was out of the question. His father William, Billy, worked on the railway and, as long as his role as the breadwinner was respected, and his seat by the fire was not usurped, he was a benign figure. The real power in the house was his mother Elizabeth, Liz or Lizzie, who managed the house efficiently and stood no nonsense. Since I was to live with my grandparents for a year when I was five years old, I will be able to give a first-hand account of the experience in due course.

My father left school at fourteen being required to supplement the family income as soon as it was legal to do so. John loved school and frequently used the cliché of school as the best days of his life. But for him it wasn't a cliché and the regret he felt from having his education cut short was tangible and poignant. This must have been a common experience for intelligent children from his background at this time and a dreadful waste of intellectual talent. He was apprenticed in a tobacco factory in Liverpool and acquired engineering skills.

Scouting and sport were the principal leisure activities of my father. Scouting allowed him a sound excuse to get out of the house and he remained in the scouts as a young man, as a ranger scout and troop leader helping in the induction of boys into the scouting movement. Football was also one of his passions both as a player at a moderate level and a supporter of Everton, one of the top teams in the first division between the wars with their famous centre forward, Dixie Dean. Golf was another strong interest, though unsurprisingly, his family were not members of a golf club. But the Lancashire coast (between

Liverpool and Southport) boasts some of the most famous golf courses in the world: Hoylake, Formby, Southport and Ainsdale, Birkdale and, just up the coast below Blackpool, Lytham, all of them championship courses and three regularly hosting the Open Championship. Any lad with sporting interests couldn't fail to notice the significance of golf in the area, and the dunes which provided the classic links terrain for golf were on his doorstep. Golf clubs were begged, borrowed or pilfered so that the young Lloyd brothers (and sister) could practise their skills for nothing on the local sand hills and beaches. Occasionally there were opportunities to caddy and even get a round on a public course. However limited the opportunities, John became an extremely proficient golfer eventually becoming captain of his club in Kent and a respected committee member.

Despite his outside interests, life in Ainsdale was very constricting given the continued high expectations of his contribution to home life and caring for siblings. His ambition was to get right away. This he achieved in his mid-twenties when he obtained a position with The Burroughs Adding Machine Company in Nottingham. This American firm, the forerunner of computer manufacturing, had opened a factory in England in 1888. Nottingham represented freedom to John and he would tell tales of The Trip to Jerusalem, one of Nottingham's famous pubs, and the joy of at last being a free young man.

At the end of 1937 John transferred to London with Burroughs where he lived in a flat in South London with his sister, Hilda, who was a dental nurse. He hadn't realised how significant his employment with a manufacturer of calculating machines was until, when war was declared, he was informed that since he was in a reserved occupation he wouldn't be permitted to enlist. John ignored this embargo and went anyway to join up at his nearest enlistment point. His boss somehow got wind of this and telephoned the local recruitment office and informed them that Burroughs engineers were a reserved occupation, needed for servicing adding machines used in a variety of war effort locations such as the war office and other civil service departments. This meant that my father didn't see active service, much to his disappointment. Nevertheless, he lived through some of the most dangerous times in the middle of London throughout the war, once receiving head injuries in a bombing raid and surviving numerous other raids during the blitz and later when the V1s and V2s were hitting the south of England.

He met my mother Irene through his job when he was visiting the office at which she worked as a comptometrist. He clearly fancied her at first sight and managed to get a date quite quickly, probably wangling other visits to her company so that he could see her more often. Irene was higher up the social scale than John being the daughter of George and Amelia Jenkins, from Deptford, South East London. George was a draughtsman, a decent job in those days. He was a larger than life character, a strong swimmer with a medal for saving a man's life, and also a keen cricketer. He also loved a drink and a gamble on the horses. In addition, he played the piano and was a popular socialite in that part of London. Amelia was a quieter person and probably a steadying influence on Irene. Irene had an older brother George Junior, usually known as Georgie, who did see active service. He featured in the Normandy landings in 1944 and was injured and repatriated to his home in London where he had a wife and two small children. After being patched up he was returned to France and was killed in August, 1944. (However, it was not until 1992 that we took my mother to visit his grave in Normandy).

Irene was a good-looking young woman, keen on dancing and swimming. She represented London at swimming and was selected for the Great Britain Olympic Team for 1940. Sadly, there were no Olympic games in 1940 and by the time the war ended my mother had no time for serious swimming and so missed her opportunity for fame. She was the apple of my grandfather's eye and as an only daughter was undoubtedly spoiled. I recently learned that she was engaged to a young Jewish man when she was only 18. Close enough to the wedding for wedding presents to have been received, the young man called off the engagement. Apparently, my grandfather said it was probably a blessing in disguise. Despite this experience, Irene's parents entrusted her to John Lloyd, the dashing young man from the north with a little sports car. They married in April 1942, a dark time in our history when Britain was hanging on against the might of Germany. Thanks to the attack on Pearl Harbour by the Japanese, the USA had also joined the allies and it was no longer Britain and the colonies alone. Nevertheless, it was some time before the tide turned. Meanwhile the newly married couple settled in Clapham, South West London, and like thousands of others made their best of life in war torn London. Initially they lived in a flat in Cavendish Road and later moved to a small house in Rudloe Road where they were living when I was born.

Infant years

My memories of my pre-school days are few. I can remember banal details like walking to the end of Rudloe Road up to the junction with the main road (now the South Circular) with my mother and baby brother, Allan, in a push-chair, to catch a red London double decker bus. If we stayed on the same side of the main road, we were just catching a bus into Clapham town centre to do some shopping. If, however, we crossed the road we were on a more exotic journey, usually to see my mother's parents in Deptford, a journey that involved a number of bus changes.

War-time and immediate post-war Britain was an austere place. Most things were rationed, in short supply or completely non-existent. It's hard to imagine in these times of relative plenty that mundane things like bananas were seldom to be seen. Meat, cheese, eggs, and butter were rationed which meant that when your coupons or 'points', as they were known, for the month ran out you did without. For a child the rationing of sweets was hardest to take, limited to 3oz a week and this continued until 1953 when I was ten. Toys were also a scarce commodity and I can't remember having any toys other than those my father made including a pedal car, a toy fort and soldiers, and a bus conductor set. I realise I was very fortunate to have a father who had the ability to make such amazing toys. The soldiers, for instance, were cast in lead but I have no idea where he got the lead, not to mention the moulds. Probably better not to know. I can clearly remember playing with the fort and the bus conductor set. The latter was my favourite toy since I was keen to become a bus conductor when I grew up. It was a power thing! Punching tickets and handing them out to imaginary passengers seemed to represent a level of authority that a little boy could only dream about. The pedal car was unpainted, that is gun metal grey, but I'm not convinced that I really remember 'driving' it. There is a picture of me in it and family snaps often cloud the memory rather than facilitating it. Do I really remember being in this car or is it the stories of my father's cleverness in making it along with the picture of me in it which I'm really recalling?

Much clearer is a change in my circumstances when I moved north to Ainsdale to live with my grandparents while my parents and Allan stayed in London. This was nothing to do with moving to the country to escape the dangers of London under bombing since by now the war was over. The reasons were never clear to me and really never concerned me. It turns out, I discovered sixty years later, that my parents' marriage was going through a difficult time made worse by the fact that my father had gone to live with my mother's brother's widow, Daisy. I remember Daisy as a smiling face with a prominent nose. She had two daughters, my cousins, called Irene and Miriam. Irene had a soft face and fair hair and resembled me while Miriam had curly hair and looked like my brother. That's virtually all I remember about them yet clearly they and, more especially, their mother had a significant effect on my young life. They also affected my mother since she spent much time looking after Irene and Miriam, no doubt feeling sorry for widowed Daisy, while she and my father were having an affair. Eventually an agreement was reached whereby my father left home, leaving my mother and Allan to go and live with her parents in Deptford. My father claimed me but since he wasn't in a position to look after me, he persuaded his mother to take over my care. In retrospect this was a very sorry state of affairs, unfair to me and my mother and brother. It's never a slight thing to split up a family and remove young children from their attachment figures, their loved ones, and not an easy action to forgive. But, at the time I accepted the situation for what it was and got on with it. My brother being even younger, only three, clearly did the same and was even less aware of what was going on.

Life with Grandma Lloyd was strict. I felt wanted and cared for but there were few frills and she ran a tight ship. At that time she still had two children at home, Ken and Dorothy, the twins, who must have been about sixteen. I was in awe of Ken who seemed like the big brother who could do everything that I couldn't. He sometimes teased me but was essentially kind and funny. Dorothy enjoyed spoiling me and provided the affection that was probably in short supply from Grandma Lloyd. Dorothy, I now realise, was going through adolescence which helped explain her moods. When she was seeing David, her boy friend, she was in a good mood and would buy her mother flowers and give me sweets. When for some reason David was not around she could become irritable and storm around and play the piano loudly. (When in a good mood she would play Debussy's Clair de Lune and it's still one of my favourite pieces of music).

Looking back, I'm surprised at how easily I adjusted to life in the north with my surrogate family. In some ways it was a livelier community. As well as Ken and Dorothy, there were also regular visits from the next older brother, Stanley, who was in the navy doing his national service. Then there were visits from the other brothers who lived in the north, Peter and Harold. Peter, my namesake, had a girl friend called Trudie who was also delightful towards me. She had a lovely smile and I remember telling her that she had small teeth. 'Not half as small as yours,' she said laughing. Ken had a good friend called Barry McFarlane whom I met again recently at Ken's funeral. It was more than fifty years since I'd seen him but he really hadn't changed much; still good looking and comfortable in himself.

When Barry used to arrive at the house and say: 'Good evening Mr Lloyd, good evening Mrs Lloyd. My, Mrs Lloyd you look lovelier than ever. Are you going out tonight?' she used to tell him off but loved his flattery. And sometimes Barry would arrive with a couple of young women and the four of them would then go off to the pictures and I would think, that looks a good life.

I started school in Ainsdale and also piano lessons. School seemed pleasant enough. Though I must have started by being taken by my grandmother, I soon began to do the journey on my own, sometimes accompanied by other children. (Unthinkable today, to cross the main Liverpool-Southport road at only five without an adult). Two names come to mind. One, David Bueb, was larger than me and rather dreamy. He liked to walk by the brook on the way home and try to catch tiddlers in a jar with a bit of string on it. Billy Garner was more dangerous. One day he invited me into his house on the way home from school. His mother was out. He took down his shorts and pants and knelt down with his bottom in the air. 'Smell my bum', he said. I did as I was told though with little enthusiasm. He then commanded that I let him smell my bum and, again, I did as bid. This experience carried no frisson and I did wonder who or what had given him the idea. Perhaps he spent a lot of time observing dogs.

There was a routine at Grandma Lloyd's. Granddad Lloyd went off to work early taking his lunch with him including a billycan of tea. When he got home in the evening he would plonk himself in his fireside chair, take off his big black lace-up-to-the-ankle boots and say, 'I'm ready for a cuppa, mother.' He would typically pour the tea when it came into the saucer and sip it noisily. Grandma was a good cook and we'd eat simply but well. At weekends we'd have a roast which would be chicken on special occasions. Grandma kept hens and I remember Uncle Harold chasing and catching a fowl and wringing its neck one Sunday morning. It was plucked, drawn and cooked within a couple of hours and enjoyed by a large gathering. Grandma's puddings and cakes were celebrated and I got my fair share, sometimes not being able to finish what I'd taken which always earned the admonishment: your eyes are bigger than your belly.

Granddad Lloyd seemed essentially kind with a ready smile but was not a great talker. He would sometimes get upset if he felt he was being teased by his children. He complained once about his sore hand which he called a bet hand. 'What are you talking about?' said Ken. 'There's no such thing as a bet hand.' 'Oh yes there is,' he said hotly and they proceeded to have an argument which eventually led to Granddad clipping Ken around the ear. There was also a dog in the house called Prince who was very attached to Granddad. He was sitting on Granddad's lap one evening after a big family meal and I went over and stroked him whereupon Prince snarled and grabbed my ear in his jaw. I screamed and everyone got excited. I think Ken said the dog should go if it was going to be a danger to children and got a clip round his ear again for daring to suggest that Granddad's dog should be turfed out.

I got a reputation for being a bit of a mimic. One of Grandma's friends was Cissy Mumford, a large lady with a stupendous bust, a loud voice and a lop-sided face which with hindsight was probably due to a stroke. There was also Mrs Hoskins who had a cleft palate and spoke in that distinctive voice which such misfortunates did. There was an occasion when I'd been with Grandma when she met Cissy and Mrs Hoskins in the village and passed the time of day with them. I was seen and not heard. Later, I recall Grandma telling Dorothy how she had found me on my own rehearsing the conversation I'd heard earlier in the day, including acting out the expression of Mrs Mumford and the voice of Mrs Hoskins with remarkable precision.

Another part of the routine was being allowed to listen to 'Dick Barton, Special Agent' at 6.45 every weekday evening as long as I was washed and ready for bed in my pyjamas and dressing gown. It was a highlight of my day as, seated by the radio, that wonderful music – *The Devil's Gallop*– would come thundering through the airwaves on the Bakelite box. The adventures of Dick, Jock and Snowy had me so enthralled that on Saturday morning I would listen all over again to the omnibus edition. Imagine my disappointment, then, when Dick Barton came to an end to be replaced by something called The Archers. I suspect there is a generation of boys who have never quite forgiven the BBC for killing off Dick Barton. Another distinct radio memory is hearing some strange music which I did not understand but which fascinated me. It was on Saturdays in the early evening. It must have come on after Sports Report because as soon as anyone noticed it was on, it was turned off. The music was jazz and it intrigues me that I was susceptible to it even at the age of five. Mention of Sports Report brings back that stirring signature tune, *Out of the Blue,* which always returns me to the parlour at 78 Salford Road. I have a clear recollection of the 1949 Cup Final when I would have been six. I can still hear the excitement in Raymond Glendenning's voice as he described the goals by the Wolves forward, Jesse Pye.

Did I ever see my mother and father during that time with my grandparents? The only memory I have is of a visit by my father. One late afternoon I was sent to the corner of Leamington Road and Liverpool Road to await the arrival of my father who was coming by motorbike from London. A trip of 250 miles on a motorbike on the roads of the 1940s was arduous. Eventually he arrived, all covered up against the elements; I seem to remember it was raining. I guess we were pleased to see each other but I've no recollection of what we did during his visit or how long it was.

My only other firm memory of that period of my life was playing the piano. My piano lessons were with a lady called Mrs Elias. She had a son called David whom I was led to understand was the sort of boy I should be keeping company with rather than the likes of Eddie Bagshaw, let alone Billy Garner. I think David's father might have been a professional man. David was nice but a bit dull. I loved playing the piano though I probably resented practising at times. Later I resented even more the fact that my parents never got me a piano teacher when I returned to live in the south. By the time I left Ainsdale I had a grounding in the piano but sadly it was never continued.

Although I was never a part of any gang while at Salford Road, I hung around with some of the neighbouring children including the aforementioned Eddie Bagshaw. I was aware that he was a bit of a rogue and his older sister Eunice a bit of a flirt. I recall Uncle Stanley referring to that Bagshaw kid 'with his snotty nose and his arse hanging out of his trousers'. There was also a boy called John on adjacent Leamington Road who astounded me when he said he didn't go to bed until nine o' clock. With me it was up the 'apples and pears' promptly at seven when Dick Barton finished.

School in the South

I've no recollection of returning to live in the south again though my brother says he does remember us being reunited. It may have coincided with the acquisition of a council house in St Paul's Cray near Orpington. In the post war years much of Britain was characterised by large new housing estates built by local authorities. They were an efficient way of meeting the huge demand for housing and, in this case at least, the environment was pleasant enough with plenty of green spaces as well as adequate front and back gardens in the semi-detached style. By this time my father had taken a job with the Anglo Iranian Oil Company (later BP) in Abadan and was therefore absent. My mother worked for Swan Biro in London and I would take my brother to school. He was six, I was eight and the journey entailed a walk of about a mile to catch the 61 bus to Scads Hill where his school, Shirley Lodge, a private prep school, was located. From there I'd walk on to Chislehurst Road School, a state 'elementary'. These days the idea of two small children going backwards and forwards alone daily to school on a six-mile round trip in a suburban area might appear irresponsible behaviour. It seemed nothing of the sort then. This isn't to say there weren't child predators around in those days, it was that the fear factor wasn't as strongly heightened as it is now.

The school memories are hazy – I went to another school in Cray Valley for a while but why I'm not sure. At Chislehurst Road my routine was to fetch Allan after school and complete the return journey by bus and walking. Sometimes I called in at a local sweet shop which sold gob stoppers, liquorice sticks and an amazing chewing gum which came in various colours and could be mixed like an artist's palette. So, for example, when you mixed the blue and yellow in your mouth, the resulting goo was green. Add red and you got a sort of purple colour.

Lack of continuity in schooling is rarely a good thing and when I started Brabourne House, it was my fourth school in three years. Brabourne House was in the Crofton area of Orpington and was a small, boarding preparatory school taking children from five to thirteen years. My recollection is that the pupils were between five and ten, though there may have been the odd older student being prepared for entry into public school. There was a mixture of day and boarders, the boarders being predominantly boys. The reason for sending Allan and me to board is unclear. Presumably, with our father being abroad, there was the availability of funding from BP for private education. Perhaps our mother felt we'd be better educated and cared for in a boarding establishment while she was working in North London which involved a lot of travelling time. 'Boarded children are better off than latch-key kids' could have been the thinking.

I have a strong recall of the journey by taxi from the house in Clarendon Green, passing along Crofton Lane with snow on the ground suggesting we were starting in the New Year rather than in September. Our mother, a smart, attractive woman, was anxious but tried not to show it. We were driven along an unadopted road and then up a drive to a large old house with substantial grounds. After introductions to the Headmaster we took our leave of mother and prepared to discover what awaited us in this strange new world. I was better prepared than my brother. First, I was older and second, I'd been used to living away from my parents in a strict household. In contrast my brother had been surrounded by his mother and grandmother as well as a doting grandfather. This isn't to say he was spoiled, though it's quite likely that he was, but that he'd been used to being the centre of attention in a house of loving adults. At the tender age of six, to be plucked out of the bosom of the family to a boarding school must have been a dreadful shock to his psychological system.

These years are related in a fictional account – *Tales from Torrington* – but one that is strongly based on the actual experiences.

The Abadan Experience

In 1947 my father took a job with the Anglo Iranian Oil Company, subsequently BP, in Abadan. The position certainly represented advancement for him in terms of salary and job satisfaction but it also meant the break-up of the family. 'Break-up', however, is a misnomer since there had already been the disruption which led to my moving to live with my grandparents in Lancashire. The move to Iran may partly have been a solution to an ailing marriage but there is no doubt that my father enjoyed his time with Anglo Iranian.

I've never been sure what his precise employment was in Iran. He was based at the oil refinery in Abadan but he occasionally went on visits in a small plane to the oil fields at Masjid-i Suleiman which were about a hundred miles up country. I had always assumed that his experience in working with adding machines for Boroughs was relevant. What is undoubtedly the case is that his aptitude for golf served him well. He became the honorary secretary of the Abadan Golf Club and seemed to spend as much time there, virtually running the place, as he did working in the office. Golf was a pastime that the Europeans valued and Head Office regarded it is an important facility to offer to visiting dignitaries. Accordingly, my father was frequently to be found arranging such occasions and obviously being there to front them up. A by-product of this was that he developed relationships with the Iranian staff including green keepers and caterers and used to receive letters from them, written in amusing English, long after he returned home.

We visited my father in 1950. It was intended to be a six month stay but my mother became seriously ill and we returned home after three months. We had to have vaccinations against diseases such as cholera and yellow fever and I remember my arm aching for some time after the injections and being annoyed that my brother seemed to suffer no ill effects. We flew by Swissair at a time when a journey to the Middle East by air was a major undertaking. The first day we flew from London to Geneva and stayed overnight in a hotel by the famous lake. I remember my mother complaining about the meat that we were served at dinner that evening – 'this is so tough it must be horse meat.'

Next day all the passengers had to sit in the rear of the aircraft to assist the take-off over the Alps. Our next destination was Cairo and I saw the pyramids as we came in over the city. After a night in Egypt we flew on to Basra in Iraq. A man called Ross Dunseith became friendly on the aircraft. He knew my father and was agreeable to my mother and us boys. After a short break in

Basra we finally made the short hop across the Shat el Arab River to Korramshah and Abadan where my father greeted us at the airport.

We lived in pleasant quarters in a new residential suburb called New Braim. We had a servant whom we called Nanny who seemed old. This was partly because she had few if any teeth but she was probably only in her forties at most. We played her up at times and there was an occasion when our parents were out and we ignored Nanny's request for us to get out of bed. We took it in turns when she wasn't looking to dash into the kitchen to help ourselves to a pile of fresh dates, which, for those who had only had the boxed variety, were a revelation.

We had no schooling during this idyllic time, spending half of virtually every day at the swimming pool which was a popular gathering place for ex-pats. Daily attendance at the pool was encouraged for health reasons. Not only was swimming regarded as good exercise but time spent in the water out of the heat was also considered a good thing. It was very hot with temperatures over 100 degrees Fahrenheit most days. When we arrived in Abadan I wasn't a swimmer. My Dad, who was not a strong swimmer himself, tried to teach me crawl but without success. It would have been better if my mother had been the teacher since she had been a champion swimmer. In any event, Dad gave up on me but offered me an incentive. At that time I was fascinated by circuses and he said he'd buy me a book on circuses that I coveted if and when I could swim the width of the pool unaided. One day I was at the side of the pool, staring at the water when I felt a push in the middle of my back and I fell into the water. I was frightened but found that I was able to make some movements which kept me afloat and indeed moved me back to the side of the pool. The outcome was that soon after this incident I did manage to swim a width, using breast stroke rather than crawl, and I duly earned my circus book prize. By the time we returned to England I was a decent swimmer and loved diving. When I started my new school I discovered I was an exception in this since virtually all the other boys (and girls) didn't swim. This is in contrast to the generation which followed where most children took early swimming lessons and were comfortable in the water when they started school.

The other social facility was the golf club where, as I've indicated, my father was the secretary. As well as his administrative role, he also played a lot. I would walk round with him on occasions. When you arrived at the club, as you left your car you were surrounded by a posse of young men all clamouring to be your caddie. My father would ignore them and signal to a silent boy at the back of the group and Hassan would come forward and take charge of my father's clubs. Hassan was his regular caddie and a quiet, dependable fellow. One day we went up to the golf club for tea with my father after his round. We waited on the terrace and then I saw Dad emerging from the 18th green. I ran to meet him and failed to see a barbed wire fence, perhaps a single strand, about a metre above the ground. I ran into it and it caught me across the throat. There was a lot of blood. But it had a happy ending as one of Dad's friends allowed me to 'drive' his car back home, that is sitting on his lap holding the steering wheel.

One day Nanny took my brother and me to the Bazaar. This was regarded as forbidden territory and spoken of in hushed and rather shocked tones by the European population. Perhaps this coloured my impressions but what remains most vividly, along with smells, noise and gaudy stalls, are the beggars and the disfigured people including absent limbs, eyes, ears, digits and so on. When one of my mother's female friends learned that we had gone to the Bazaar, she was dismayed.

'There are some very frightening sights and bad things going on in the Bazaar,' she said. 'It's not a good place for children to go.'

This attitude is unsurprising given that the ex-pats spent their time attempting to avoid 'native' life assiduously. In order to feel safe in this hot, dusty, troublesome land, where the natives spoke a strange language and indulged in many unusual customs, including their religion, it was necessary to maintain one's own standards and culture as actively as possible and to generally live a separate life. It is difficult to blame them, certainly at this distance in time and space, but such attitudes undoubtedly contributed to the distrust that continues to exist between Iran and the United Kingdom. However, these prejudices pale in comparison with the political chicanery that was practised by the governments of the UK and the USA in their dealings with Iran in 1953.

Our visit to Iran was cut short when my mother became ill with a gynaecological condition. We were met by my mother's parents at Northholt Airport, then a civilian airport, and returned to humdrum normality and, even worse, school. My father remained in Abadan until the democratically elected government of Dr Mossadeq failed to come to an agreement with AIOC about the distribution of oil revenues. This signalled the end of his time in Iran, and my father returned to England and got a job with Dictaphone who made small office recording machines. He was later offered a job in Kuwait by BP but by that time he had settled back in London and declined to go abroad again.

Not unreasonably, Iran requested a 50% share in its own energy resource. This was rejected by AIOC and it is salutary to reflect how different history would have been if BP had not been so greedy. My father would almost certainly have remained in Abadan. In the event, on May 1st 1951 Mossadeq effectively nationalised the Iranian oil industry.

Soon after, the AIOC technicians were evacuated and Britain blockaded Abadan causing a virtual standstill in Iran's oil production and therefore much hardship in the country. Meanwhile, Time Magazine named Mossadeq Man of The Year in 1951. Two years later, thanks largely to a coup organised by the CIA and British intelligence, he was deposed and the Shah was reinstated as an autocrat. Thus ended Iran's experiment with democracy and a shameful episode in British and American history continues to reverberate to this day.

Chapter 2
Bromley Grammar School

Two years in a small boarding school was not a good preparation for the rough and tumble of a state grammar school. This was even more the case for my brother who not only spent longer in the prep school but was unlucky enough not to pass his 11+ exam and was therefore consigned to the scrap heap, otherwise known as secondary modern education. Those who advocate a return to grammar schools and selection at 10 years either have no idea what failure at the 11+ meant for the majority who found themselves in this situation, or else they don't choose to care about a system that determines life chances at the age of ten.

In my case I was lucky enough to pass this pernicious exam and found myself in the position of being offered a place at Bromley County Grammar School. I had also had an interview at Eltham College, an independent school which seemed not unlike a larger version of Brabourne House. I decided that this is where I wished to continue my schooling and had convinced myself that this was going to happen. I was therefore disappointed not to get into Eltham. I had also had an interview at Bromley during which I remember being tricked. The Head at Brabourne had coached us a little in interview technique saying, for instance, that when we were asked about the books we read we should talk of authors such as R M Ballantyne, R L Stevenson and Louisa M Alcott.

At all costs, avoid mentioning Enid Blyton. Sure enough, at the interview by the kindly head at Bromley, I was asked this question and dutifully mentioned Coral Island, Alice in Wonderland, etc. 'But what do you really like reading?' was then the next question. I relaxed and said, 'Enid Blyton'.

The move from a school of about fifty pupils to one of over seven hundred was a massive change that took a long time to adjust to. I was sensitive and somewhat alienated from most of the other boys who seemed rough and ill mannered. There were boys that I liked and with whom I developed a good relationship, such as Dick Gilbert, but the main consolation was that I liked the work and felt stretched for the first time. A lasting influence was our form teacher Mr Drake, known as 'Quacker'. He was a kind man but more than that he was a gifted English teacher. Instead of restricting himself to a narrow curriculum, especially devoted to parsing sentences, his approach was to cultivate an interest in literature. He would read to us and I wish I knew the name of one of the books about a prehistoric tribe which I found enthralling. Even better, he got us to read aloud plays such as Agatha Christie's *Ten Little Niggers* (since retitled for a more sensitive world *And Then There Were None*) and *The Shop at Sly Corner* by Edward Percy. Mr Drake recognized that in order to engender a love of literature it was first necessary to engage the class in the activity. He chose popular plays for this purpose where we were encouraged to act the part, at least in terms of voice and intonation. I always coveted a part and was delighted if I was selected.

There were plenty of very clever students at Bromley but also some rough diamonds. This was the age of the teddy-boy and, within the confines of the school uniform, some boys tried to cultivate their teddy-boy image. One such was a mixed-race boy known as 'Blackie' Phillips. I cringe at the name now but that was what everybody called him and he didn't demur at the name. A rumour went round that Blackie had a gun and I was once shown it. It looked mean and threatening but, of course, it could have been a mere air gun. Gatherings of teddy-boys in rival gangs armed with bicycle chains, knuckle dusters and coshes were not uncommon and I remember once that it was forecast that there would be a major incident one evening at St Mary Cray Station. This was the station I used to go to school and I remember the nervousness we felt as we came home that early evening. Fortunately, I was well away from the scene of the action, which certainly ensued, later in the evening.

Even more seriously, there was an event which brought police to the school. An elderly lady had been battered over the head and had her handbag stolen on a footpath near the school. An assembly was called and we were addressed by the headmaster and a plain clothes policeman about this incident to see if anybody could throw any light on it. Eventually we learned that a third-year boy (MH) was arrested and eventually charged with the woman's murder. It transpired that MH had incurred some gambling debts and in order to meet them had become desperate and decided to rob a suitable victim. The story went that the old woman only had a pittance in her purse which made the crime all the more terrible. MH was not a friend of mine, he was in the year above, but I vaguely remembered a large, awkward, red headed individual. What an awful start to a young life not to mention the fate of the victim and her family.

My years at Bromley were mixed. After an uncertain start I began to feel comfortable in the company of most of the year group and enjoyed playground games such as Weak Horses and Chain He or Release. As we got older we could lord it in the playground and play football with a tennis ball. I once got into a fight with a boy called Ferguson. I can't even remember what it was about but there must have been a difference of opinion and a crowd gathered around and started shouting, 'Fight! Fight!' We more or less got pushed into some fisticuffs but I don't remember getting hurt or properly hurting Ferguson before some prefects arrived and marched us to the headmaster's study. There we sheepishly stood, the subject of stares by passing pupils and staff. The headmaster,

Mr Cheney, was not averse to giving the cane, but we were let off with a warning and an imposition. Subsequently, Ferguson, who was half Icelandic, became something of a friend.

My main problem at Bromley was that I didn't work hard enough. I can make excuses for this. I was one of the youngest students in the year at a time when the calendar year determined entry rather than the academic year. This meant that I was ten when I started whereas some other boys could be as much as eleven and three-quarters. Moreover, since my brother was not at an academic school it affected the environment at home. Although my parents worshipped education, because they were not from a professional background, they didn't appreciate the amount of homework that was expected. It was too easy for me to skimp homework and watch The Lone Ranger, The Cisco Kid and other children's television fare with my brother. I remember this as a happy time at home. We were in a new house, a house my parents owned, in a village called Pratts Bottom on the A21 half way between Bromley and Sevenoaks. I did well enough academically in the first year to get into the advanced Q stream in the second year which did a second language, in my case Latin, a choice made purely because my best friends had elected to go into that class rather than the one that learned German. But I struggled in Q, and in the fifth year, when O levels were taken, I passed only English and French. Because I had actually passed these subjects well, excelling particularly in English, I wasn't asked to leave but invited to repeat the year, this time going into the German class but not actually taking German. I did very well in the repeat year finishing second in the class and picking up another seven O levels which convinced me that I was merely a late developer!

I mentioned my first English teacher as a positive influence. The styles of teachers, or masters as they were known, in those times were various and frequently idiosyncratic if not eccentric. Masters wore gowns and many were skilled at putting the fear of God into their charges. Having been used to a strict regime at Brabourne, the discipline did not worry me. I was more fearful of the boys than the masters. Nevertheless, I was no rebel and preferred to toe the line. On my first day I was whispering with a boy while we were being lined up to go to our classes when a loud voice bellowed in my ear, 'Be quiet, boy, when the headmaster is talking.' This was Mr Lewis, known as Bolo, and who taught me Maths in my first year. He seemed a terrifying figure in his winged collar and bowler hat and severe countenance beneath a shock of white hair and his loud, deep, almost gravelly, voice. But as a teacher he could be warm and understanding. He had his own approach to the teaching of algebra. He would tell us to make ourselves comfortable, resting our heads on our arms on the desk if we preferred, as long as we didn't fidget. He would then say: 'Close your eyes and think of a blue sky. Put two sets of brackets onto that sky in white and then put the following numbers and letters.' He would then set a simple problem and, in the process, induct us into one of his algorithms for dealing with this branch of maths. One I remember was MOCE which he pronounced Moke. This referred to the effect of the minus sign outside the bracket on processes within the brackets – Minus Outside Changes Everything. Such acronyms, or perhaps more accurately mnemonics, were valuable and his interesting approach which engaged our imaginations meant that I always found this aspect of maths enjoyable. In contrast, geometry which was taught exclusively from the blackboard by my next maths teacher, a certain 'Sticky' Richardson, always remained an uncomfortable experience.

Building on the beginnings set by Mr Drake, English remained my first love. Being introduced to poetry, drama and other literature was fascinating. Conducting a close analysis of plays such as Richard II, Macbeth and Merchant of Venice opened up the world of Shakespeare. Extended pieces of creative writing were also encouraged, something that I enjoyed. I remember being held up as an example to boys who were being excoriated for their poor output. Unfortunately, there was a sting in the tail as I had made what you might call a schoolboy howler. 'Lloyd has produced a twenty-page account of 'The Dairy of a Dog' intoned the master, nicknamed Nemo. Images of a dog running a shop selling milk and butter came to mind in my red face but at the same time I was pleased that my writing was being recognised.

Although I was competent at languages (apart from Latin) and humanities – what were called modern subjects at Bromley – my record in science was mixed. I was able to excel at biology and chemistry because up to O level you were able to shine simply by reproducing facts to order. Where a clearer conceptual knowledge was required, such as in physics and the more demanding areas of maths, I struggled. Weaker science students took an O level called Physics with Chemistry. My problem was that I was good at chemistry and dreadful at physics. Fortunately, I was put in for both subjects and obtained a good pass in chemistry and a miserable fail in physics. I fear that my antipathy for physics would have led to me failing the joint paper and so by this ploy I at least had one science subject along with maths.

The chemistry master was called Taylor and he had a lugubrious approach to the subject with an acid wit, no doubt appropriate for a chemist. On one occasion, a boy was daydreaming during a lesson and failed to answer a very simple question about, let us say, what happens to a base when an acid is added to it. Not satisfied with simply castigating this boy, he proceeded to embarrass him by insisting that we relive the lesson over the past ten minutes while this wretch had not been paying attention. 'I started by asking the formula for hydrochloric acid, you answered this question Stannard – let us hear it again. Then I asked what happens when you add sulphuric acid to copper oxide. Who answered this? And then what did you do Ingram? Yes, you dropped your ruler you nincompoop. Go on then, drop it'. And thus it went on, including every interruption, cough and sneeze until the point at which the unfortunate was asked his question again. Needless to say, this boy didn't daydream in Taylor's classes again.

*

Taylor might have been sarcastic but he was entertaining and he certainly wasn't a physical bully. This capacity was exhibited in spades by the woodwork master Mr Osborne. Osborne frightened me since he was completely unpredictable and prone to lose his temper with grave consequences. Not only would he hit pupils, he would also throw whatever came to hand at those who displeased him. In a woodworking environment some rather dangerous implements were available as missiles. Even worse than making things with wood were the geometric drawings which we had to produce in advance of being let loose with what are now called resistant materials. I'd no talent in the domain of geometric drawing. I was always making mistakes on angles and lengths with the result that I was constantly rubbing out the lines I made which tended to detract from an already poor effort. We were required to show Osborne our drawing for him to approve before we moved to the wood preparation phase. I remember Dunning, a small pinched, thin faced boy taking up his drawing to Osborne. The master took the offering, held it out in front of him and growled, 'There's enough muck on this to sink the Queen Mary. Take it away and clean it up.' Meanwhile I cowered, knowing that when it came to my turn a similar epithet, or worse, was bound to come my way.

We each shared our benches with another boy and my companion was Shepherd, sometimes known imaginatively as 'Bogbrush' because of his short sticking-up hair. Osborne got to our bench and glared at Shepherd's drawing. 'What are these measurements supposed to be?' He pointed at the widths of some struts. 'One and a quarter inches, sir,' said Shepherd. 'No, one and a half.' And he cuffed Shepherd round the back of the head. 'Please sir,' said Shepherd, 'they are one and a quarter, Mr Gardener told us.'

'What did you say?' snarled Osborne. 'Mr Gardener told us...' Before he could complete his reply Osborne slapped him viciously across the face, almost knocking him over. Quickly a red weal came up on the side of the unfortunate Shepherd's face leaving the imprint of Osborne's hand. Bravely, Shepherd still tried to protest his innocence but Osborne told him to shut up. Trying hard not to cry, Shepherd said he was going to see the headmaster and left the room. I was impressed at Shep's bravery but fearful of the consequences. Sometime later the Head appeared in the woodwork shop and talked to Mr Osborne. I overheard some of their conversation. They seemed to be discussing those boys in the school who represented a threat to authority. The Head mentioned a boy who was difficult to handle and Osborne scoffed and said that he wouldn't give *him* any trouble. As they continued to chat, I realised that far from reproving Osborne for his disciplinary methods, the Head used him as a reinforcer for boys who were perceived as a threat. Osborne was probably a law unto himself but he appalled me to the extent that I dreaded Friday mornings and did everything I could to miss his classes, including feigning illness.

Shep became a hero of mine having the sort of courage that I knew I lacked. As for the results of my woodworking classes, which we were allowed to take home at the end of the year to our admiring parents, there were two. One was a 'pencil sharpener' which consisted of a piece of wood with a sort of handle to it, like a small chopping board; stuck to it was a piece of coarse sandpaper. The idea was that you could use it to put a point on your pencil by rubbing it across the sandpaper. I do not recall anyone using it for this purpose. The other triumph was a 'table lamp'. This was a major project which I worked on for weeks including the laborious technical drawing phase. Unsurprisingly, it was not completed but nevertheless I presented the half-finished enterprise, a wooden tower about a foot long attached to a wooden base, to my underwhelmed parents. Who'd have thought that I had a grandfather who was a draughtsman and a father who was a skilled cabinet maker?

Apart from the miseries of woodwork and the futility of physics, I mostly enjoyed schoolwork. But I was aware that bullying played a significant part of school life, a part from which the teachers themselves were not immune. To redress the balance with the horrific Osborne, there was the treatment of Mr Nation, known as Natty, a diminutive bespectacled geography teacher. This poor man had ineffectual class control which led to him suffering terrible treatment at the hands of 5Q. There was one lesson where a boy brought a frog or toad into the class and let the animal loose. At a given signal, a boy screamed and shouted, 'There's a frog jumping about!' whereupon everyone stood on their chairs, as though we were nervous women in the presence of a mouse. Natty tried to restore some control. But then someone said that we should call the frog and it might come, and someone else said, 'What's his name?' and a third said, 'Natty'. Any hope of a normality returning to the class was lost. I don't know why Mr Nation was picked on other than that he was slightly bumptious. The real reason, I suspect, was that he was ageing and weak. It later transpired that an order of a lorry-load of logs was delivered to his house and dumped in his drive and his house was also put on the market. Both these actions were carried out by students who no doubt thought they were being amusing.

Boys were also bullied and these were typically students who were afflicted in some way or different in a way that wasn't thought acceptable. An example of the latter was Newman who was a quiet, well behaved boy with a gift for music. He was an accomplished pianist and violinist. For this he was punished by the other boys. I now realise that he was also Jewish and I hate to think that anti-Semitism played any part in his treatment but it's a possibility. The other sad character was a boy called Palette. His problem was that he was immature. He looked a bit of a milksop, walked with a feminine gait and spoke with a lisp. He was unmercifully bullied by some, not including myself, and I knew it was wrong but did nothing to stop it and occasionally joined in the laughter at Palette's expense. There were many clever young minds at Bromley Grammar but intelligence appears to be no bar to the ill treatment of others. Arguably it makes it worse because the perpetrators can think up more imaginative and unpleasant forms of making someone's life a misery. David Green, one of the principal bullies of Palette, was someone with whom I later came to share a flat.

More happily, the old grammar schools could be places of culture. One of my O level subjects was Art and we had an excellent teacher called 'Danny' Drew, an appropriate name for one in his profession. Drew had his favourites, one of whom was Michael Johnson who later became better known as the film star Michael York. On one occasion Mr Drew was giving an illustrated lecture on classical painting and among other paintings and sculptures were various naked women. This elicited some perspicacious questions from Johnson but also laughter and whistles from others in the audience. Every time a nude appeared there were titters and eventually Mr Drew lost patience and stopped the lecture. As the lights were put up he said, 'You'll be interested by Kenneth Clark's new book, Johnson. It's called The Nude. Come to my office after the class and you can borrow it.'

Another bully was 'Killer' Thomas, the PE teacher. He took a particular dislike to an effete boy called Anthony Dear. Dear was an intellectual interested in music, literature and the arts generally but uninterested, let alone gifted, in games. He seemed to upset Killer who frequently victimised and ridiculed his tall, thin, unathletic figure. It became known that an anonymous letter had been sent to Killer calling him, among other things, 'born out of wedlock', a phrase one would have associated with Dear. Sure enough Dear was identified as the culprit but he avoided, as far as I know, being expelled.

I was never particularly close to the group that comprised Johnson, Dear, Peter Fenwick and Dick Vane-Wright. (The latter became an academic and occasional broadcaster, well known for his work on butterflies.) Typical of this group was when Fenwick and Vane-Wright devised what they called a sex formula. They had dreamed up an equation of some sort which was supposed to indicate how much sex appeal you had. You had to provide them with certain details about yourself, one of which was the length of your aroused phallus. Since I did not know what a phallus was at this time, I asked Fenwick what the average measurement was for this ingredient in his formula. He told me and I told him to enter that value for me. He eventually came back with a meaningless number to represent my sex appeal.

More interesting were the odd occasions when I was invited to go to London by Danny Drew as part of Johnson's clique. We were given a guided tour of parts of The National Gallery or The Tate and then invited back to Drew's flat (or possibly his mother's flat) in Kensington. There we had toasted tea cakes and played charades. This all seemed highly sophisticated and enthralling to an impressionable sixteen-year-old. On the journey home, one evening, from Victoria Station, I was travelling with Mike Johnson. We got into an old-fashioned single compartment and were soon joined by a man in a raincoat and small brown case. He proceeded to engage us in risqué conversation and mentioned that he had some interesting pictures in his case. Mike Johnson, using his 'O'level Latin, said 'senex sordidus' (dirty old man) to me which set me off giggling. We moved to another compartment.

Sixth form

Life at Bromley significantly improved with the advent of sixth form. I went into the modern sixth and took economics, geography and French. Economics seemed a new, trendy subject but it was a mistake. I found it dry and mostly unenlightening and I wished I had taken my first love, English. In some ways I might also have been better taking history rather than geography but I nevertheless enjoyed both physical and political geography. I'm not a natural linguist but I didn't regret taking French. Not only did my language improve but I acquired a knowledge of

French literature and philosophy through the works of Corneille, Moliere, de Maupassant and Voltaire among others.

The best thing about sixth form was the freedom and intimacy it provided. Class sizes were small and one wasn't required to spend the break periods in the playground. Because I'd distinguished myself neither academically nor in the sporting field, I never became a prefect. I suppose this was shameful but I can't say I missed the responsibility of handing out impositions and generally lording it over junior students. I think prefects may have been allowed to smoke in their common room but that was no hardship since I was not a serious smoker. Another person that shared my non-prefect status was Angus Wells. We became firm friends sharing a delight in reading and writing, in music, humour, drinking and girls. Angus lived in Green Street Green, a village between Pratts Bottom and Orpington, and therefore pretty close by. His parents ran a newsagent's shop in the village. His mother was kind and friendly, like Angus, but his father, Toby, was something of a brute. A stocky, shambling figure he was not unlike Osborne in appearance and behaviour. He and Angus seemed to have a perpetually antagonistic relationship which didn't surprise me. Toby's only recreation seemed to be drinking in the Rose and Crown. To be fair, the life of a newsagent was hard. Up very early to take delivery of the papers and make up the paper rounds, followed by a daily morning visit to Orpington Hospital to take papers round the wards and then manning the shop until the early evening. The Wells had a house in Romney Marsh and I was invited to spend the odd weekend there. This was the only time that I found Mr Wells in a convivial mood, especially in the local pub. This happened to be next to the police station and it was instructive to be drinking after hours in this pub, under age, with Toby who was very generous when it came to buying drinks. Romney Marsh was a remote place which perhaps enabled it to flout conventions easily.

Other friends at school in those days were Nick Tryhorn and Fred Greyer. Nick lived in Orpington and had a much older sister and parents who seemed almost as old as my grandparents. He played for the first eleven at football as a dashing winger and cricket as wicket keeper but later he started to join us at youth clubs and parties in the area. Fred was the first eleven goalkeeper and lived locally to the school at the top of Hayes Lane. His mother was French, or half French and used to call her son Freddy. His father was Dutch and he, too, was much older than my parents and rather a remote figure that Fred called Pa. There were also a couple of younger sisters. Ferd, as he became known, always seemed hard up and when we played cards he often ran out of money and either had to be subbed or else volunteer to look after someone else's stake. Fred had a bad stammer but I never remember anyone teasing him about it. Like a lot of stutterers, the handicap disappeared when he was drunk or when he sang to his guitar.

The other great friend at Bromley was John Knight. John moved to Kent from Sale near Manchester when he was fifteen or sixteen. He went into what was called Five Shell which was a class made up of those who had performed poorly in their O levels, something which I mysteriously escaped. Bromley probably shoved John there in order to assess him since he had been educated in the north! I may not have got to know him if we'd not shared the same bus in the morning. John lived in a neighbouring village, Badgers Mount, and caught the 402 a couple of stops before me. The first thing we shared was an antipathy to Ken Turpie who also lived in Badgers Mount. Initially I was friendly with Turpie who ingratiated himself with me once he discovered that we were on the same bus. Coincidentally, he was also from the north, Leigh, though he'd come south earlier than John. I put up with Turpie's foibles – he was a know-all and a bore – because he was a neighbour and shared an interest in sport. We used to play football and cricket together in a local field often with my brother. John soon got on the wrong side of Turpie, who was a prefect, because he ignored the school rule of wearing a cap to and from school. Sensible prefects realised that sixth formers (and the shell) only put on their caps when in sight of the school. Turpie reported John to the authorities about this heinous misdemeanour and thus was the start of a beautiful enmity. In my case it was the start of a beautiful friendship which continues still and the beginning of the end of the relationship with Ken. Much later Ken Turpie intruded again into my life because he was working in Manchester at the same company as a good friend of ours. I resisted any attempts to meet up with him and then he died suddenly and I relented and went to his funeral.

John was straightforward, immediately likeable and a lot of fun. By his own admission he had found it difficult to integrate into a new life at an age when he had already formed a peer group at Sale. Moreover, he'd moved from a rugby playing school. Nevertheless, his sporting prowess enabled him to play for the school as a centre forward and an off spinner. He was also a champion shot putter. Until he met me, his leisure pursuit was drinking at the Black Eagle in Halstead with a dubious crowd. John could easily pass for eighteen even though he was underage. I introduced him to Angus, Nick, Ferd and my brother and the local youth club and he didn't look back.

Chapter 3
Leisure and Holidays

My parents were not particularly hands-on in encouraging structured leisure activities for which one should probably be eternally grateful. Initially there was Scouts, an activity I started at Brabourne House, and later I was urged to join the school scout troop at Bromley. Living under canvas in the close company of other adolescent males, let alone learning to tie knots and worst of all what were called 'lashings', unfortunately far removed from the daydreams of the Marquis de Sade, was not my idea of fun which probably disappointed my one-time ranger-scout father. But ballroom dancing classes, though occasionally embarrassing, had the advantage of allowing you to put your arms around a girl without getting arrested. The Frank and Peggy Spencer School of Dancing was famous in South London. Their formation dancing team were regularly on television when a programme called 'Come Dancing' was popular.

Classes were held in the civic hall in Orpington and Allan and I used to go together in the early evening, often with our neighbour Jane Boullin and her cousin Pauline. As well as the traditional ballroom dances – waltz, quickstep and foxtrot – we also learned Latin American dances like the tango, samba, rumba and cha-cha. Jive was also taught and daring new-wave dances like the Madison and the Twist. The teachers were magnificent but the pupils' competence varied considerably. Boys would line up on one side of the hall and girls on the other. Initially we were taught our respective gender roles and then paired up with the girl who happened to be opposite, or next on the line, and attempted to look the part. You hoped for a gazelle but sometimes ended up with a hippo and prayed that the dance would not go on too long. At the end of each lesson there was a short period when you were permitted to choose a partner and try out a few dances, hopefully corresponding to the music being played. This was an opportunity to link up with a girl that you fancied. You risked being rebuffed, of course, but it was a question of nothing ventured, nothing gained. Allan outshone me which was fortunate since he eventually married an accomplished dancer and he and Meryl still look good on the floor together.

At a time when the opportunities for leisure are legion, it's not easy to convey the tedium which was Sundays in 1950s Britain when I was a teenager. There was no daytime television, let alone sport on TV, and the radio had to serve as the entertainment medium. 'Family Favourites', a programme of listener popular music requests for the armed forces, who were mostly stationed in Germany, was followed by the 'Billy Cotton Band Show'. Billy Cotton was a jovial Londoner who revelled in corny music and even cornier jokes and had execrable singers like Alan Breeze. The next offering was 'Ray's a Laugh', a lame comedy show starring Ted Ray. After that there might be the cringe-inducing 'Life with the Lyons' or 'Educating Archie', starring Archie Andrews who was, would you believe, a ventriloquist's dummy. It was a common joke that Archie's 'vent', Peter Brough, was so bad that radio was the only place he could perform. Nevertheless, Educating Archie was the recruiting ground for later stars like Tony Hancock and Harry Secombe.

This is not meant to be a diatribe against radio comedy since I spent many happy hours listening to Jewel and Warris in 'Up The Pole' and then the surreal humour on 'The Goon Show', with the incomparable Peter Sellers and Spike Milligan. 'Take it From Here',

'Hancock's Half Hour' and later 'Beyond Our Ken' and 'Round The Horne' were other classic radio comedies. Nevertheless, popular entertainment was restricted in the 1950s and I was too young to watch what decent programmes there were on evening television once we acquired one. The Queen's coronation in June, 1953 was the event that triggered a large sale in televisions but my family watched the famous occasion at my Aunt Hilda's in Beckenham who was blessed with a TV. As a ten-year-old, I found most of it boring and began to long for it to be over so that I could watch something else on the TV. When at last it finished, what should come on but tennis, something I then found even more boring.

Exotic holidays were not part of life in the forties and fifties and I didn't go abroad until 1959 when I was sixteen. A typical holiday before that was to go to Southport to stay with grandma or one of our uncles and his family, in particular Uncle Peter and Auntie Trudie and their two children Sue and Tim. My early memory of Peter and Trudie is their flat off Lord Street in Southport. They had a talking blue budgie, Mickey, who was so tame that he flew down the stairs to greet them when they came through the front door. One day, unfortunately, he flew right past them and out the front door and was never seen again.

In those days Southport had an allure for young boys and no doubt rather older young people. It was a popular seaside resort in the heyday of the British seaside town. Smaller and much more sophisticated than Blackpool, it boasted about eight cinemas along one side of Lord Street as well as a commercial theatre (The Garrick) where I saw Eve Boswell, Derek Roy and Tommy Cooper in the summer show in 1952. Boswell was a popular and very talented female vocalist of the time with a major hit called Sugar Bush. This caused her to be known for a while as the Bush Girl. Derek Roy was a rather vulgar comic with his own radio show and everyone knows who Tommy Cooper is though at that time he was a newcomer. There was also a professional repertory theatre, The Little Theatre, where my father's brother Stanley was a star turn.

More interesting to young boys was the stuff of seasides: the promenade, the pier, boating lake, miniature railway and, above all, Pleasureland. I couldn't get enough of Pleasureland at a certain age but wasn't allowed to go into it unaccompanied until we were much older. All was grist to the mill: the helter-skelter; ghost train; dodgems; big dipper and umpteen booths with the possibility of winning tacky prizes for a few pennies. On top of that there was popcorn, toffee apples and candy floss made in those amazing machines that spun sugar. The first time I went to Pleasureland alone with my brother was both exciting and slightly dangerous. The stallholders and purveyors of attractions would call out to you in enticing ways, eager to relieve you of your modest sum of money.

Pleasureland, boating trips and rides on the little railway were treats. More typical was to go down to Ainsdale beach to play in the sand hills or perhaps cricket on the beach. Ainsdale beach was a magnificent stretch of firm sand which had been the setting for a number of land speed record attempts and was where Henry Segrave set the land speed record of 153 mph in 1926. At low tide it was usually impossible to see the sea. Christmas was sometimes spent in Ainsdale. The tradition was to hang a pillow case at the end of the bed and one year, in the morning, poking out of the pillow case was a real bow and arrow. This was deemed a far too dangerous activity to enjoy in Grandma's back garden and so we had to take the bow, arrows and the heavy big circular target into the sand hills supervised by my father and one of his brothers. As I recall, no one was injured.

Smoking

Smoking could be considered a leisure activity or a vice but for the child, that is anyone who looks clearly below the age at which smoking is legal in this country, it is fatuous to regard smoking as merely leisure. Imagine yourself saying at the age of thirteen to your father when he asks you where you're going, 'Oh, I thought

I'd just pop out to the garden for a smoke.' The attraction of smoking to the young child, and I guess I am thinking principally of the young male, is that it is a forbidden pursuit that looks as if it might be exciting. Ours was not a smoking household and my father was a confirmed non-smoker. His father had smoked Woodbines. My mother's father had been a heavy smoker and had died of lung cancer in 1956 when he was barely sixty. My mother did smoke from time to time but knew that my father disapproved and was therefore an occasional social smoker.

Smoking was depicted as glamorous while we were growing up in the fifties. All film stars seemed to smoke, unless they were playing Robin Hood or Ivanhoe, and the activity of constantly handing out and lighting cigarettes was a staple of films and TV drama. Smoking was also taking place everywhere, not least in the cinema where films were always viewed through a haze of blue smoke. In the current era of stringent anti-smoking it's hard to believe that cinemas, theatres, concert halls, cafes, restaurants, buses and trains (in the designated areas) were awash with smoke. It seemed sexy, adult and enjoyable. So, it's not difficult to understand why two young lads would want to participate in the pastime. The problem was how to get hold of them. You couldn't go into a tobacconist's and buy them since it was illegal. This didn't stop thousands of youngsters going into shops and saying that they wanted ten Player's Weights for their Mum. Very often this strategy worked and sometimes it was a genuine request. Our approach was different.

There were two solutions: steal them or pick up dog ends in the street. The quality of the former was definitely preferable but there were risks and this is portrayed in *Tea Leaves in the Local Shop*. The more disgusting approach (perhaps not morally) was perpetrated on one holiday in Ainsdale. My brother and I were staying on our own with our grandmother. We'd made the journey by steam train together from Euston, a big adventure. Grandad was in the house, puffing away on his Woodbines and we became desperate to join him, if covertly. I hit upon the idea of surreptitiously collecting discarded dog ends from the gutters. This did not mean any old spittle covered, ground down butt. We were more discriminating than that. We looked for fag ends in fairly good condition with a substantial amount of tobacco still to be consumed. And don't think that we simply smoked the end of the cigarette once we got our grubby hands on it. Again, a more sophisticated approach was adopted. From somewhere we acquired some small tin boxes – I think we told Grandma that we were collecting old bus tickets – and we put our haul of butts into these tins. After traipsing the streets long enough to fill a tin, we went into the sand hills to sift through our haul.

The next phase was to empty out the tobacco into another tin and discard the old papers and corked tips if these were present. In this way, I reasoned, we would be avoiding contamination from germs, an appalling word in one's lexicon at that time. However, still required were the materials to make use of this random pile of shag, namely cigarette papers and matches and, ideally, a cigarette rolling machine. Our pocket money stretched to all three of these items and having acquired them from the appropriate shop in the village, we once more retired to the sand hills. We settled down out of the wind and I prepared a paper and put it into the appropriate compartment of the machine – something I'd watched my granddad do when he couldn't afford woodbines. Allan was charged with pouring some tobacco into the paper. He opened the tin that contained the golden shavings and started to tip some gingerly onto the paper. Just then there was gust of wind which blew all the tobacco out of the tin onto the sand. I'm not sure what oaths I was capable of in those days but expletives were certainly uttered and Allan did well not to cry. We managed to salvage enough to make a couple of roll ups and lay back to enjoy the great moment.

It took a while to get them alight and I noticed that almost half my brother's 'cigarette' had disappeared in the act of lighting it. Eventually we got them both drawing and savoured our first drag. 'Ugh!' said Allan. 'Don't you like it?' I responded, trying to look suave as I inhaled deeply. 'It's horrible,' he said, and threw it in the sand. I wondered if there was a term to describe a cigarette made of discards that was itself discarded. At first, I wouldn't admit that I also found it revolting. I tried to reassure myself that this wasn't because smoking, in itself, was an unpleasant activity but it was the nature of the raw materials we were using that accounted for the disappointment in the experience. This subsequently proved to be at least partially true since when we got hold of the real thing we were, for a while, hooked.

Paradoxically, it was my brother who smoked for some time once we were of an age to do so legally. Two things served to discourage me. One was when my father discovered some cigarettes in my pocket when I was underage. I think my brother may have had some as well. 'I see you're smoking,' he said. 'Go on, have one,' he continued, handing them to me along with some matches. 'No,' I said. 'Go on,' he repeated, 'I want to see what big men you are.' We felt very uncomfortable and refused to acquiesce to his request which, of course, was his intention. After that humiliation I didn't smoke again until it was legal.

What finished off my smoking career was a trip to Austria by train with Ken Turpie. I was sixteen and we were heading to a youth camp in Graz in the East of Austria. The first leg of the journey was the boat train to Oostende via Dover. On the boat we were amazed to see the price of duty-free cigarettes and both bought a pack of two hundred Peter Stuyvesant. For the rest of the journey, on the boat and on the train, we smoked more or less nonstop. I think I'd finished most of them by the time we got to Salzburg. However, instead of feeling like a cool dude I felt terrible, my tongue parched, my throat burning, my head aching and a disgusting taste in my mouth. After that I was uninterested in cigarettes again, though I came to appreciate that nothing complemented a brandy or port like a good cigar.

The last time I saw Grandma Lloyd was when I visited Ainsdale with some friends at the age of twenty-two. It coincided with Churchill's funeral which dates it as January, 1965 when I was working for Harris and Hunter in London. I remember the funeral being on her black and white television and feeling slightly embarrassed because she hadn't long been a widow, her husband William having recently died. She seemed pleased to see us and made a fuss of me and friends as usual. While there we drove down to the beach in our hired car in cold, frosty conditions and did some foolish things on what was virtually a skidpan.

Sport

My sporting activity at this time could be described as dilettante. I never had the confidence to try for school colours and was content to represent my house at football and cricket and even, foolishly, cross country running for which I had no natural talent. Once, when playing cricket for 5X against another year group, I found myself opening the bowling with Derek Tennant who was a feared fast bowler with the first XI. Quaking members of the other side asked Tennant to go easy on them. 'Don't worry,' he said, 'Pete is bowling faster than me.' He suggested that I go for a trial with the second XI. My batting was also sound in those days and it was a pity that I didn't take up his suggestion. I did later play a few games for the Old Bromleyans after leaving school but after getting a fearful blow on the temple while fielding at slip (the bowler thought I had caught the ball and was momentarily jubilant and then completely lost interest when he realised I'd only taken a hit on the head), I decided there were better things to do with my time.

My parents were close friends with Ray and Chris Boullin who had a tennis court in the garden of Greenshoots, their house on Halstead Lane. It was about two minutes' walk from us and so it was inevitable that Allan and I got to use the facility as long as we were prepared to mow the grass and mark out the court. We had many happy hours playing there, sometimes with Chris and Ray's daughter Jane, and her cousin Pauline. Later, we played with the Kemp brothers, Martyn and Geoff, who lived next door to the Boullins and later still, school friends like John Knight and Nick Tryhorn joined, increasingly supplemented by various other girls. Playing on grass is still the best experience in tennis but one that is increasingly difficult to find.

For a while I joined a tennis club at Goddington Park in Orpington but the club situation was not to my taste. It's difficult to elucidate the reasons for this but it has remained a feature of my sporting life ever since. Perhaps it's something about being expected to take part with strangers or engage in social activities that go along with the role of being a member of a club that don't resonate with me. Or is it a fear of failure?

The same thing happened with golf. My father was a fine golfer and captained his club (West Kent) and was a regular member of the team, of committees, and won numerous trophies and competitions. My mother sometimes said that he 'lived at the golf club' and this may have had an off-putting effect. I was given every opportunity to take up golf, with a set of junior clubs provided. I also caddied at West Kent and earned useful pocket money at the weekends pulling the trollies of affluent members. In the sixth form, when we had free Wednesday afternoons, I'd go up to the club and caddy for matches against other clubs and get quite handsomely rewarded. All this taught me an appreciation for the game and I used to enjoy playing. However, I had no aspirations to be even a good club player, let alone competition winner and never pushed to join West Kent as a junior. Perhaps I was never offered the chance as money was always a consideration in our household.

Nevertheless, I remain grateful that I was introduced to golf as a boy. I've spent many happy hours on golf courses and it has helped to cement good friendships. Golfing holidays still play an important part in my life. But, ultimately, I've still resisted the lure of golf club membership. This isn't quite true as I've twice been a member of golf clubs in the Manchester area – Northenden and Heaton Moor. On both occasions the experiment was short-lived as I discovered that I wasn't playing enough to justify the membership fee. And I was also a bad member as I didn't turn up to play with other members and nor did I take part in social activities at weekends or during the evening. Essentially, I like playing golf when I feel like it with certain friends. This suits me fine and doesn't require membership of a club. In truth, golf clubs are strange places where lurk misogynists and sticklers for rules of all sorts. I don't feel comfortable in such an environment.

As a footnote, I should mention that we joined as a family the West Heaton Bowls and Tennis Club when it was but a few yards away on Princes Road where we lived. This allowed our children the opportunity to learn the game and Virginia and I also took advantage of membership. But again, my pattern of play has been to restrict my playing to games with a dozen friends on Sunday mornings and certain other times. Although we've been members for more than 30 years, I doubt if many of the members of a similar standing even know who I am as I rarely venture into the place for social reasons. It doesn't help that the club isn't open for refreshments on Sunday morning. I fear I may have passed on this phobia of clubs to my children since none of them has ever shown much interest at excelling at sport let alone joining a club!

Delinquency

Delinquent acts are not confined to youths from poor environments, homes where children are unloved and uncared for. I have committed or participated in my share of stupid, not to say criminal, actions, and I can't blame my parents for this failing. Rather, I think it's more or less normal for children, especially young males, to engage in daring, risky activities some of which turn out to be harmful to others. (There is a difference when there is no intention to harm others although it might not constitute a successful defence in a court of law). It amounts to a phase that most traverse without any adverse harm resulting. This isn't intended to be a defence of criminal behaviour but rather to point out that some do bad things and get away with it while others are less fortunate. The age-old cry, 'it's the poor what gets the blame', is pertinent if simplistic here.

Making fires is a primitive activity that humankind has engaged in since the ability evolved with obvious benefits. Responsible adults know that lighting fires wherever and whenever you feel like it is a foolish and potentially dangerous pastime. Boys do not necessarily appreciate this distinction and making and lighting a fire was a popular thing to do among our gang. And where better to carry out this game than in the woods since there's an abundance of fuel. Our nearest woods were very close and we spent a fair bit of time there, climbing trees and also getting up to less innocent activities.

Two incidents come to mind that were particularly reprehensible. The first came about through allowing a game that was essentially benign to get out of hand. In other words, it was a question of scale. You light a little fire because it is a fun thing to do and perhaps you also want to warm yourself up. There were three or four of us and we got carried away collecting fuel, which, obviously, was freely available. Once the fire was lit, the obvious thing to do was put on a little more wood. Twigs gave way to branches, then large limbs until were virtually dragging whole, dead trees onto the fire. The inevitable result was that a conflagration ensued that started to set fire to some of the surrounding trees. What we didn't realise is that this blaze could be seen from the main road a couple of hundred yards away. And who should be travelling along that road in his Landrover but the owner of the land. We were suddenly aware of a vehicle drawing up in the field adjoining the woods and a man shouting. We may have been stupid but it didn't require great intelligence to see that this man wasn't happy with us. We abandoned the fire and beat a rapid retreat. We weren't apprehended because the farmer was more concerned about putting out the fire than catching us. By the time that he'd done that and driven his jeep back to the road, we were safely indoors.

The second idiocy was even more dangerous since it involved explosives. It was common knowledge that the combination of weed killer (sodium chlorate) and sugar was a powerful mix. Put these two ingredients in a confined space, such as a metal tube, and ignite them and a satisfying bang would result. Sadly, all sorts of people with a far more malign motive than us are currently in possession of this information as many victims of terrorism can testify. In our case the single reason for combining sodium chlorate and sugar was to make an impressive firework. The usual technique was to make up the inflammatory combination, pour some into a tin or tube, seal it and then place it on the ground. A trail of the mixture was then made away from the 'bomb', rather like a fuse. I should point out that we were not idiotic enough to do this in a place where innocent bystanders might wander but in the aforementioned woods. It was exciting to watch the flame lick along the fuse, once lit, until it reached the metal container whereupon the explosion dwarfed even the loudest firework banger. It never occurred to us that the blast might make neighbours think that troops were on manoeuvres. Although we were never discovered 'playing this game', it didn't last long, either because we realised that the resulting pieces of shrapnel could be lethal or, more likely, we didn't have the resources to keep buying the weed killer. These days it is impossible to buy the critical component without a licence but those were more innocent times in the 1950s before the advent of an element who thought it was appropriate to further their political cause with bombs.

I mentioned earlier in this narrative that a valued Christmas present was a 'real' bow and arrow. Even more exciting was when, some years later, we were given an air rifle. It now occurs to me that having exculpated my parents of any responsibility for my delinquency, I might be wrong about this. What were they thinking of, allowing a firearm in the hands of (irresponsible) teenagers? In the beginning we were responsible, only firing the weapon at a paper target which allowed us to ascertain our level of skill. But this obviously became boring because we started firing at small birds and when Allan, to his chagrin, actually hit and killed a chaffinch, we looked for alternative targets. I remember we fired on the birds from our bedroom window and when my brother hit the unfortunate bird, we rushed downstairs to the stricken animal only to be in time to see it breathing its last.

We next turned our attention to the main road on the other side of the house. Here there were plentiful targets in the shape of cars, vans and buses. Again, what were we thinking of in firing pellets at moving or, in the case of the bus, sitting targets containing people? I can offer no defence. It was a lark and the possibility of anyone getting hurt didn't enter our heads. What was satisfying was to see heads turn on the bus as a lead pellet struck the bus loudly enough for passengers to be aware of it. This particular game came to an end when we were heading up to the woods one afternoon after school with the rifle jauntily placed over my shoulder. A white van suddenly came to a halt beside us. The passenger wound down his window and enquired if we were the owners of the rifle. When we nodded, he told us to look at the mark just below the window on his van. This, he said, had been done by an air rifle. With the window open and a foot or so higher, someone could have been hit in the face. Naturally, we denied all knowledge of such a stupid and dangerous action and said we only used the rifle in the garden or in the woods. The driver asked if there were any other people around with rifles in the neighbourhood and we affirmed that, indeed, there were. The implication being that these others were less scrupulous than ourselves and would probably do a criminal thing like shooting at a moving vehicle. Once again, it seemed, we'd got away with delinquent behaviour without any adverse consequences to ourselves. But we did learn the lesson: no more shooting at traffic.

The most serious piece of delinquency concerned the local railway line from London to Hastings. Our nearest station was

Knockholt and between Chelsfield, the next station up the line, and Knockholt was a tunnel taking trains beneath part of the North Downs. On one of our walks we discovered a point that directly overlooked the southern entrance/exit to the tunnel. We enjoyed watching the trains leaving Knockholt station and coming towards the tunnel whereupon we would wave to the driver who would wave back. Someone, I forget who, had the bright idea of lobbing a stone on to the train below when, if we scored a hit, came a satisfying dull thud. The odd pebble on a large train may not have mattered if it had ended there. But, of course, it didn't. Over enthusiasm, to put it euphemistically, took over and we started chucking ever larger missiles until great clods of earth and small boulders were being heaved on to the trains below. Once or twice the projectile landed on the whirring fans that were part of the diesel engines on some of the trains which caused a satisfying plume of dust and grit to fly into the air.

Once again we were fortunate that before any serious accident occurred, we were stopped in our tracks when a group of railway police were seen walking along the line from Knockholt station looking up to where we were situated. I think they were shouting up at us and waving sticks or truncheons. And once again, we scarpered rapidly and were never apprehended. This warning was enough to make us give up the stupidity before we, not to mention any innocent party, suffered any adverse consequences. Now, whenever I hear of someone being arrested for throwing missiles onto motorways or railways from a bridge I have a twinge of sympathy for the perpetrator, however misplaced, since I know how easy it is to be in that situation and that the intention may not have been to maim or injure, let alone kill. Thoughtlessness is a feature of human behaviour that, for the most part, doesn't have serious consequences. Hopefully we learn from our mistakes and, in this respect, I've been fortunate while others have been less so.

Ironically, the last example of delinquency, which did lead to a police arrest and charge, was one of which I was mostly innocent. It happened on my 21st birthday, when I should have known better, and involved five friends, two of whom were girls. The incident is described in full in the story in Part I, *Key of the Door*. In brief, it involved a nocturnal drunken spree, driving around the Kent lanes, pinching signs – one from RAF Biggin Hill and one a street sign – and putting them into the car boot. The street sign was so large that we were unable to close the boot. This left it hanging out which almost certainly alerted a passing police car. It was a silly prank and we got caught. But, given the number of stolen signs I've seen in student flats and the like, it represents a national pastime, almost a rite of passage, that young males in particular pass through at a certain stage of their lives. It left us with an appearance in court, a police record, and a fine of £5 which at that time was almost half a week's wages. And no trophy to show for it!

My paternal grandparents – William and Elizabeth Lloyd (nee Hughes). He worked on the railways and she had been in service before her marriage.

Maternal grandparents – George Alexander and Maria Amelia Jenkins (nee Hollands). He was something of a dandy while she was more reserved.

In my first year.

My parents in the 1950s, John Noel and Irene Amelia Lloyd.

Polyfoto at age three.

In the pedal car made by my father, aged about three. I was lucky to have a Dad who was a supreme handyman even when resources were limited in wartime.

On my paper round in Chelsfield with brother Allan. Taken by the proprietor of the village shop. He made it into a calendar which was for sale in the shop.

The model pupil at Bromley Grammar School.

On the tennis court at Greenshoots.

Male friends at my 21st party at West Kent Golf Club. Back, l to r: Trev Rising, Perce Parker, John Andrews, Bob Neve, me, Derek Tennant, Angus Wells, Allan. Front, l to r: Dick Wythe, Steve Wythe, Fred Greyer, Nick Tryhorn.

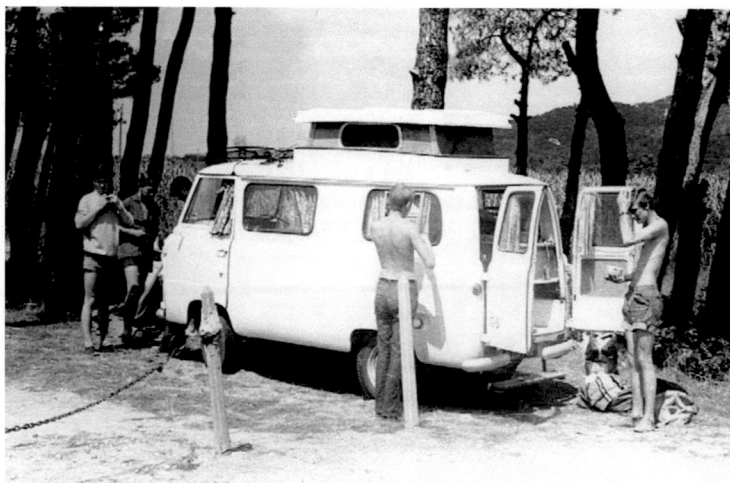

Camping in dormobile outside Playa de Aro, Costa Brava. Martyn and Nick on the left and Angus and me on the right.

In the garden at Pratts Bottom.

On Heinz's boat on Chiemsee, Bavaria.

At masonic ball with Susan and Linda Calder and Angus.

Photo shoot with Susan for PR client (Youngs Potted Shrimps). Professional models were available but we cost nothing.

With Martyn Kemp, behind, and Dave Green on the balcony of our flat in Sinclair Gardens, Shepherd's Bush.

Best man to Nick Tryhorn, Farnborough, Kent, January, 1969.

Best man to Martyn at his wedding to Moya, Torquay, August, 1966.

With Nick and Ruth Tryhorn and brother Allan.

Editor of Aien, University of St Andrews student newspaper, with the editorial and production team. Note the dearth of women and how many are wearing ties. (1967)

With Isabel at University Faculty Ball, 1968.

Graduation Day, University of Dundee, 1969.

Taken at Cognition Project, Edinburgh University, where I was Research Associate to Margaret Donaldson, 1971.

Wedding day, Edinburgh, April 3rd, 1972.

Chapter 4
Foreign Adventures

Graz (1959)

My first foreign adventure was a trip to Graz in Austria under the auspices of an international youth camp organisation, via UNICEF. I went with a Bromley Grammar friend and near neighbour, Ken Turpie. Turpie and I gravitated together through propinquity rather than anything else and at times I found him irritating. Nevertheless, we planned to spend a large part of the summer holidays in 1959 hitch-hiking to Austria to take part in the youth camp that would provide us with board and lodging and a chance to meet with other young people in exchange for some work for the local forestry commission.

We bought some stout walking boots and rucksacks and went on a couple of practice walks. Eventually we set off in July by train to Dover to catch the Oostende ferry. Our efforts at hitch-hiking were unsuccessful and we returned home two days later. I like to think that Turpie was responsible for this ignominious beginning, throwing in the towel far too early just because the first car we thumbed didn't stop. In truth I'm not sure but, based on later hitch-hiking holidays the following two years with different people, or alone, I suspect that my suspicions might be accurate. In any event, we booked the journey by train – I suppose parents coughed up the money – and we tried our luck for a second time shortly after.

The main recollection of that outward journey was the purchase of the duty-free allowance of two hundred cigarettes and then smoking the lot on the journey to Graz, something I have already referred to in an account of my smoking 'career'. We must have looked a sight. Two youths sitting in the railway compartment, lighting up cigarette after cigarette if not lighting one from the stump of the other. At least it had the beneficial effect of putting me off fags for life.

In Graz we met up with a number of other young men, a mixture of Germans, Austrians, British, French, and so on. Rather surprisingly, the three English boys were put together and dropped off by minibus at a farmhouse about two miles from a village in Styria called Obdach. The other young man was called Jim and was somewhat older than us and had a motorbike. I was impressed that he'd driven all the way from England by motorbike. Later in the evening, a French boy joined us by the name of Jean who came from Nice and was close to Jim in age. At sixteen I was the youngest of the group and Jim and Jean were nineteen. I must have seemed callow but they did not make me feel unwanted. What we all agreed, however, was that my companion was a pain with his whinging and frequent negative demeanour. They were puzzled as to why I had teamed up with him and I had to admit that I also didn't understand it.

Our lodging was in a wing of a farmhouse. I shared a room with Ken, and Jim and Jean shared. We had breakfast and dinner together, usually alone, and occasionally with the family. The food was uncomplicated. Breakfast consisted of black bread with cold meat or cheese, jam and a bowl of hot milk into which one could sprinkle coffee or chocolate. On Sundays we got sweet white bread and a huge pat of butter. I wondered why we were given such a large amount of butter on Sundays rather than spreading it out more economically over the week. We were told that this was simply the way that it was. Lunch was a sandwich, drink and apple, to take with us to have in the fields. The evening meals were usually meat and two veg, plainly cooked. On one weekend, we witnessed a piglet being chased round the yard before it met an untimely end. Later that day as we were eating the unfortunate beast we agreed that it tasted peculiar. This was not only for emotional reasons but because it hadn't been hung for the period that we were used to.

We didn't work for the farmer but for the forestry commission and our job was to plant conifer trees. This meant preparing the ground, digging out the holes and then putting in the saplings. For anyone not used to physical labour, it was back breaking work. We used to start at eight in the morning, have a break for lunch at midday and then continue to four in the afternoon. Herr Hiertler, our boss, was a jolly individual who corresponded to the Austrian stereotype by going around in lederhosen and a hat with a feather in it. Jim and Ken spoke some German but, on the whole, Herr Hiertler communicated in heavily accented English. As Jean remarked, it was as well that his first name wasn't Adolf. Once he had shown us what to do, the boss sometimes worked with us but more often left us to get on with it while he went about his business elsewhere. Occasionally we were asked to help out on the farm with harvesting which made a change and allowed us to fraternise with the natives who included some shy farm girls.

Three weeks was a long time in close proximity, essentially in the middle of nowhere. Initially we were tired after a day's work but as we got used to it we looked for things to amuse us in our spare time. The nearest village, Obdach, was an hour's walk, but we went in on a number of occasions. It had a bar with a juke box and I remember that one of the tunes it played was 'Peter' (pronounced 'Payter' in German) sung by a female vocalist. At weekends, activities were on offer from the youth camp organisers. One Saturday we climbed the highest mountain in the region, something like 8,000 feet, and another time we went into Graz which made an agreeable change. On another weekend, Jim and Jean went off for a couple of days to Trieste on Jim's motorbike which left a difficult gap for Ken and me to fill together. On the final weekend we discovered that there was a motor racing event in a town called Zeltweg, not too far away. It turned out to be quite a big race and was won by a British driver called David Piper whom we were able to meet in the pits after the race. The security then was far less than it would be now. Zeltweg has since been the home of the Austrian Grand Prix on many occasions. We were elated at both the racing and the British win and secured a huge BP flag as a souvenir which I kept in my possession for many years.

On our first visit to Obdach I tried to buy a pack of playing cards but only German skat cards were available. This was a disappointment to me since we'd plenty of time to kill in the evenings. I decided that there was nothing else for it but to make a pack of cards and to this end we managed to procure some thick card. The resulting pack was huge – at least six inches high – and impossible to shuffle in any conventional way. Nevertheless, we had many happy hours playing with that pack and I taught the others variations of whist and rummy as well as Switch. My parents were amazed when they saw the pack since I took it home. They showed their friends and I think the feeling was that we'd been in a prisoner of war camp.

Jim and Jean, being three years older than I, enjoyed their own company. Nevertheless, they were very likeable companions and made me realise that the next time I went abroad I'd have to find friends with whom I was compatible. Our return journey on the train was an ordeal as we had spent up what little money we had on presents. Some cheese and a loaf of bread soon ran out and we were starving when we reached Oostende. The smell of an English cooked breakfast on the boat was almost more than we could bear but our appetites were sated when we got home. Overall, I felt proud that I'd survived a month away on my own at the age of sixteen and was grateful for the independence it had given me. From then on, all my holidays were abroad without parents.

Montpellier and the Midi (1960)

Two of my sixth form A levels were French and Geography and in the summer following my first year in the sixth, I looked to go to France. Two friends, David Parker – known as Perce – and Fred 'Ferd' Greyer were keen to come with me. It was another international youth camp, this time organised by UNESCO. Again, the purpose was to bring young people from different nations together. The camp was situated in what amounted to a sports university (CREPS) – rather like Loughborough – in the southern French town of Montpellier. The task for the inmates of the camp was to build a volleyball court.

Below is my verbatim diary entry of our first day of this trip. I offer it not because it's a good example of travel writing. On the contrary, it is very much the scribbling of a rather naive 17-year-old but it has a simplicity and a certain charm. Moreover, it was actually written at the time and therefore, however banal, it accurately records the sort of features and episodes that I must have considered significant.

July 8th
Commenced trip 08.30.
Arrived Folkestone 10.20
Boarded boat safely 11.00. Sailed 11.20
Had ½ light ale (last English beer!)
Changed some stirling (sic)
Arrived Boulogne 12.45.

Met chap from Burnley. Walked to hostel, dumped our bags in baggage office. Walked to beach and had meal. Bought postcards. Had beer in café and sent postcards. Returned to hostel at 17.00 hours. Bought some Vin de Bordeaux et Vichy water. Had smack-up meal of beans, pork luncheon meat + vin de Bordeaux + bread and butter. Peaches to follow + coffee and biscuits.

Went with Swede named Tedde to a café in Boulogne. Had a game of pool and two glasses of very refreshing beer. A very enjoyable time. Came back to hostel to play table tennis. Perce beat us both. I beat Ferd. Ferd washed some socks. Later found I had left my jacket at the café. Perce and I belted back and retrieved it. Ferd had a fright – thought he had lost passport and money – he had dropped it in passage. To crown eventful day Perce broke my surgical spirit. In bed by 10.30.

An exciting entry the next day included this earth-shattering episode:

As we came out of the station Perce slipped over and broke our Vichy bottle. It also soaked the food and ruined his card home. At this moment our luck seemed right out. Then Perce made up for this blunder by seeing a railway agency office.

Perce's vigilance allowed us to get 30% tourist discount on the fare to Montpellier.

My first visit to Paris was initially taken up with finding the right station for our onward journey to Provence. A porter at the Gare de Nord said we needed the Gare de Austerlitz. We did this by bus only to find that we should have been at the Gare de Lyon. This required a hectic journey by metro during which 'we claimed about five victims with our rucksacks'. It then transpired that the train didn't leave until past 11.00 pm and so we had about six hours to kill. We had a picnic down by the Seine, using Ferd's guitar as our table to the amusement of passers-by. Later, the diary reminds me, we had a sing-song and were entranced by Paris at night especially the fairy-lit bateaux mouches on the Seine.

Because we had a week before the Camp began, our plan was to spend the time in the Montpellier area. Our first stop was to be Nimes with its famous Roman amphitheatre. The journey to Nimes took more than twelve hours and little sleep was had. While going through the Massif Central we excitedly pointed out to one another the features of a volcanic landscape that we'd learned about in our geography course. It was unbearably hot in Nimes and after taking an eternity to find the youth hostel, we decided we would take the train on to the small coastal town of Sete, about 12 miles west of Montpellier, as the place for some sun, beach and swimming. We aimed for the youth hostel and it was an eye opener. A large house in a dominant position on the hill above Sete, to us it seemed like a hotel. We were delighted when the very laid-back warden said we could stay the rest of the week.

The diary records that 'we met some English girls from a college in Manchester' and that the days were spent swimming and sunbathing and the evenings at local dances, one organised by the Communist Party which seemed rather risqué to us. An American discharged soldier, named Frank, with a penchant for gambling, also latched on to us. Sete is notable for its canals which feature in its famous sports event – 'les joustes'. Since we were there on Bastille Day – quatorze juillet – we were treated to a major jouste. Large rowing boats with a raised platform at the back, on which stood a jouster armed with a shield and a long lance, would row towards each other with the intention of trying to knock the other combatant off the boat into the water. To add to the atmosphere, each boat had a small band – reeds and percussion – on board which sounded its fanfare as it rowed towards the enemy.

The entertainment lasted all afternoon on an elimination basis and we enjoyed the sight of huge men being tossed into the water. In some cases both lost their balance and were deposited into the canal. The winner was a colossal guy known as Le Gros. Some unfortunates were obliged to carry him through the town on their shoulders. At the dance in the evening I was conscious of a special, rather peculiar smell in the air which I took to be the local soap or perfume. It was somewhat later in life that I realised that I'd been smelling garlic!

The UNESCO camp was better organised than the one in Austria in as much as we were a large group. This enabled friendships to flourish across nationalities. The majority of the boys were French but there were also some Germans, an Algerian, a Vietnamese as well as we English. My French reached a peak on this holiday and I never spoke it as well again. A contributing factor was that wine was served as a matter of course at meals, even if in metal cups, and this helped to loosen tongues and, inevitably, French was the lingua franca in all activities.

It was a happy time. The atmosphere was convivial and in exchange for our labours on the volleyball court we were allowed to take advantage of the many facilities that a sports university, a new concept to us, afforded. In addition, there were tours in the surrounding region, a rich area of Provence. We made visits to Nimes, Arles, Les Baux, and the Camargue including Aigues Mortes and St Marie de la Mer. Montpellier town centre was also within easy reach and proved a fun city for adolescent males. We realised, with envy, that our French counterparts were far more adventurous with the opposite sex than we reserved Anglais. During the coach trips, when we were going through towns, one of the lads would stand at the front of the coach keeping an eye out for girls. 'Attention la droite!' he would shout to indicate that there was something for our delectation on that side of the bus.

One particular friend I made at the camp was a German from Hannover called Fritz. At the end of the camp we exchanged addresses and subsequently he came and had a holiday with me in England. Our popularity, such as it was, was mainly because of Ferd. He needed little encouragement to lead a sing-song with his guitar. Although Ferd had a bad stutter, with a guitar in his hand and a song on his lips it disappeared. He and I did a double act with an Everly Brothers routine including Bird Dog, Be Bop a Lula, Wake up Little Susie, Poor Jenny and Cathy's Clown.

When the camp finished Ferd and I decided to stay on in the south of France for a week or two. Perce had become friendly with a French boy called Pierre and stopped off at his home in Fontainebleau on the way back. Meanwhile Ferd and I went to the youth hostel at Nimes. In the evening I took myself off to a bar and got in conversation with a young German named Heinz. I bought him a drink and he apologised for not being able to return the complement as he was completely skint. The bar was putting on an outdoor film show and Heinz and I found ourselves watching it. It was one of those bad B movies that the French do so well. Supposedly a crime mystery, it was full of slapstick and silly chases and had us laughing uproariously. We exchanged addresses at the end of the evening and promised to keep in touch.

While we were eating in the hostel kitchen one evening, an Englishman named Fisher appeared announcing that he was looking for help at the local fruit market. He named the hourly sum he was paying and Ferd and I looked at one another and decided that this seemed a good opportunity. The work consisted of loading boxes of grapes on to lorries. Mr Fisher fetched us, and some other recruits, from the hostel each day and drove us to the market. After a couple of days, Fisher said he was suffering a temporary cash short-fall and that we would be staying at his house rather than the hostel. Since we were relying on Fisher's income to pay our hostel bill this seemed a sensible decision. Fisher had a farmhouse in the country. He'd created a dormitory to accommodate the temporary workers. We also ate at Fisher's house – simple food – and learned about his former life. He'd been involved with the production of The Goon Show, a famous radio comedy of the 1950s starring Peter Sellers, Spike Milligan and Harry Secombe. When he heard we were fans, Mr Fisher produced a bunch of old scripts that were in his possession. I've no way of knowing if his story was true and, if not, how he came to have these carbon copies of typed Goon Show scripts. What did seem to be true was that Fisher was down on his luck and it increasingly became apparent that we were unlikely to get any money off him.

As Ferd and I wanted to see and do more in the South of France, we bade Mr Fisher goodbye – I can't remember if any money changed hands but I rather think not. Ferd had some friends of his mother who lived in Toulouse and who were half expecting us, or at least him, to look them up. Having little money there was nothing for it but to hitch-hike. Because we were two, each with a large rucksack plus a guitar, it was optimistic to expect many to stop to pick us up. With a series of lifts, we eventually got to a place called Mazamet, south of Castres in the Montagne Noir. There was no youth hostel in this place and we couldn't afford a hotel. After a drink and jambon in a bar we decided to sleep rough on the mountainside. It was a clear, warm night and as we got into our sleeping bags in the heather we thought: this is the life! Half an hour later it began to rain. Soon it was pouring and we trudged back into town and went to the police station asking if they would let us sleep in the cells. The policeman looked at us quizzically and shook his head. We must have looked desperate because he told us to take a seat. Twenty minutes later a *curé* in a cassock appeared and beckoned us to go with him. We accompanied this priest to his house in the town where he gave us some milk, bread and cheese which we wolfed down. He then showed us to a comfortable pair of beds. It was not a Damascene moment but it did make me reflect on the kindness of Christian people.

We weren't far from the famous walled city of Carcassonne and thought that we'd make this small trip before moving on to Toulouse. Even so, we had no success travelling as a pair and therefore split up arranging to meet in Carcassonne. In Carcassonne I enquired for directions to the youth hostel. I ended up in a place that appeared to be a camp site and slept on my own in a marquee that had dozens of beds. In the morning there was no sign of Ferd, and of course, long before the days of mobile phones, no way of getting in touch with him. I decided to get on the road for Toulouse and as I was walking out of town who should appear coming from a different direction but a familiar figure toting a rucksack and guitar. It transpired that he'd found the proper youth hostel and had spent a more interesting night than I had.

Again, we split up and I got a lift to the other side of Castelnaudry and then spent ages in a lay-by failing to attract a lift. A little Simca pulled into the lay-by and a family got out to have their lunch in the shade of some nearby trees. All through their lunch I continued to stand, vainly trying to get someone to stop. The French family completed their meal and returned to the car. The woman came over and offered me a lift. I was amazed since there were already two adults and two children in a small car. But I was not about to refuse and they managed to get me in and take me most of the way to Toulouse. So often it was those who had the least who were prepared to give the most. I lost count of the number of limousines that passed with only the driver in them. Yet this family made a sacrifice, even if a modest one, to get me on my way.

This time Ferd and I did manage to find the same hostel. The next day we bought a map of the city and set out to locate the business owned by Ferd's mother's friends. By the time we found it, we were told that the owners were at lunch. We must have looked disappointed because they explained that it was only two minutes' walk away. We found the restaurant and the couple we were seeking who were with some acquaintances at a large table. They greeted us like long lost cousins and told us to join them. It seemed to go on forever; my first experience of a magnificent French lunch. Afterwards they took us back to their house and later to the youth hostel. The next day they took us out in the evening to another super restaurant, my abiding memory being the Martini Rosso on the rocks that we had as an aperitif. Another first, an aperitif. This was followed by the North African dish, couscous, also a novel experience. These people were clearly very close friends of Ferd's mother and they seemed to have shared significant experiences in the war. At this time, with memories of the war still fresh for many, the British were popular visitors. We were asked if we had any plans. Our vague idea was to return to the Mediterranean, perhaps the Cote D'Azur.

It was our good fortune that M Blanc (not his real name) was driving to Cannes on business the next day and offered to give us a lift. We stopped for an al fresco lunch on a glorious day, cicadas chirping, and M Blanc produced some bread, cheese, tomatoes and a bottle of rose wine. This simple meal made me realise the joys of good food, however modest, if the quality was evident. As we neared the Mediterranean, we passed through the town of Frejus where, the previous winter, there had been an appalling disaster. A dam had burst at Malpasset following record rainfall and a swollen River Reyran. It caused a wall of water 40 metres high travelling at 70 km an hour which devastated two villages as well as the downstream town of Frejus. The death toll was 421. We were able to see the all too visible scars some seven months later. We were dropped off at St Raphael and stayed at the Frejus hostel which, as they so often seem to be, was at the top of a hill.

We had a lazy, delightful few days swimming, sunbathing and surviving on what money we had left. Eventually the money ran out and some seven weeks after leaving home we used our return train ticket to Boulogne. My surviving memory of that journey is getting off the train at Knockholt station and walking home to our house in Pratts Bottom. I felt pretty good about myself. At the age of seventeen I'd spent seven weeks abroad, mostly obliged to rely on my own resources to survive, and had come back if not wiser, then certainly richer for the experiences I'd undergone. Back home I was received like the prodigal and much envied by my brother for my prodigious tan. After a summer spent mostly outdoors in the Midi sun it wasn't surprising that I was very dark. Not only my brother but also my friend Angus was envious of my appearance. When he and I spent a few days in his parents' bungalow in New Romney, Angus bought himself some fake tan so as to compete in the female stakes. It looked a vile orange colour and wasn't easy to remove. But, as I recall, my success rate with women was not vastly superior.

France and Spain (1961)

In the school year of 1960-61 I got to know John Knight. John had joined Bromley Grammar the previous year when his parents moved south from Sale near Manchester. He lived in the nearby village of Badgers Mount. (The relationship between Pratts Bottom and Badgers Mount is one that has puzzled anthropologists for years). We frequently caught the same bus to and from school. I remember walking with him from the bus stop at Hayes Lane down to school, only a five-minute walk, but in that time, I knew he was someone I'd value as a friend: straightforward, loyal, amusing and generally fun to be with but with a strong integrity. When John learned of my French holiday the previous summer, we began to make plans to repeat the experience.

At that time, I was beginning to read Hemingway which brought with it a fascination for Spain and bullfighting. Our intention was to travel through France with San Sebastian as our destination. Hitch-hiking was to be our mode of travel. There is a school of thought that hitch-hiking is tantamount to begging which, of course, it is. However, it's hardly begging in any menacing sense since no one is obliged to pick up the individual on the side of the road. Having spent many frustrating hours failing to get a lift, I always vowed that when I was a car owner, I'd unfailingly stop to pick up hitch hikers if I were in a position to do so, a promise I didn't keep. It seems hard to credit now that hitch-hiking was such a popular mode of travel in the '50s and '60s. We live in a more fearful, less trusting, age and the overwhelming view is that only fools stop and pick up complete strangers. Perhaps significantly, the so-called A6 murder of Michael Gregston and the shooting and rape of his lover Valerie Storie, took place in August, 1961. The murder had been committed by a stranger who'd come to their car while they were in a quiet lay-by. This received a great deal of publicity at the time and eventually led to the conviction of James Hanratty, coincidentally born in Bromley, who was hanged after appeal in April 1962, the last victim of capital punishment in the UK. The danger of picking up strangers on the road became self-evident to many.

John and I set off from Folkestone to Boulogne on a morning ferry in early August. We were in no particular hurry and soon found a bar in the port area, sat at an outside table and ordered some red wine and a sandwich. After our third red wine, we began to think we should consider getting on the road. At that point a young man in a smart suit asked us if we'd like a lift to Paris. Would we?! It seemed that he was tired and wanted company to keep him awake on the road. His car was nearby and we finished our wine and performed our public duty of assisting this man in need. He turned out to be a dreadful driver, halting and so slow that it was dark by the time we got to Paris. Bizarrely, as soon as we got into the Paris traffic his driving became confident. He accelerated and drove at a speed that sometimes alarmed us. He insisted on finding us a small hotel before setting us down. As I recall it was the first of a number of double beds but we were tired and intoxicated and it didn't worry us.

Next morning we took a metro to the southern side of Paris and then proceeded to get a series of mostly short lifts. The preferred route was to Biarritz via Tours, Poitiers and Bordeaux. Initially this worked successfully and we spent the next night in a hostel in Amboise on the Loire, near Tours. Leonardo da Vinci ended his days in Amboise and after one night there I knew how he felt. Once again I was in a hostel that was completely empty apart from us. During the night we had been aware of insects buzzing about but we were not prepared for the sight that greeted us in the morning. We were both covered in bites, with our faces, being the part most exposed, particularly affected. Mosquitoes were not something that troubled us in Kent and I realised how fortunate we were. From then on 'mozzies' became public enemy number one and the high-pitched whine of a mosquito is a sound that I still dread. At least we now understood why this particular dormitory, next to the river, had been deserted.

The main worry now was whether any motorist would stop for two young men who looked as if they had the plague. We did get lifts but increasingly got blown off course so that, by the end of the day, we were in the seaside resort of Les Sables d'Olonne, north of La Rochelle. We had with us an ancient army tent of John's which meant that we could stay more cheaply in camp sites as well as hostels. There was a pleasant site by the sea and, with not a little difficulty, we eventually pitched our tent and placed some possessions inside. It looked a little pathetic against the smooth lines of the substantial French tents that surrounded us, but we convinced ourselves that it had a certain character. Satisfied with our work we rewarded ourselves with a stroll along the front and a few beers. When we returned to the tent a couple of hours later it was completely flat and looked even more pathetic. Nevertheless, we liked the area and thought we deserved a couple of days recovering from our Amboise experience.

We got to Bordeaux a few days later where we shared another double bed in a *logis*. The barmaid here was to die for and John and I spent the evening propping up the bar and working our way along the top shelf which had a selection of exotic liqueurs of varying colours and tastes. There was a loud group of English tourists, two 'middle-aged' couples, also at the bar. They were friendly enough but appeared uncouth to us. As a result of that experience two phrases: 'We're from Hemel Hempstead' and 'Trois coca colas' have always caused considerable mirth to John and me. I know it sounds not at all funny but, believe me, in a certain context it is hilarious.

Next day we were hung-over and needed to get out of Bordeaux on to the Biarritz road. We got to the suburbs on a bus and flopped down, dehydrated and with sore heads. Nothing stopped and we concluded that perhaps we were in a bad spot and so walked further out of town passing, depressingly, plenty of other aspirant hitchers. It was getting very hot by now and we were getting hungry. We thought our luck had changed when a car stopped but only to ask for directions to somewhere. What sort of idiot asks English hitch-hikers for directions? After relieving our frustration a little by swearing at all the empty cars that passed us, we finally had some good fortune when a large Mercedes towing a boat stopped. Towing a boat, must be going all the way to Biarritz, we thought excitedly. I'm not quite sure how it happened but one of us started to open the back door of the car whereupon the driver, a bald bull-necked German, said: 'Do you usually get into a stranger's car without being asked?' I muttered something about since he had stopped, I assumed he was offering us a lift. He retorted to the effect, 'Not with your manners!' and drove off.

We were shattered but there was no attempt to apportion any blame. No rudeness had been intended; we were simply relieved, I suspect, that someone had stopped and this led us to make an unwise inference. By now we were so hot, tired and fed up, that we took it in turns to put out the thumb while the other rested in the shade. It was by now the middle of the afternoon when a small Citroen Deux Chevaux stopped just down the road from us. It was full and so when someone got out and came towards us I took little notice. But the young man, himself a hitcher, was coming to ask if we'd like a lift. 'Have you got room?' I asked. 'Well the *curé* seems to think so,' he replied. We gathered our effects and walked down to the little car. The driver was a priest and he had two hefty Dutch hitch-hikers with him. John got into the back with one of the Dutch lads and, because I was the smallest (!), I sat in the middle in the front. I say the middle as if the car had a bench seat. Anyone familiar with the Deux Chevaux will know that it had two canvas seats slung in a metal frame at the front. By sitting in the middle, I actually had part of a buttock on either seat with everything else, including my rucksack, swinging free in the centre. It was one of the most agonizing journeys I've had. At times, despite the dispiriting wait we'd suffered, I just wanted to stop and get out and wave them goodbye. When we did stop for a break, the cure produced a more or less black banana and John and I, both famished, looked on longingly. Unfortunately, this kind man did not have a banana for us.

The stay in Biarritz was memorable. Again we camped and, again, the tent collapsed a few times before we finally got it securely erected. The day after our arrival, having recovered a little, we were interested to learn that there was a festival in the neighbouring town of Bayonne. When a tall, blonde-bearded American called Tom announced in the dining area that he was able to give a lift into Bayonne in his jeep, we jumped at the chance. We were a little aggrieved when Tom relieved us of five francs as payment for the lift but mollified a little when he said it was a return 'fare'. He would pick us up from the same spot at midnight. There then ensued a night to remember, at least it would be if one could remember it.

Bayonne is an attractive town and *en fête* it was even more delightful. Everyone was friendly and we joined in the celebrations with gusto. One memory is of a bar where much communal drinking was going on. We were in the Basque country and many of the revellers were carrying leather pouches or *porrons* filled with wine. These were passed around and you got a cheer if you could hold the *porron* away from your mouth and allow the thin jet of wine to enter it. The further away the better. Of course, the consequence was that you often got your face or front drenched but this was all part of the entertainment. At one point it was suggested that a lady's slipper should be filled with champagne and passed round. In the absence of the necessary footwear, a soldier removed his boot and this was filled with some fairly disgusting liquid and passed round. John and I had our share.

We drifted out of the bar with our new friends and went through the town holding hands. Every so often we would form a large circle. Someone would shout 'La Guitare de Manuel' and a guitarist would perform a flamenco flourish on his instrument and we would all cheer. Then there was a round of porrons to celebrate. After a while we were running as a group, all shouting 'La Guitare de Manuel' and adding others to the circle. There came a point where I was desperate for a pee and so John and I lurched into a bar. The bar was heaving with hot sweaty bodies and the patron told us they were *complet*, full. I shouted 'I need a piss' but this cut no ice. As we left the bar I half fell against a pile of beer crates causing them to fall over. John and I found this very amusing especially when the patron started cursing us.

We were having a wonderful time but became vaguely conscious that we had to get back to the square where Tom would collect us to return to the camp site. When we arrived at the spot where we expected to find the bearded American, there was no sign of him. After cursing his no show, we drifted around and my next recollection is of rolling in grass beside the river. It was beautifully cool. Eventually we realised that we would have to get back to the campsite under our own steam. That is a slight exaggeration. I had little if any steam left and John ended up virtually carrying me on his back and, although Bayonne is not far from Biarritz on the map, it is a hell of a long trek on foot. Since I've no personal memory of this journey I am in the debt of someone who has remained a close lifelong friend.

The sun was well up by the time we got back. I never thought I would be so pleased to see our little camouflaged tent. We crawled in and fell deeply asleep. I scarcely left the tent for the next few days. The hangover was enough to put one off alcohol for life. Strangely that did not happen. I was grateful to John, who also felt rough but who had a stronger constitution than I, for keeping me hydrated and administering the odd aspirin as I lay in the baking tent. Lawrence of Arabia wasn't in it. When I finally got on my feet we made a point of looking for Tom. He was entirely unapologetic saying he'd waited until gone midnight. So three days of my holiday disappeared in a blur but when I was fit we struck camp and set off for Spain.

We'd been advised that it wouldn't be a good idea to enter Spain as hitch-hikers. We could get a train to San Sebastian via St Jean de Luz and without expending too much. At the border we had to vacate the train and board another because the gauge of the track was different in Spain. San Sebastian is a beautiful city with a bay shaped like a sea shell and known as La Concha. One of the first things we did was go up to the top of Monte Igueldo for a drink in a bar with a glorious view over the bay and the town. We set off back down the track to the city centre and then became aware of someone calling us. The large female proprietor was waving something and for a moment we thought we'd not left enough money. We were just thinking of making a run for it when I realised that it was my wallet that she was waving. This was the first of many experiences I've had of the inherent honesty of the Spanish.

We stayed in a little pension in one of the backstreets of San Sebastian. I was now determined to see a bullfight and we discovered that there was a *corrida* in two days' time. I was very excited since, as well as Hemingway, I'd also been reading a number of other accounts of tauromachy and felt well versed in this remarkable, if savage, sport. It proved an amazing spectacle, at times beautiful, at times stomach turning. I was prepared for the blood and brutality but not for the very real danger in which the toreros, horses, and especially matadors put themselves. The programme we saw included a *rejoneador* in which the bullfighter is mounted on horseback throughout the encounter up until the moment of truth. The way in which a man is able to control two animals, the horse and bull, is astonishing. A horse is inherently frightened of the bull and its natural inclination is to flee. Not only does the training inhibit this action but the horse, which is unprotected, constantly puts itself into life threatening situations passing just inches from its fierce aggressor time after time. The juxtaposition of acute danger and beautiful movements sums up the aesthetics of bullfighting at its best.

I'm not sure that John shared my liking for the *corrida*. As we left the bullring and drifted among the crowds outside, I was aware that John had gone very quiet and then suddenly he collapsed in a heap against the wall of a building. I looked for help but most of the passers-by seemed to think he was drunk, an easy mistake to make. A woman looked more concerned and I said 'enfermo' which was my limited Spanish for 'ill'. The woman placed John's head between his knees and he came to. He soon felt sufficiently well to walk to a bar for some tea. We puzzled as to what had caused him to faint. Was it the bullfight experience or the heat? Perhaps both.

The next day we moved down the coast to the small town of Zarauz. There we were able to take a room in a hotel with a sea view. Prices in Spain were much cheaper than France and this enabled us to live a little better. Not that we were sufficiently flush to afford to eat in the hotel. Instead we'd buy food and smuggle it up to our room and effectively camp there. This finally got too much for the management and we were asked to leave. Presumably we were taking up space that other guests could use, guests that would be more profitable for the hotel. We were a little put out but we couldn't really blame the hotel. We had one night at the next town along the coast, Zumaya, which was as far as we got before beginning our return journey which we made by train.

Twenty-five years later I passed through Zarauz and Zumaya as well as San Sebastian travelling in our camper van with my wife and family on our way back from the sabbatical year we'd had in Barcelona. I fancied I recognised the hotel in which John and I had 'camped' but didn't reliably locate the spot where John had fainted. Summer 1961 was a terrific holiday and firmly cemented my friendship with John. We still talk about those times. Happy days.

Austria, Italy and Germany (1963)

I had maintained a correspondence with Heinz, the German I had met in a bar in Nimes in 1960. He proposed a canoe trip down the Danube which sounded romantic and exciting but never came off. Instead he suggested that I come to Innsbruck where he was at university and from there we would do a motoring tour of the Austrian and Italian Alps. Accordingly, in July 1963, I took a train to Innsbruck and with the aid of a map managed to find his digs in the town. I was dismayed to discover from his landlady that Herr Heinz was away but that he'd return in a few days and, meanwhile, I was welcome to use his room. In the room was a note from Heinz saying that he'd been called away suddenly back to his home in Dinkelsbuhl, Bavaria because of the death of a friend. He would join me in a day or two.

This wasn't a good start. Innsbruck is a beautiful town but when you know no-one and don't speak the language it becomes a lonely place. Filling the day was difficult on a limited budget and was made worse without anyone to share activities and perceptions. I've always been happy in my own company but realised that I wouldn't choose to holiday alone. I was at the point of wishing I'd not come when Heinz finally appeared. One of his close friends had been killed in a car accident and there was no question that he had to go to the funeral.

The next day we set off for our alpine adventure. Heinz had a Skoda two (+ two) seater sports car. It was quite nippy and made a magnificent throaty roar as it went through small villages. But it was a heavy vehicle and it was no surprise to learn that Skoda also made tanks. We saw many magnificent alpine panoramas. First, we went south through the Brenner Pass and then to Cortina in the middle of the Italian Dolomites. Visible for much of the time was the highest peak in the Dolomites, Marmolada, with its red tinged rocks. The Italian civil engineering was impressive as we did mile after mile of mountain roads. We then returned to Austria and Klagenfurt with its warm lakes which were delightful to swim in. The next highlight was the Grossglockner, the highest mountain in Austria at 3,800m which was a long climb for the car. At the top we walked to the glacier that had plentiful snow and ice even in the summer. The final stop in Austria was Salzburg, an enchanting place and very significant for Heinz because of its Mozart Festival. Close by was Hitler's mountain retreat in Berchtesgaden, spectacular but also grim. While there we visited a salt mine which required that we dressed in a black overall and a black fez. I still have a photo of this in which we are clearly amused by our garb. We boarded a little train which took us deep into the mine and then on to a boat which crossed an underground lake.

Then we were in Bavaria, Heinz's homeland. He took me to Chiemsee where his family had a chalet and a boat. We had good fun on the boat, sailing in complete safety in lovely weather. But when a storm did blow up, I was surprised how difficult the boat was to handle. At Chiemsee, in a tavern one evening, I discovered that Nazism was not dead. A group of local men were having a good time reminiscing about the war and fondly remembering, so Heinz told me, the days of the Third Reich. This part of Bavaria was the location of King Ludwig's fantasy castles and we visited a number of them including a replica of Versailles. 'Mad' King Ludwig was Wagner's patron and therefore something of a hero to Heinz. We ended up in Munich, an exciting city, especially the haunts that Heinz took me to.

The plan now was to go to Heinz's home in Dinkelsbuhl, an attractive little town north of Ulm near Ansbach and there pick up some friends and drive to England. Heinz was good company; small, highly intelligent, with a dry, sometimes cynical, sense of humour. His English was excellent and spoken with an American accent thanks to time spent with local American military. I think he had an American girl friend at one time. But he was disposed to depression and was clearly unhappy with his current relationship. He was infatuated with a girl who didn't seem to share his feelings and perhaps liked to amuse herself at his expense. His parents seemed charming to me though Heinz didn't have a good relationship with them, especially his father. As they didn't speak English, he had to translate when necessary. One evening at the dinner table, his father, who was managing director of a local firm that manufactured brushes, produced an impressive wooden box. In this box was the complete range of the company's brushes. At the end of the meal, Herr Werner opened the box and took out the brushes one by one explaining to me the function of each. Heinz of course was translating and he kept interjecting things which I knew his father hadn't said, causing me to laugh inappropriately. At one point he said: 'I think he must think that you're a real dusty guy.'

The family were well off and Heinz was spoiled but didn't show much gratitude. He took himself off from time to time leaving me to amuse myself. He was disappointed that I preferred his few jazz records, such as Brubeck, instead of his own favourite, Bartok. In the town he had his own club to which he invited friends. It was a sort of cellar with a bar and chairs and tables and a juke box. One evening I was there along with a number of Heinz's friends including Erich Bauer and Peter Sommer who were coming to England with us. Heinz drank a lot and became very maudlin. Eventually he became angry and started shouting and throwing bottles around. He soon started smashing up the place. Erich said, 'Let's get out of here and leave him to it. You can't reason with him when he's like this.' I began to wonder if I wanted him to come to England with me.

Next morning we loaded up the Skoda and somehow got four people and their luggage in. Heinz and I continued to share the driving. We didn't arrive in England until quite late and I remember the Germans being impressed as I handled driving on the wrong side of the road with some aplomb. It was after midnight before we got to Broke Farm Drive and everyone was in bed. I asked if anyone wanted anything before we went to bed and Heinz spotted some brandy on a shelf and asked if he could have a spot of that. I told him to help himself. The following day he met the family including my brother who was excited because he could see that someone had taken some of the brandy. 'Why should that amuse you?' I asked. 'Well, because it was empty but I half filled it with cold tea', Allan replied. I could see the joke especially since Heinz had not said anything. Perhaps he thought there was such a thing as English brandy that tasted almost like tea.

I can't remember if we accommodated all the Germans. I have a feeling that a couple of them stayed with Chris and Ray Boullin.

They didn't stay long as their ultimate destination was Ireland which is a popular place with Germans. My friends enjoyed meeting them and it soon became clear that the warm, engaging Erich was preferred to Heinz. They called in for a night on their way back to Dover and told us about their adventures in Ireland. They had loved it and described the incident where they decided to catch a lamb to have for supper on the camp fire. They had chased some sheep and driven them over a cliff. This wasn't very edifying and they seemed surprised that we weren't impressed.

Postscript

I kept up correspondence with Heinz for a while afterwards and in 1964 he came to England and stayed with us until my father got fed up with him and he found digs in London. We went to see *Oh What A Lovely War*, the celebrated Joan Littlewood theatrical musical, which was then showing at Wyndham's Theatre. I recall being concerned that, as a German, he would resent the choice of play. I needn't have worried as he thought it superb and, after all, an anti-war, not anti-German, work. After he returned to Germany I lost touch with him.

This was not the case with my other German friend, Fritz, who had visited earlier in the year. He was charming and impressed my mother with his manners. He was a good tennis player and somewhat disappointed with the grass court that we played on in our neighbour's garden. He called it the meadow. At that time a popular pastime for John and me with our girlfriends was to mess around with a tape recorder recording songs and other nonsense. Fritz must have been amazed by these weird goings-on but if he was, he didn't show it.

Fritz had a friend who was in England to improve her English and was working at a health farm near Stratford on Avon. He suggested we go and see her; he'd been told that they would be able to provide accommodation for us for a couple of nights. We hitch-hiked to Stratford, not without some difficulty of course, and made it in time for the evening meal. Marie Luise, always known as Didi, and her friend Doris were delighted to see us. We had a happy couple of days with them. When they were working we were free to use the facilities such as the table tennis. I remember one of the guests complementing me on my graceful play! The meals were unusual, being vegetarian. All sorts of unusual cereals and yoghurts were on the table at breakfast, commonplace now but then very strange. Following this visit, Didi became a good friend, visiting me the following year and also keeping in touch with my parents. After I was married, Virginia and I had a holiday in Northern Europe visiting Holland and Germany when we saw Fritz and his wife Angelika in Hannover and Didi and Franz in Bremerhaven. They are good people and we still keep in touch with both families. Sadly, Fritz died suddenly of a heart attack while visiting Paris in October, 2012. His funeral was on my 70th birthday.

Spain (1964)

The previous summer, while I was with Heinz in the Alps and Bavaria, my brother and Angus, Nick and Steve had hired a camper van and taken it to the Costa Brava. They came back full of stories about the superb holiday they'd had and I determined that I would join them the following year. This time we were six: Allan and me, Nick, Martyn, Angus and Steve, who had been at school with Allan. We took a small tent with us as well since the van only slept four. In order that we'd not starve, we loaded up with cans of fruit, rice pudding and luncheon meat. This demonstrates the way unsophisticated minds operated in those days of relative ignorance about the Mediterranean. A haven of delicious fresh fruit, vegetables and sea food, and we choose to take canned food! Nevertheless, there were times when a tin of Winnie Wilts's rice pudding went down a treat.

The journey down to Spain was notable for one incident when Angus fell out of the moving van. We'd stopped for lunch somewhere in Southern France and were motoring along a quiet twisty road. Angus was sleeping off lunch on the floor in the back of the vehicle. Suddenly those in the front – either Allan or Steve, both under age, was driving – heard a shout and an oath. 'Christ,' Martyn said, 'Stop! Angus has fallen out.' We couldn't believe it. Going round a bend, one of the back doors had opened and the prostrate, sleeping Angus had just slid out on to the road. We came to a halt and rushed back to see how the casualty was. He wasn't a happy bunny but the cause of his misery was not so much the bruising he'd received as the hole in his new treasured sweater. Quite why Angus was wearing a sweater in July in the heat of the day in the south of France is unclear but it may have cushioned the blow and saved him from serious injury. More important was the fact that he was asleep and fell 'softly'; even more fortunate was that no vehicles were behind us at the time. Anyway, the time that Angus fell out of the moving van at forty miles an hour, a distinct exaggeration, joined the list of tales of the holiday.

We crossed the Spanish border in the late afternoon and found a camp site at Port Bou. It was very windy and we struggled to keep our feet as we walked along the beach in the evening. The next day Allan discovered he'd lost his wallet with all his holiday money in it. We assumed that he'd dropped it the previous evening in the strong wind. A search and a visit to the police station produced nothing and we headed south a little subdued. Our destination was Playa de Aro, a new resort between Palamos and San Feliu de Guixols. The boys had been there the previous year and had liked the town. They had made friends with the waiters in a place called the Mont Bar and this was our immediate target. They greeted us effusively: Paco, Tony, the manager, and Soltero who'd become their special friend. When Tony heard the story of the lost wallet he asked how much Allan had lost. We told him and he disappeared soon returning with the precise sum that had gone missing. 'You can pay me back when I come to London in October,' he said. Astonishing generosity from someone who was nothing more than a brief acquaintance.

Instead of paying for a proper camp site, we camped on a bit of waste ground by a dried-up river about a kilometre inland from the coastal resort. Camping off-piste saved money but it had drawbacks, most obviously in the hygiene department. We kept reasonably clean by swimming in the sea every day but we could not have survived without making use of the waiters' showers in the Mont Bar. Since we fell into bed most nights after a surfeit of drink, we tended to wake when the sun was too hot to remain in the van or tent. One morning I awoke to the sound of someone shouting. It was a man with a horse and cart. He'd been loading the cart with sand from the river bed. He was now attempting to leave the scene with his load but the horse was having trouble hauling the now much heavier cart up the side of the river bank. The man whipped the horse unmercifully and the animal's distress was pitiful. Eventually the horse managed to get up the bank and away but it was my first experience of the Spanish unsentimental, not to mention cruel, approach to domestic animals.

The beach at Playa de Aro was magnificent and we spent a lot of time there swimming and lying in the sun, determined to get a tan and to meet girls if they came within our circumference. A popular view was across the bay to Palamos which seemed forever bathed in sunshine whatever the weather in our resort. 'It's always sunny in Palamos' became one of our catchphrases. We called our resort 'Playa' for short which seemed reasonable to us. But, some French girls we became friendly with referred to it as 'Aro'. They were right, of course. Calling it 'Playa' was as sensible as calling Camber Sands, 'Sands' or Southend-on-Sea, 'Sea'. Playa means beach and every resort along the Costa Brava has a beach and so as nomenclature it has its limitations. The French girls consisted of two sisters, Annie and Dominique, and their cousin Maite. All three were beautiful and we couldn't believe our good fortune when they asked us if we'd like to play volleyball with them. It seemed that they normally holidayed in Laredo on the Atlantic coast between Bilbao and Santander but it was our luck that this year they'd switched to the Mediterranean. We met up most days and played volley ball, swam and generally enjoyed their company.

The nearest large town was St Feliu de Guixols. We went there one evening during a fiesta. There was a large fair in town and we discovered that we could win bottles of 'champagne' or cava at the hoopla stall. You had only to throw a ring over the neck of the bottle to win it. The stalls were designed with short Spaniards in mind. With my long legs and long arms I could quite easily 'ring' the bottle, and if someone held my legs I could lean over and virtually place the hoop over the bottle. Later in the evening we went to a cabaret. We arrived early and picked a table right by the stage. Our tactic was to get friendly with a waiter by tipping him generously at the start of the evening, so ensuring we got good service. This was particularly important on this particular evening as the cost of the ticket, quite expensive, included as much drink as you liked with no restriction on type of drink. This is just the sort of situation that the British abroad can abuse and, of course, we did. The variety of drinks we had that evening was preposterous including rum, gin, tequila and brandy, sometimes altogether. The cabaret was wonderful and Allan fell in love with the top-of-the-bill singer called Maria Dolores. She was actually quite a celebrated Spanish popular artist and must have been surprised when half a dozen young English men invaded her dressing room after the performance. We were sent on our way with a signed photograph.

It would be a surprise if anyone was sufficiently sober to drive but we made the 10 kilometres or so back to Playa D'Aro and, though it was one in the morning, went immediately to the Mont Bar. There we had a nightcap and entertained our waiter friends with our evening in San Feliu. We left the bar and Angus announced that he was going to drive. Both Nick and I realised that Angus was probably the most intoxicated of any of us and

Nick the least. We suggested that he let Nick drive but were ignored. The engine sprang into life and Angus shot off and drove straight into a stationary vehicle, another van, less than twenty yards away. We were horrified but also vastly amused. Angus was now removed from the driving seat and Nick got us home to our riverside site.

The waiter we were especially friendly with was Soltero. He spoke little English but I'd been doing some night classes in Spanish and was able to converse with him a little. He came from Barcelona and when we learned that he was going back to Barcelona for a few days we suggested that we drive him there as we wanted to visit the Catalan capital. Before going to his family, whom he'd not seen for some time, he insisted on showing us some of the sights of the city including the Sagrada Familia, Las Ramblas and the bullring. I was keen to see a bullfight and he helped us to get tickets. We were impressed by Barcelona but little realised what it would become much later in the century, one of the major tourist centres in the world. Nor, of course, did I have any notion that I would one day spend a sabbatical year there at the University of Barcelona.

Spain in 1964 was very different from what it is today. In the first place it was a Fascist country, controlled by the dictator Franco. This made very little difference to holiday makers looking for sun and cheap food, drink and entertainment. We did, however, encounter the Guardia Civil, Franco's own police force, detested in Catalonia, who sported the weird hard hats with the upturned brim at the back. One lovely warm evening it was so enchanting that Angus, Martyn and I decided to sleep on the beach in our sleeping bags. We lay on the beach and fell asleep to the sound of waves softly breaking on the shore. We awoke to the rising sun and the prod of a rifle in our ribs. The Guardia Civil had found us and were not amused. Fortunately, they let us off with a warning not to repeat the 'crime' and we packed up our things and adjourned to the Mont Bar for breakfast.

It was difficult leaving Playa. We'd had a wonderful couple of weeks and there were fond farewells to Tony, Soltero and the gang at Mont Bar. We'd arranged to meet the French girls for a last goodbye. I'd become particularly fond of Maite, a dark, brown-eyed beauty, who lived in Pontoise just north-west of Paris. We exchanged addresses and agreed to keep in touch. The girls decorated the van, which they christened 'Hector', and wrote messages in pink lipstick. We looked quite a sight as we set off home. As we drove north we became aware that the brakes on the van were defective. Only by pumping them energetically were we able to come to a halt. It became something of a skill to control the vehicle. There was a particularly bad moment on the N7 approaching Lyons. A policeman suddenly appeared in the middle of the road holding his hand up in classical police 'stop-traffic' mode. I was driving and remember frantically pumping on the brakes to get Hector to stop. We came to a halt a couple of yards in front of the policeman who, fortunately, didn't realise that he was in any danger. In Lyons we found a garage that carried out some repairs on the van and the rest of the journey was relatively uneventful.

Italy (1965)

The final summer holiday abroad with friends essentially from my school days comprised a trip to Venice by car with Martyn, Allan, Dave (a school friend and later flatmate with Martyn and Ferd) , Steve and Dick (Steve's brother). We went in two cars, a mini belonging to Dave and a hired car. I was insured on Dave's car.

All went well until we got to Wurzburg in Germany. We'd arrived late and it was dark and raining heavily. I was driving and we were looking for the hostel where we were booked in. Someone told me to turn left and as I was making the manoeuvre I was suddenly aware of some lights bearing down on us. A motorbike collided with us and the rider flew over the handlebars. The guy was on his feet by the time we got to him, albeit limping a little. A witness to the accident had called the police and I ended up in the back of a police van being charged with careless driving. I was fined a long-forgotten sum of Deutsch marks on the spot. That was bad enough. I felt bad about hitting the motor cyclist, though fortunately he had escaped with bruising, and about damaging Dave's car. The latter proved the long-term problem. Dave went on about the damage to his car for the rest of the holiday. He insured his car through his father's insurance company and he seemed more worried about what his father would say than anything else.

We were renting a villa for a fortnight in Lido de Jesolo on the northern end of the Venice lagoon. It was a great spot and the villa was unaccustomed luxury after holidays in a camper van. We did quite a lot of cooking as well as eating out and found the locals friendly. One evening we were invited to sample a proper spaghetti bolognese by a neighbour which was absolutely delicious. Mario, the proprietor of the local Pizzeria, also became a feature of our lives. We patronized his place a lot and he was also a familiar sight on the beach in the late afternoon, gazing up and down the ranks of sunbathing females for a likely conquest. When he noticed us looking at a particularly attractive girl as she walked past with her equally attractive mother, he boasted: 'I've had her. And the mother!'

We found a Go Kart track in Jesolo and it became a regular haunt of ours. It offered the thrills and spills of racing without, apparently, putting anyone in danger. We were warned to avoid collisions but Steve managed to park his kart head on with another vehicle putting both out of commission. When we came to leave, the management demanded compensation from us for the damage we'd done. An argument developed which became quite heated and I saw some mechanics looking menacing with crowbars. Steve, who was at the centre of it, held his hand up and said 'Calmo,' which was the nearest Italian he had for 'calm down'. He then said to us, 'Come on, leg it'. At that we dashed away from the track with some mechanics in pursuit. But they soon gave up the chase and we got away with it.

Being so close to Venice it was inconceivable that we would not visit the immortal city. There was a regular ferry from Jesolo to Venice which allowed us the special pleasure of arriving by sea. The famous landmarks were visible from some distance and gradually materialised as we drew closer. Venice in a party of six blokes is not the ideal way to enjoy this unique place, but the romanticism was not quite eliminated by the company even when we went in a couple of gondolas. What it did achieve was make me vow to return, hopefully with a sweetheart.

The remainder of the holiday was not especially memorable and this probably explains why it was the last trip I did with my old school and neighbourhood friends. In future I either went away alone, with a girl friend, or with one good friend. Because I went to University two months after returning from Venice, I was able to undertake longer trips in the long summer vacations. Two of these are recounted as stories set in Russia and South Africa.

Chapter 5
The World of Work

Eventually came the day when full time education ended. I'd left school in the summer of 1961 and managed to pass my three A levels if not with any great distinction. I did, in fact, gain the best grade in Geography but didn't receive the prize as, presumably, another student who got the same grade as I, had been awarded a higher mark. Since my academic career was now over, this lack of distinction didn't concern me. I'd no intention of applying to university, even assuming my grades would have gained me a place. In fact, most of my close friends – Angus, Nick, Ferd and Martyn – didn't go to university though John did get a place at Dartmouth Naval College much to his joy.

The world of work beckoned but I'd little clear idea of what I wanted to do. When asked by my careers masters what career I intended, I usually said journalism or advertising. This seemed a glamorous, supposedly creative job which didn't require too much in the way of additional qualifications. Nick decided to pursue a career in accountancy and got a place as an articled clerk with a firm in London. Similarly, Martyn wanted to become an architect and was engaged as a junior by a firm of architects. Both Nick and Martyn were destined for a long haul of night school, and some day release, to obtain their professional qualifications, a much harder route than university though they were earning some money.

When I did a little more research, I discovered that pay for apprentice journalists was pitiful and the thought of working on the Kent Messenger in Maidstone was hardly exciting. Experience on a provincial paper seemed essential before one had any chance of breaking into Fleet Street. I also made an attempt to get interviews with advertising agencies in London and got one interview with a large agency called Foot, Cone and Belding but without success. Since I could no longer expect to live at home without putting something towards the household expenses, I signed on at a temp agency and got a position in the post room at The Otis Elevator Company in the City of London. This was diverting enough for a while as I got to make special deliveries in various parts of London, sometimes taking one of the chauffeur driven cars that existed in a pool. But I had my sights a little higher than working in a post room.

I was rescued by George Towers, a good friend of my parents, who was a director with a leading advertising agency and had been responsible for some famous advertising campaigns, most notably for inventing the baby deer that featured in the Babycham campaign. It had made the manufacturers, the agency, and George himself, a lot of money. Through his contacts, George got me an interview with the advertising firm, Mather and Crowther. There I was interviewed by Ernest Lough, the famous 'Oh for the Wings of a Dove' choirboy. That recording, which became the first million selling record, was made in 1927 and the Ernest Lough I met was far removed from the cherubic choir boy. In any event, he didn't give me a job.

I then got a phone call from George asking if I'd be interested in working for a public relations agency. I had to admit my ignorance and George explained that PR was related to advertising but instead of placing paid advertisements in the media, PR agents obtained publicity gratis in newspapers and other media by presenting their clients as news stories such as in the launch of a new product or service. It turned out that Harris and Hunter, one of the larger PR agents, was looking for a promising junior to train up as an account executive. I was interviewed by Eric Harris, a quietly spoken, slightly overweight man, and the interview seemed to go well. Next day I was offered a job at £500 a year and I was exultant. The idea of writing about products and companies rather than producing advertising platforms was more congenial for me. It meant that I got a training in journalism and in magazine and newspaper production.

Harris and Hunter were on the second and third floors of 69 New Oxford Street, quite close to Tottenham Court Road tube station. There was an old-fashioned lift at the entrance and also a postal room which was manned by a retired noncommissioned officer, in an army dress uniform, whom one addressed as Sergeant, or more commonly, 'Sarge'. Sarge was a cheerful fellow who seemed to know most of the gossip going on in the building and neighbourhood. On my first morning, he insisted on taking me up to the second floor in the lift and personally presenting me at Harris and Hunter's reception. I was greeted by one of the secretaries and told that Mr Hunter wanted to see me but that he wasn't in yet. I sat rather uncomfortably on a hard chair until eventually W R "Bunny" Hunter arrived. Still I was obliged to wait while he saw his secretary for some ten minutes. Finally, I saw the great man, who was also on the podgy side but shorter than Eric.

Bunny was very much the senior partner and obviously wanted to give me the once over himself before I was assigned a desk and some work. He told me that I would learn the trade by being attached to various account executives. The big accounts were Tesco Stores which was exclusively handled by Eric Bennett, Aspro Nicholas which was Mike Morley's terrain, and Petfoods, makers of Kit-e-Kat, Lassie, etc which was under the direction of Bunny himself. My main initial duties were to acquaint myself with the accounts by reading the clippings and looking at the files containing recent press releases. I was given a desk in a large room with two other desks in it. Off this room was an office for two secretaries, Marian and Janice. Marian looked after Mr Harris and Janice was available for everyone else. Also on this floor were the offices of Mike Morley, Eric Harris and Eric Bennett. Upstairs was another domain, one I rarely encountered and run by a formidable woman called Joan Price who had an almost equally formidable and beautiful assistant called Audrey who had long blonde hair. They were responsible for the beauty and fashion accounts and were seldom seen on the second floor.

By the end of the first week, the job was taking shape. Initially my responsibilities covered two main areas: house magazine production and keeping clippings books up to date. In addition, I was asked to accompany some of the account executives on visits to clients to familiarise myself with the role of account executive since, in due course, I was expected to take on my own account load.

Keeping clippings files up to date was not demanding work. In common with all PR agencies, Harris and Hunter employed a cuttings agency whose job was to scan the written media to detect all mentions of Harris and Hunter clients and their products. Scores of these would come in the mail every day and my job was to sift through them, checking what was definitely due to our efforts and then to paste the clippings into the relevant clippings book. There was a large scrapbook with hard covers for each client and such was the volume of newsprint we provoked, and therefore received, that it did not take long to fill a scrapbook. From this activity I soon realised what a vast range of outlets were available to PR agents. The great prize was to get a piece in a national newspaper and, after that, a daily provincial paper such as the *Western Mail*. Then there were local newspapers with particular emphasis on those that were adjacent to the factories of our clients. The *Leicester Mercury* was important because it was relevant to Petfoods based in Melton Mowbray. Similarly, Slough newspapers were significant because there was the home of Mars, Petfoods' parent company. I became almost intimately acquainted with the *Eastleigh Advertiser* and the *Southampton Evening Echo* because of the proximity of the pharmaceutical giant, Warner

Hudnut Lambert, in Eastleigh. A separate category was magazines. Particularly prized were weeklies with large circulations such as The Economist and New Statesman but prestigious monthlies were also valued, especially the vast array of women's magazines for their focus on fashion, beauty and domestic matters. Finally, there were trade newspapers and I soon discovered that getting a piece in leading trade papers, such as the weekly *Grocer* or the *Grocer's Gazette*, was highly coveted.

Something else I became intimately acquainted with was the Directory of Newspapers and Trade Magazines. The early 1960s was a time when almost everyone had a daily paper delivered to them, and sometimes an evening paper, not to mention a weekly local paper. Now, most local papers are free and little read while daily regional papers are in decline. Back then, sending out a press release even to all national and regional dailies meant a large postal bill. The big red Directory was something I was constantly consulting as a source of information including circulation figures and, among the trade papers, their specialisms. Targeting your press release was important. Any fool could send a blanket release to all newspapers but the trick was to identify those outlets which were likely to bring the best coverage for the money allocated to the exercise. On occasions a press release had to be rushed out. Tesco were fighting the retail price maintenance legislation at the time in their attempts to undercut other traders. This brought them into conflict with the courts and Eric Bennett was frequently called into action to put out a statement on behalf of the supermarket. In such situations the press needed to be contacted urgently and yours truly was pressed into service as a glorified messenger boy. I'd take a taxi to Fleet Street and have it waiting outside as I dropped in our significant statement to the Daily Express, Mirror, Mail, etc. In the coming months I became very familiar with the route round the national dailies and Sundays.

I was pleased when I was given the opportunity to try my hand at writing press releases. Usually it concerned a new product by such as Aspro Nicholas or Warner Hudnut. Fields of Bond Street were a cosmetic house owned by Aspro Nicholas. They launched a new perfume called Manhattan, during my first year, with dramatic black and white packaging intended to evoke New York by night. I don't remember whether the perfume was any good but the box was terrific. I was given the task of writing a release for the fashion pages of the dailies and weeklies and also a piece for the appropriate trade press. You might question my qualification for this role, and you would probably be right. This was really a job for Miss Price and Audrey but presumably Fields were not paying enough. Anyway, I managed to produce a piece that, with suitable editing, appeared in plenty of newspapers.

It came as a surprise to me how much newspapers and public relations officers, as they were originally called, worked hand in glove, a type of symbiotic relationship. It was obvious that PR consultants needed the assistance of the press but it turned out that papers were also dependent on PR people to provide much of their copy. This was particularly true of the regional and local newspapers and trade press who could not afford to run a large body of reporters. Of course, there are bodies like the Press Association and Reuters who have a good reputation for covering news events all over the country and throughout the world. They are invaluable to the media but they cost money. When, essentially, you want to fill space with something you think will entertain the readers why not use the free service of PR people. Someone like Joan Price would be writing a weekly fashion and beauty column which was syndicated throughout the country for local papers and even some regional dailies. This was not a crude sales plug but an informative article about something like coping with sun on holiday, and it would artfully include mention of a sun cream manufactured by their client. Even if the name was deleted, as long as your product had a reasonable proportion of the market, its sales would be increased. It would be erroneous to think that press releases were set up in type just as delivered to the media. They were almost invariably edited and the name of the product was often removed and called, say, 'a new perfume launched by a Bond Street perfumers'. When, from time to time a cutting turned up with your press release published unedited, it might have been a time to celebrate even though you slightly despised the person who could not be bothered to tailor the piece for their newspaper.

Life in a big PR agency, and H&H was big for a PR company, was fun and sometimes glamorous. At this time Tesco were opening a new store every week, most of them in the south of England, and each opening was an opportunity to give the firm some publicity, certainly in the local press. Once or twice I attended an opening to give Eric Bennett a hand. When a store opened, it was the PRO's job to engage a celebrity to come along and cut the ribbon and press some flesh. The Tottenham High Street store was opened by Bruce Forsyth, a big name then just as he remained until recently. There is nothing like a 'name' to attract a crowd and I was amazed at how many people turned out to catch a glimpse of Brucie. I've no idea how much he got paid but he was around for barely an hour and it seemed money for old rope to me. Of course, becoming a 'name' is the clever bit.

The most useful skills I developed at H&H were how to write quickly and concisely, usually under time pressure, and how to produce and edit a magazine. The computer age has simplified publishing and print production but back then there were special techniques to be mastered. In the first place, I achieved the ambition of becoming a cub reporter, something I had entertained when trying to determine my career towards the end of school. This happened because, as editor of 'The Tesco Tatler', 'Petfood News' and 'Warner Hudnut News' – house magazines for the respective corporations – I was obliged to seek copy. Since I did not have a staff of reporters to minister to my every need, or *any* need, I had to get off my backside and do it myself. H&H convinced Tesco, Petfoods and Warner Hudnut, and no doubt others, that a regular house magazine served to give workers some stake in their company. It gave them a warm glow to learn that Vera, in the Tunbridge Wells store, had celebrated her 25th wedding anniversary or that Nellie in the canteen at Warners had won first prize in a cake baking contest.

I look back fondly to my trips round the Home Counties, sometimes by train and sometimes in my Morris Minor Coupe to talk to the staff of Tesco supermarkets. Those were the days of relatively small high street shops before the out-of-town giant stores took off. As well as eliciting little stories from the staff, I also recruited 'reporters'. It was comparatively easy to obtain the help of someone who was sufficiently nosey and literate to supply me with information of the hatches, matches and dispatches kind as well as the more noteworthy human interest story: 'Jeff Nobbs of Warehousing swims round Isle of Wight to raise money for homeless budgies'.

Once you had the copy it had to be turned into a magazine. Eric Bennett and Mike Morley showed me the ropes. I learned how to mark up a page so that the printer knew what type face and size you required and also the print proof signs so that I could correct galley proofs. The next stage was to produce appropriate headlines and set up the page design. This was nothing like as demanding as that required on the Tesco Times, the newspaper that Eric Bennett produced and which was handed out to the public in stores by the thousand. Nevertheless, I acquired enough knowledge and became sufficiently au fait with the world of printing and publishing to take on the production side of the St Andrews weekly newspaper as soon as I arrived at the University some years later. And, there is definitely a feeling of achievement when your 'baby', your magazine, appears fresh from the press. There may also be the odd embarrassment when you see a howling 'typo' you missed or some crass piece of editing but, on the whole, it was a very positive and enjoyable experience.

One day Bunny Hunter took me with him to visit Petfoods, the manufacturers of canned food for dogs and cats. It was pleasant sitting back in his large Rover as he retailed stories of his early days in PR. When Petfoods arrived in the UK from the States they encountered a fair amount of hostility. British pet owners fed their animals on real food, not inferior stuff from tins. This made Petfoods very sensitive and initially they engaged H&H to keep them out of the news since they assumed that any publicity was bound to be bad publicity. After working for them for twelve months, Bunny went to the client review with an empty clippings book.

'Look,' he said, brandishing a series of empty pages, 'I've kept you out of the Daily Express, the Mail, the News of the World, The Mirror, and so on.' He might have been in danger of doing himself out of a job but his point was that it was possible to perform a more positive role. Despite the prejudice, canned pet food was catching on. Busy people look for time saving options and opening a tin is quicker than providing your own 'meal' for the dog or cat. One of the wheezes that Bunny came up with was to picture the sales force eating pet food from the tin. When, say, a new line of Pal or Kit-e-Kat was to be launched, a gang of salesmen in smart suits would be paraded in front of the press and given forks with which to eat the product straight from the can. I've no idea if this stuff was disgusting or not though I was assured that it was perfectly palatable. Certainly the sales team attacked it with gusto and it made a hit in the press. The other thing that Bunny pointed out was that more than half all tinned food for cats and dogs was a Petfoods product. This meant that as the pet population of Britain expanded, the profits for Petfoods would do likewise. This led to a series of articles about the value of pets to a family's general welfare.

One I remember was about budgerigars because I had a hand in it. Trill was the leading budgie food brand and a Petfoods line. From somewhere I discovered that a lot of elderly people had budgerigars and from there it was but a short step to claiming that budgies were a vital source of comfort to lonely old people. There was usually a rent-a-quote gerontologist prepared to say that companionship was vital to promoting the welfare of elderly and single people. If a person was not available, then a dog or cat could make a difference. And if quadrupeds were not feasible, then the humble budgie could also be a 'friend'. The article we prepared, complete with a picture of a charming old lady with 'Charlie', her budgie, appeared in many newspapers and did, I understand, promote the popularity of budgies and, of course, Trill.

Harris and Hunter had its fair share of characters. Eric Bennett was an ex Fleet Street man who had moved to PR when he could no longer hold down a newspaper job. As is well known, Fleet Street is tolerant of boozers but Eric stretched that tolerance to breaking point. In my early days in the company I began to notice that Eric was conspicuous by his absence after lunch. On one occasion I needed to consult Eric and asked a colleague if he knew when Eric would be back from lunch.

'Eric is rarely back from lunch and if he is, it is not appropriate to discuss anything with him. Eric is a morning person.' This turned out to be true as I found out when I ignored this advice. One day at about 4 o' clock I observed that Eric was in his office apparently on the phone with, as usual, a cigarette burning in the ash tray. I knocked on his door and he waved me to take a seat. When he came off the phone, he said something to me which was completely unintelligible. I realised that I'd made a mistake in trying to engage with him but I had to find an excuse for coming in to his office so I asked if he'd had a chance to look at the proofs of the forthcoming edition of the Tesco Tatler.

'Yesh, ole boy. Great stuff, g- g- go ahead.' He had a slight stammer.

Having rather denigrated this grizzled newspaper veteran, I did learn a lot from him and marvelled at his grasp of things when on top form, which he was before lunch, and on days when he knew a big story was brewing when he would miss his liquid lunch. Eric was slightly built with thinning sandy hair and always wore a dark suit, white shirt and cufflinks. Virtually a chain smoker, his suit or waistcoat was invariably spotted with ash. His writing was indecipherable and I sometimes had cause to look in his diary to see where he was. I could never make anything out. I dreaded him leaving messages for me though Marian, his secretary, had learned to decipher the code. At Christmas, Eric received many bottles of scotch from those who felt that they owed him something. He looked at the label and commented on the quality, sometimes negatively, but he always took it away with him.

Mike Morley was absurdly handsome and charming and used every inch of his persona to obtain favours. It was hard to resist Mike and I enjoyed his company but I heard less good reports about him from some of the females on the staff. I used to accompany Mike on trips to Eastleigh where Warner Hudnut was based. He had a habit of bursting into a line from an advertising jingle. We'd be driving along and he would be talking quite seriously about an issue to do with a particular product we were helping to market when he'd suddenly break out into:

'Summer County, Summer County!' sung to a tune from Franz Lehars's Merry Widow.

It used to amuse me which I'm sure is what Mike intended. I was too inexperienced to know if Mike was really good at his job but he seemed plausible with his public school accent and debonair appearance and that was probably enough to get him by in those days. But he used to take liberties with the secretaries which eventually did not endear him to them.

David Hann joined the firm a year after me and seemed worldly and, if not wise, an amusing cynic. He was one for the telling phrase and anecdote, often concluding his tale about an acquaintance who'd had an unfortunate experience with the expression: 'Ah, love his bum.' Hann was a betting man and claimed to know a lot about horse racing. As someone who followed the sport a little, I listened to what he said. One day he came into the office and said there was a sure thing in the 3.30 at

Kempton. I looked in the paper – there were always lots of papers in the office – and found his selection was distinctly unfancied.

'Ignore the coconuts, someone's given me the nod.' By coconuts he meant all the zeros signifying an unplaced finish in the horse's past six races. He eventually took a bet off nearly everyone in the office which he said he would place at the best price he could get at the local bookie. We never saw Dave again that day but we soon learned that the horse was once again unplaced. In the morning, Hann was quite unapologetic. 'Sometimes, they don't come up,' was all he said and I wondered if he'd just pocketed the money knowing that the horse had no chance.

H&H had a Christmas ritual. On the last day before the holiday, the secretaries would buy in some food and drink, put up some perfunctory decorations and provide a tape recorder which could produce music to dance to. At about 3.30 Mr Hunter would appear with a bunch of envelopes and address the staff. After a little speech thanking everybody for all their hard work, he would hand round the envelopes which contained a card from him and Eric Harris and one's Christmas bonus in the form of cash, the amount depending on one's position. He would then invite all present to partake of the food and drink. This was an excuse to get drunk on the firm. At probably my second Christmas party, after some time on the booze, I got a message to go to Mr Hunter's office. I knocked on his door and found him alone with Marian.

'This young lady has specifically asked for you. You better take her home.'

I realised that Hunter was pretty drunk and that he had been forcing his attentions on Marian. I took her back to the main room of the party where she said she was OK as long as she was away from Mr Hunter. This was the beginning of a relationship with Marian that was strictly conducted only on Harris and Hunter territory. It also made me see my boss in a new light though at least he had the decency to desist when his advances were unwanted.

When the term 'spin doctor' has become almost a term of abuse, it is appropriate to reflect on the value of public relations. Ideally, the individual promoting a product or service should believe in what he or she is doing and avoid exaggerated, let alone fallacious, claims. In politics this is virtually an oxymoron but in the work I carried out, I like to feel that ethical lines were not crossed. However, as I started to question the worth of what I was doing – did I want to spend the rest of my life 'puffing' consumer products? – I considered looking for a job with an organisation like Oxfam where the integrity of the exercise could not be questioned. I discussed my concerns with Angus over lunch one day. He worked for Sphere Publishing in Holborn and was sympathetic since he was not greatly enamoured with his own job.

I mulled over this problem for some time before finally deciding to apply for a place at University to read psychology and philosophy. Since my application was after the UCCA deadline, I had no great hopes of getting a place. Meanwhile I had become friendly with Anne, Mr Hunter's secretary, probably due to another liaison at a Christmas party. Anne was 'dangerous' since she was married, even if unhappily, to a policeman. She would pour out her problems to me and I was a sympathetic ear. One day she discovered that I was making a trip up to Melton Mowbray to do some business with Petfoods. This was her home town and she said she would like to make the trip with me so that she could see her parents. I was happy to have company, especially with the beautiful Anne, and I picked her up at Hammersmith in my car at 8.00. She said she had rung Marian to say she was unwell and would not be in that day.

We had a memorable day including a stop for coffee in a handsome pub on the A1 at Eaton Socon. I dropped Anne off at her parents' house and went on to have conversations with the work force at Petfoods for the house magazine. Later I returned to Anne's house and had tea with her and her mother before we set off back to London. By the time we parted in the evening, it was clear that I was falling for Anne and she made me feel I had become indispensable to her.

I was invited to an interview at Liverpool University where the entire procedure was conducted by postgraduate and senior undergraduate students. It was really just an Open Day and we were fodder for student experiments. But it didn't put me off the idea of being a student. I finally got a letter from UCCA to say that I'd been unsuccessful in my application but that I would be placed in the clearing scheme. I was deflated but not altogether surprised given my late application and modest A levels.

By September I had given up any idea of doing a degree when another letter from UCCA arrived informing me that I'd been awarded a place on the Social Science course at the University of St Andrews. It was embarrassing that an A level geography student had to get out a map to find out exactly where St Andrews was. Well north of Edinburgh, I discovered, but I didn't care. The job at H&H had gone stale and I was ready for a new life. Things had moved on with Anne, literally. She announced that she'd left her husband and asked if she could move in with me.

I broached the subject with my flatmates. We'd moved from Sinclair Gardens in Holland Park to a house in Barnes. I'm not sure that they were enthusiastic about the idea but it was not totally vetoed. I explained that it would only be for a short time. So Anne moved in and I gave no thought to whether I might subsequently be cited as a co-respondent for divorce. That was the swinging sixties for you. It all seemed rather unreal because I knew I'd only a few weeks before I'd be leaving London for a very different world in Queen's College, Dundee, a constituent of St Andrews and the location for degrees in psychology and philosophy.

I now had to inform H&H that I was leaving and I asked to see Bunny Hunter. He was very gracious, wishing me all the best for the future, probably realising that I didn't have the brashness, the cut and thrust needed for the job. But I was very grateful to him and Eric Harris for giving me the opportunity and knew that the many skills I'd acquired in the areas of journalism and publishing would hold me in good stead. I still have the card that everyone at H&H signed on my last day and I've no regrets about my time there. It was exciting to be young in a reasonably glamorous job in the middle of '60s London.

I let it be known that my friend Angus would be interested if a position became available at H&H because of my departure. And he duly moved to the company. It was from Angus I heard that Anne survived my absence and that he himself became one of her lovers and that she subsequently became Mrs David Hann.

The World Outside Work

My life outside work in the years from leaving school to going to University, covered by the period 1961-1965, was dominated by the social circle I was in. This consisted mainly of old school friends plus a few other acquaintances that became significant. These were people I met with in the pub, went to football matches with, played cards with, partied with, played tennis with, went to the theatre, cinema and concerts with, and generally engaged in a variety of leisure and cultural activities.

John Knight invited me to a youth club in Badgers Mount where I met Brenda with whom I had an immediate bond. She had failed her 11+ but had the gumption to work hard and get into the 'grammar school' stream and she eventually took O and A levels. She had a lovely, shy smile and we were well suited with many common interests including books, theatre, music and sport – Brenda was a keen hockey player. We also enjoyed walking together. Brenda had lost her father some years earlier and she had a slightly difficult relationship with her stepfather. I got on well with her mother and her brother Joe and the Yorkshire terrier they were infatuated with, and which I thought slightly silly. Since Brenda lived only half a mile away, we saw a lot of each other and she became very well received in my family with my mother particularly fond of her.

Friday nights were spent with male friends. As we were now legally able to enter pubs, we didn't hesitate to take advantage of the opportunity. Our allegiance switched between pubs over the years including the Queen's Head at Green St Green, The Bull at Pratts Bottom, The Harrow at Knockholt and The Cock at Halstead. The Harrow was probably the most popular venue even if the licensee was temperamental. Angus, Nick, Ferd, and John (when on navy leave) were the core Friday stalwarts, later joined by Martyn and his brother Jeff, and later still, when they were old enough, by my brother Allan and his close friend Steve and his brother Dick. The Friday night session, which almost invariably led to us drinking more than was sensible for driving (and one or two were always driving), was followed by a card session. Our house was the most popular venue because my parents were the most tolerant, but we sometimes went to one of the other houses. We played poker but never for large amounts. Even so, Ferd seemed to be continually financially embarrassed and was sometimes reduced to acting as someone's money minder if loans from others ran out.

My starting salary at H&H was £500 per annum which sounds ludicrous today but ten pounds a week was a good income for someone starting work as a school leaver in 1961. I was in fact better off than most of my friends who were effectively in apprentice schemes. It enabled me to buy a car after I passed my driving test. I had six lessons, starting on the evening of my seventeenth birthday, and each was at night. Apart from that, my parents took me out as a learner regularly and on some occasions I went on the road with my father as his driver when he was visiting clients in Kent, Surrey and Sussex. When I took my test a few months later I was a confident driver and passed first time. The car didn't come along immediately but eventually I bought a convertible Morris Minor for £100 with the registration KOT 119. It was always known as KOT and was shared with my mother and brother.

My interest in jazz came from listening to the radio initially and then we were given a record player one Christmas. This was a prize item even though the record that came with it, an LP by Winifred Atwell, wouldn't have been my choice. The first record I bought was Raunchy, an instrumental by the Ken McIntosh Orchestra. Stupidly I bought a 78 as I didn't like the look of the new little 45 records that were coming in. They looked insubstantial to me and I thought they would never catch on. I was right; they only lasted until the advent of CDs twenty years later. My obsession with 78s abated when one got broken. Although I purchased a few pop records – I liked Elvis, Buddy Holly and The Everly Brothers – I was already looking towards music with more depth. My first jazz album was The Atomic Mr Basie which came out in 1957 and which I bought in Bromley on the way home from school. I proudly put it on the turntable and was immediately blown away. My mother's friend Chris was visiting at the time and I could sense that they weren't impressed. However, Chris said: 'Well, he can certainly play the piano,' in response to The Kid from Red Bank.

Angus shared my interest in jazz and bought a Thelonious Monk and I felt I was launched on a life-long interest. Live jazz was available at The Marquee in Oxford Street and at The Bromley Court Hotel. It was at The Marquee that I saw The Alexis Korner Blues Band with Cyril Davies on harmonica. During the interval it was announced that a young man from the audience would come up and sing a number with the band. That young man was Mick Jagger. He was full of himself but didn't particularly impress me. My favourite musicians in those early days were Tubby Hayes and Ronnie Scott, Joe Harriet, Ronnie Ross and Stan Tracey. The musicians were very friendly and would even give the time of day to a callow youth like me when playing at Bromley Court. Trad jazz was all the rage still and we would sometimes go to dances, often in the back room of a pub, where bands like Chris Barber, Humphrey Lyttleton and Alex Welsh were playing. It was good dancing music but it never caught my imagination like bebop or the big bands of Ellington and Basie.

One year, Brenda gave me the perfect birthday present. She got tickets for the Melody Maker Jazz Awards concert. It was held at

Kilburn Empire and started early, about 10.00am. I think we went with Angus and his girl friend Rita. It was a marvellous occasion with all the British stars with whom I was familiar, and a few not, performing. Particularly memorable was the Ronnie Ross Quartet appearing on a dais that rose from beneath the stage. Ross was a lyrical swinger and my gateway to Gerry Mulligan. Later when I moved into a flat in London, we became aware of The Bull's Head in Barnes. This was a venue that featured most of the visiting Americans that played at the new Ronnie Scott Club in Soho but at a fraction of the price. There I saw Zoot Sims, Mark Murphy, Sonny Rollins, and Annie Ross among others. Of the local bands and artists, Bill le Sage, Dick Morrissey, Bobby Wellins and the remarkable prodigy, Roy Budd, were regular visitors. On one occasion we invited Dick Morrissey and Roy Budd back to our flat after the gig and I felt privileged at being able to chat freely with these jazz icons.

Perhaps because of my interest in Hemingway and his passion for bullfighting, I got it into my head that I wanted to learn Spanish and enrolled for some evening classes in Bromley. I found the language exotic possibly because of the Moorish influence. My attendance at classes didn't survive the year but it sowed some seeds and I maintain a fascination for the Spanish language. Angus and I, both being in public relations, decided that we needed to improve our public speaking and enrolled in some other classes, also in Bromley. They are a dim memory but I feel they gave us some confidence in speaking in front of others on a subject of our choice, or one prepared in advance, or, much more difficult, off the cuff. In any event it probably assisted a little in my subsequent career as a lecturer.

Because we both worked in London, Angus and I also had access to courses and activities in the big city. We were both dabbling in philosophy and an advert in the Underground caught our attention. It was a course of lectures on the big philosophical questions including the meaning of life itself. We enrolled and only realised later that the course was run by the Theosophical Society.

This has interests in spiritual concepts supposedly opening up the nature of the universe and the mysteries of human nature. Initially we found the course interesting – we were fans of existentialism – but steadily we realised it wasn't for us even though we recognised that they had some charismatic speakers. Colin Wilson's book *The Outsider* was a big influence at the time. Wilson didn't have an academic background but he was bright and had a big hit with this compendium on existentialism. It introduced me to many writers including Shaw, De Beauvoir, Sartre, Hesse, Rimbaud, Dostoyevsky, Hemingway and Camus. Wilson had an enormous success with *The Outsider* but it seemed to go to his head and he never produced another book that was as well as received. Indeed, he began to produce ever more extreme books on the topics of murder and sex and it became embarrassing to admit to reading him. Nevertheless, I have no regrets of having read *The Outsider* which seems to have had an impact on many of my generation. I was a voracious reader at this time getting through books at a great rate and recording my thoughts in a black book using a star method to indicate my rating of the book. I also wrote about my opinions of books in the diary I kept in 1964 and 1965.

I mentioned that my parents were tolerant when it came to welcoming my friends into our home. Nevertheless, my burning ambition was to get my own place. It seemed natural to want to have independence, to be able to do what you liked in your own space. But my desire to fly the nest was not shared by all my friends. Financial considerations meant that I needed three others to share the cost of renting. Martyn and Ferd were keen to join me but neither Angus nor Nick could be persuaded. Eventually, I met an old school friend, Dave Green, and he expressed an interest. I had some reservations about him but we were getting desperate and so it was agreed. We found a suitable flat in Sinclair Gardens which we liked to think of as Holland Park though it might technically have been in Shepherd's Bush. It was exciting moving in to our own place and, for example, leaving work in the evening, knowing that I had only to take the central line from Tottenham Court Road to Shepherd's Bush, a mere eight stops.

The house had two bedrooms, one large, and one small. Because Ferd led an unconventional life, often working late in his role as a computer programmer in the University of London, we decided to let him have the small room on his own while Martyn, Dave and I had the larger room. The business of keeping house was one we relished and we shared shopping, cleaning and cooking amicably. Instead of having to go up to London on Saturday evenings for parties, we were now on the spot and keeping our ears to the ground to take advantage of anything going. In the diary I kept at the time, I note that at one point I was tired of parties, having gone to a dozen in the past month.

Martyn and I had a number of shared interests including music and theatre. We saw the entrancing *Les Parapluies de Cherbourg* at the Regent Poly cinema and came out amazed that everyone was not singing to one another since it had seemed so natural. Jazz concerts at the Festival Hall were regular and included luminaries like Basie, Ellington and Brubeck. We also went to the popular classical concerts at The Albert Hall on Sunday evenings and stood in the gods. The National Theatre was now established, originally at the Old Vic before it moved to its new premises on the South Bank. Arthur Miller's *The Crucible* was a memorable production by Lawrence Olivier and in 1964 I saw *Eh?* by Henry Livings, with David Warner, and Peter Brook's production of *The Marat /Sade* starring Glenda Jackson and Ian Richardson both for the RSC at The Aldwych Theatre.

When our lease on Sinclair Gardens ran out we looked for a flat a little further out. By now we were spending some time at The Bull's Head in Barnes and when a good flat came up in that locality we took it. Then I heard that I'd obtained a place at St Andrew's University and so knew that my time in Barnes and London would soon be over and would require Martyn and co to find another flatmate.

Chapter 6
Scotland and University

The Undergraduate Years

I arrived in Dundee about 8.00pm after what had seemed an interminable journey from London, Kings Cross. Although weary, I was excited. This was my first time in Scotland and, more importantly, this was the beginning of a new life as a university student. My modest A-levels in French, Geography and Economics had secured me a place, through clearing, at the University of St Andrews. I didn't hear until September and so it was a last minute rush getting everything together, bidding farewell to family, friends and colleagues and arranging accommodation in Dundee. Why Dundee and not over the water in Fife, the home of St Andrews? Social Science at St Andrews was at that time situated in Queen's College, Dundee in which faculty were to be found Psychology and Philosophy, the subjects I'd opted to read. Medicine, Law and Engineering were also in Queen's College.

I alighted from the train at Dundee with my huge case, practically a trunk. A welcoming committee was there consisting of older students. I think I strolled up putting out my hand, saying 'Peter Lloyd'. No one registered a flicker of interest. Instead, they gave me the address of my digs which were not in Dundee at all but further up the Angus coast in Carnoustie, home of a golf course almost as famous as St Andrews. I was told to report to a Mrs Keith. It was late by the time I got there on the little local train but I was in time to have a 'supper' of hot chocolate and sandwiches. There I met my fellow lodgers: a ginger haired lad with a strong Black Country accent, a tall, overweight young man who was obsessed with horse racing, and the diminutive Neil Fludger, who turned out to be another psychology student. They seemed an unprepossessing bunch and more time spent with them at meals and in the evenings didn't change that view. Moreover, I soon discovered that living in Carnoustie severely hampered my social life. The last train out of Dundee was something like 8.45pm which ruled out parties, concerts, theatre, etc.

I realised that I couldn't survive any longer in Carnoustie. Not only were my fellow guests dismal, but Mrs Keith's cooking left a lot to be desired. Most importantly, I was missing an awful lot of what I had come to university for, a stimulating intellectual and social life. Furthermore, I was used to having my own flat with all the freedom that provides. However, when I made enquiries about moving in to a place in Dundee, and preferably not digs but my own pad, I discovered that first year students weren't allowed to live in flats. They had to be either in halls of residence or approved lodgings. I went to see the accommodation officer and put my case. The clincher to moving in to Dundee was that I'd become Production Manager for the student newspaper, *Aien*, which required me to be at George Outram (the printers) in Perth by 6.00 am on Wednesdays. There was no way I could do this from Carnoustie. I then had to convince him that I was sufficiently mature to be allowed to live in rented rooms rather than approved lodgings. My age and past experience got me over this hurdle and I now had only to find a flat.

Something soon turned up, only a few minutes' walk from the college. It was more expensive than I'd anticipated and it involved living on the premises with the landlord and his family. But I was independent and in the mix, even if it meant shared kitchen facilities with the other lodgers. My part of the house actually had a room off my room with a bed in it and I was told that I could sublet this if I wished. I put the word round that I was looking for a flatmate and very soon a wonderful waster called Rick Dale had contacted me and convinced me that he was my dream flatmate. Rick was, in theory, a biochemist but he had little interest in academic studies and rarely surfaced before midday. When it became known in our year that we had a 'flat' – first years with a flat were almost unknown – we became a popular venue once the union bar closed. Very often we'd play cards, Nap being the most popular game, and when that finished in the early hours I'd collapse into bed. Not so Rick; he would read crime fiction, or some such genre, in bed and it wasn't unusual to find him still reading when I got up. After that he had his sleep.

My four years in Dundee were some of the best in my life. As a so-called mature student, I had the maximum grant which meant that I didn't have to call upon my parents to help me out financially. In addition, and unbeknownst to me, my mother had saved a certain amount of my salary while I was working. Because she was chief cashier in the Bromley branch of the Midland Bank, it was possible for her to do this without my knowledge, though quite how ethical this was I'm unsure. In any event I was grateful to discover that I'd something to cushion the experience of living as a poor student after the relative luxury of living on a salary in London. Because St Andrews was regarded by some as the next best thing (and certainly the oldest) after Oxbridge – it was founded in 1413 – there were a lot of rich public school young men and women there. This could lead you into living beyond your means if you became friendly with this set and, initially, this happened to me. A summons to see the bank manager, to be informed that I was £12 11s 6d overdrawn, brought me to my senses and from then I managed perfectly well on my reduced income.

As for the academic study, I relished it. At first I was a little put out to discover that in Scottish universities it was necessary to do a foundation year in whichever faculty you were registered. This was mainly because Scottish students, who did Highers rather than A-levels, started university a year earlier than their English counterparts. The idea of the foundation year was to bring them up to degree-ready standard. I found myself doing two of my A level subjects, Geography and Economics, as well as History, Politics, Philosophy and Psychology. Effectively we only got a taste of each but I found most of the lecture courses entertaining, especially history. It was a large year, over 150 students, and we used to pack the big lecture theatre in the Tower Building to hear luminaries such as Donald Southgate and Professor Archie McDonald lecture to us in history.

In those days there were rarely hand-outs and the overhead projector was scarcely invented. The lecturer would deliver his or her talk, perhaps scribble something on the board, and you were supposed to glean enough from this, and your further study, to gain enough knowledge to pass exams. Accordingly, making notes during lectures was deemed *de rigeur*. The first time Prof McDonald lectured he looked up after he'd been speaking for a few minutes and asked a girl on the front row what she was doing.

'Making notes, sir,' she stammered.

'Don't waste your time doing that,' said the Prof. 'I defy anyone to make any notes that make sense from my lectures, anyway. Just listen, take it in, and try to understand.'

It may have been good advice since his lecturing style was to wander up and down at the front of the class, his gown flowing behind him, all the while talking about an historical period or issue. He never used a note himself and yet the output was perfectly fluent. I, like many others, did defy and take notes and later, reading them through, you were unsurprised to find that they made complete sense. More importantly, he had the capacity to make the subject interesting often by posing an intellectual puzzle and then setting out to solve it.

I was a little disappointed that my main areas of interest – psychology and philosophy – were confined to a few lectures each in the summer term and the marks that I obtained in psychology didn't match those in other subjects. I was yet to learn that as an empirical science, it was vital to support all assertions with evidence, usually of an experimental nature. The end-of-year exams were demanding in as much as we had to revise six subjects. Nevertheless, I did very well and finished sixth overall in the year out of more than 150 students. This was gratifying and confirmed in my mind that I was qualified to take a degree, something I was certainly unsure of when I began. It had been more than four years since I'd done any serious academic study and it was a relief to discover that I was not out of my depth.

Days were very full at this time. Lectures were attended diligently and when you weren't in a lecture you were usually in the library where most serious students spent their time. We'd ample reading lists and I did my best to read the recommended texts and make notes. After a day's work I would either go back to the flat to eat or have something in the Union. The Union Bar was an institution and there was always a big gathering by nine 'o clock in the last hour before closing. There were also events in the Union such as debates and visiting speakers. At the Societies Fayre at the start of term I'd shown interest in the student newspaper. I went to the opening meeting for newcomers and met a gang of 2nd and 3rd year students who were running it including Robin Rycroft, the editor, John Barker, the business manager, John Darlington, features editor and George Robertson, political columnist. When it was discovered that I had magazine experience I was prevailed upon to take the vacant position of production manager. This seemed very early promotion for a new boy but I soon discovered that my experience in editing and producing house magazines at Harris and Hunter was adequate preparation for the student newspaper. The following year I became editor and so, inevitably, working on the paper took up a lot of time. This was not a cause for regret but it meant that other activities, in which I might have indulged, such as university politics or even drama, were neglected.

The essential student experience in the 1960s, certainly in St Andrews/Dundee, was quite different to what I witnessed later as a university lecturer. By the time my own children went to university, activities like debating and entities like political clubs seemed almost quaint. The student life for many consisted of academic work (hopefully) and drinking and partying. This isn't to say that I didn't enjoy these activities. First year students, because they didn't have the locations to throw parties, had to rely on invitations from second and third- and fourth-year students. This was not as unlikely as it might sound since St Andrews had what was called the bejant system. All new students were known as bejants (from old French, *bec jaune*, yellow beak, that is, a fledgling). And all bejants or bejantines were assigned to a Senior Man or Senior Woman. My Senior Man was John O'Brien, an economist with an attractive sister with whom I later went out. Very often one of your friends had a senior man who was throwing a party and with luck you got to go along as well. Bejantines, of course, were particularly in demand, partly because young women were in relatively scarce supply in Dundee. Queen's College didn't have an arts faculty, wherein were to be found most of the female students, which meant that Social Science was the place to find women. This was good for us but less desirable for students in Science, Dentistry, Law and, especially, Engineering. There was a dance most Saturdays in the Union and this was when the guys from the less favoured faculties hoped to engage with the opposite sex. It also seems hard to believe, but photographs don't lie, that we turned up to lectures, and most activities, wearing a sports jacket and tie.

Vacation

Terms were very short at St Andrews, only 26 weeks in all. This meant that I had plenty of vacation time. Inevitably I returned to London. I was essentially based with my parents again but also spent some time with my former flatmates in Barnes. It wasn't always easy to reintegrate to a scene with which I was becoming unfamiliar just as my friends were unfamiliar with my new life. I now had two lives. My mother said I'd developed an affected accent probably due to spending so much time with public school educated folk. In the summer I went away with my girlfriend Sue on a package holiday in Mallorca. It wasn't a great success. She was very fair skinned and found the heat difficult. We enjoyed the Spanish ballet cabaret shows and met Moya Kemp's sister who'd married a Mallorcan policeman. Speedboat cruises round the Bay of Palma were popular and spectacular at night but the gut-rot 'champagne' was dreadful. Other than that, I fell back into a party routine in London. On the whole I was glad to return to Dundee in September.

Second year

Fairly early in the first year I met the person who was to become my best friend at Dundee. Colin Williams came from Alderley Edge in Cheshire, somewhere quite unknown to me at that time. He came from an affluent family, his father owned a mail order business in Manchester, and Colin had gone to Radley. Colin was tall, red haired and had a generous nature. He also liked a good argument and had a good sense of humour. Unlike me, with my burning desire to acquire knowledge, Colin seemed to have only a vague idea of why he was at university. It was the necessary next step before going into business. While economics seemed to be the obvious degree for him, he drifted into psychology perhaps because that was my chosen field. In the second year you were obliged to take three subjects and mine were psychology, philosophy and politics. In the event, I soon dropped politics, using my position as Editor to convince the authorities that I would be unable to maintain three subjects. Rather to my surprise this was accepted, a sign possibly of more relaxed times.

Most students who aspired to a good time, and that included Colin and me, determined to live in a flat in the second year. This required that you fixed something up by the end of first year. The ideal set-up was to know a group of older students who were moving out of a property and arrange to take over their lease. Most of the best flats near the College seemed to be occupied by women and we were unlucky in obtaining anything locally. Fortunately, Colin returned to Dundee in the summer term with a car, a drophead Triumph Herald. This allowed us to look further afield than Dundee. When we heard of something going in Broughty Ferry, a little town on the Tay Estuary, we decided to look at it. No 12, The Esplanade became our home for the next two years. It was an amazing student flat. Right outside the door was the beach and the Tay estuary looking on to the North Sea. It would have made a lovely holiday let but we had it permanently. What we now needed were two other students to allow us to afford the rent. These materialised in the form of Tony O'donnell, another psychology undergraduate, who also worked on the newspaper and Jim Grisdale, an engineering student with an RAF Scholarship.

The second year in Dundee was even better than the first. The freedom and excitement of our own place contributed strongly to this and it was now our turn to throw parties. When Robin Rycroft asked me to take over from him as editor of *Aien* I was flattered but wondered if I was up to it. He convinced me that I had the necessary qualities. In as much as I had management and production skills, I didn't doubt that I could run a newspaper. More problematic was that the editor was supposed to have clear views about everything, in particular university politics, and I was fearful about my ability to write weekly cogent editorials. This probably was my Achilles heel but it didn't prevent me making what I believe was a success of editing *Aien* and later becoming the first editor of *Annasach*, the newspaper of the new University of Dundee. Under my leadership the number of staff involved in the production of the newspaper reached an all-time high and sales were buoyant. What this meant, however, was that most of my spare time was spent working on the paper. One of the first things I had to do was find someone to take over from me as production manager as I didn't intend to spend my Wednesdays from dawn in Perth. When a shy young man came up to me at the fresher's fair and said that he was interested in getting involved in production I could have hugged him. It was agreed that I would stay on for a few weeks as production manager and train up Brian, before taking over from Robin.

Brian Wilson, the shy young man from Dunoon, went to the same school as George Robertson who was well known in the University for his firebrand politics and used the newspaper as his regular platform. Both were destined to end up in Tony Blair's Labour government with George defence minister and later Secretary General of NATO. If you'd suggested to George in 1967 that he would one day be the head of NATO he would have derided you scornfully. Brian went to the Scottish Office as a trade minister and also broadcast regularly in Scotland as editor and owner of a Highlands and Islands newspaper. It's nice to feel that I was something of a mentor to him in the early days. George Outram, publisher of the Perth Advertiser and various other organs, was a serious concern and it must have amused them to produce the small beer that was the university paper. On my first visit there with Robin Rycroft, I was introduced to Willie, the foreman on the print floor, and failed to understand a word he said. Robin had warned me that, being a broad Aberdonian, he was a little difficult to follow. This was a massive understatement. Try as I might I only ever understood one word in three even after more than a year working with him. But he was a patient man and put up with our naive requirements which must have been tiresome at times. Those were the days long before computing and any electronic devices in newspaper production. It was known as working with hot metal and it was very much a question of thinking on your feet as you read galley proofs as they came off the press and then constructed the paper using the relevant blocks of type. In addition, you produced the headlines as well as fitting in the advertisements. We had mocked up the paper the previous evening and so we knew more or less where everything should go but it still felt a creative achievement getting out the paper *on the day* when, occasionally, you had to write a last-minute filler.

Academically, the second year allowed me to start to get my teeth into psychology and philosophy. I proved to have some aptitude for logic and enjoyed the intellectual puzzles it posed. Moreover, I was in demand from other students who had less talent for formal logic and I would hold little tutorials for those who wanted them. But psychology became my abiding interest and I determined to take up single honours in psychology for my third and fourth years, known in St Andrews as junior and senior honours. As well as a senior man, all students were also assigned to a regent who was a member of staff. Mine was Alan Wilkes, a psychologist specialising in cognitive and developmental psychology. He was scarcely older than I but had a quiet engaging manner and a ready wit. He also had a charming wife, Judith, who was a music teacher, and two young girls. They made me very welcome on visits to their house in Newport, which was on the Fife side of the Tay. Alan wasn't particularly enamoured of the regent system but he was obliged to participate in it and he did receive some remuneration for his trouble. I remember him saying:

'As far as I'm concerned, this first meeting is to welcome you to the University and offer you my support should you need it. It's possible that we may become friends, but such a thing cannot be forced. Time will tell.'

As it happened, we did become friends and I was immensely pleased and honoured to be invited to Alan's retirement party in Dundee, many years later, which took the form of an all-day Feschrift and evening meal. After the meal, some of his closest friends (including me since I was staying with them) repaired to Alan and Judith's home to continue the party. There was, of course, only one drink to be consumed, whisky. Once upon a time I would have been too reticent to announce that I was not a whisky drinker, almost a hanging offence in Scotland. I'm sure they were unimpressed but I was allowed to drink wine instead. When he retired, Alan plunged into his antiquarian book business which he'd been running as a side interest for most of his academic life and he is still thus engaged.

Interests beyond the academic course included concerts by the Scottish National Orchestra at the Caird Hall. I persuaded a student called Bertie Lightband, who sported a bow tie with his tweed suit, to submit regular reviews (and sometimes previews) of the SNO concerts. I learnt a lot from him. There was also the Dundee Repertory Theatre, one of the best in the country, and I was a regular visitor to their productions. One of the outstanding events was Harold Pinter's *The Homecoming* which proved a powerful experience. I also recall Charmian May as Hester in Rattigan's *Deep Blue Sea*, which, coincidentally, I have just reviewed for the Stockport Garrick. For a while I also joined a dining club whose members were supposed to be gourmets. David Levy, later famous for taking on a computer at chess, was the driving force. It all got a little too precious (and no doubt expensive) for me and I resigned after a few months.

Vacation

For a couple of years I got a well-paid summer job collecting rent for Orpington Council. The job consisted of knocking on doors on the huge council estate in St Paul's Cray and collecting cash and stuffing it in a satchel and also taking note of any repairs that tenants required. After a few rounds with experienced full-time collectors I was adjudged ready to 'go it alone'. It gave me a few insights into the minds of an interesting community and is the subject of *The Rent Collector*.

My brother worked for a company called Addressograph-Multigraph and in 1967 he was sent to Durban in South Africa.

He wrote to me about the wonderful time he had on the boat over, a two-week long party. I discovered that there was an organisation that helped students spend the summer vacation and get temporary work in South Africa. I was successful in gaining a place on the trip and with my parents' help I was able to buy a return air ticket to Johannesburg. It proved a memorable experience of a country that was just beginning to attract regular adverse attention in Britain because of its apartheid policy. It gave me the opportunity to see this policy in action for myself and became the basis of the story, *Not Just Black and White*.

Towards the end of my second year I became friendly with Suzie Le Pine Powell, the sort of surname you came across at St Andrews. She lived in London and we saw quite a lot of each other. Her divorced mother lived in Kensington and was charming and took us to dinner at a Polish Restaurant. I was invited to join the family on a sailing holiday in the Mediterranean. Perhaps fortunately, as I was a lousy sailor, I had to refuse the offer because of my impending trip to South Africa. I got lots of affectionate letters from Suzie in Durban but the affair cooled off back in Dundee in the third year.

Third Year

We renewed our lease on 12 The Esplanade and Colin and I entered Junior Honours in Psychology along with about a dozen others. Because we were a small class who did everything together for two years, we became very close. When I returned in September, Queen's College had split off from St Andrews and become The University of Dundee. The birth of a new university was an exciting time and I became the first editor of the new student newspaper which we called *Annasach*. We ran a competition in *Aien* to elicit a name for the new paper but nothing appropriate was forthcoming. I decided that we should use a Gaelic name as a contrast to the Greek name used in the old university. I got hold of a Gaelic dictionary from the library and came up with a word that meant 'something new' which seemed appropriate. It also began with 'A' like the old paper. Some months later I was having a conversation with Professor Adams from the Department of Education who I knew was a fluent Gaelic speaker. He remarked that the fool who chose the name of the student newspaper obviously didn't know that it meant 'something strange or odd'.

Junior honours was an attractive year because there were no exams in the summer. This didn't mean that the level of work was any less demanding but, inevitably, it took pressure off. What it meant, however, was that we would be examined on two years of work at the end of our fourth year. But that was a long way off! Meanwhile I continued to put a lot of time into *Annasach* and Colin became Treasurer. We also recruited Isabel Simpson, a bejantine, as my secretary. Isabel was known to Colin and lived in Knutsford. We invited her to a party we had, to which my old friend, John Knight and his naval friend, Hamish Morrison, came. It was a bad taste party and there were a number of vicars, tarts and things more dubious. I was wearing a tabard on which was written in large letters: The Harry Roberts Fan Club. Roberts had recently been convicted of the murder of three policemen in Shepherd's Bush. The party was extremely noisy and spilled over into the street. At one point we had a visit from the police because of complaints from neighbours. Given the top I was wearing, it was a surprise that I wasn't arrested on the spot but we got off with a warning to keep the noise down. I was conscious of Isabel being molested by a very drunk Hamish, and John and I had to drag him off. She was very relaxed about it and I realised that I was more attracted to her than I'd realised.

I took her to the summer ball and on the way back to our flat in Broughty Ferry, I was driving her mini. Goodness knows how much I was over the alcohol limit and I was certainly over the speed limit as I raced through the quiet streets of Northern Dundee in the early hours of the morning. I became aware of a police car's flashing light behind me and pulled over. The officer was remarkably considerate.

'Where have you been, sir?'

'At the University Summer Ball, officer.' Since I was in evening dress and Isabel was in a ball gown, this must have rung true.

'Have you been drinking sir?'

'Yes, I suppose I've had a few.'

'Well, you were doing 47 in a 30 mile an hour zone. Please take it easy sir.'

With that he bid us good night and we continued our journey, still with me driving, but at a rather more sensible speed.

The students of Scottish universities elect a Rector who represents the students on the University Court. Such a figure is very often the sort of celebrity that students identify with and in recent years, Stephen Fry has been the Rector of Dundee. The first rector was a hotly contested election with the leading figures being Peter Ustinov, the actor and playwright, and James Cameron, the journalist who was a native of Dundee, traditionally known for the three Js – jam, jute and journalism. I voted for Cameron, a champion of left-wing causes, but he was defeated by Ustinov who was a very acceptable candidate. A large number of staff and students gathered for his installation in the Caird Hall including the University's Chancellor, Queen Elizabeth, the Queen Mother. Isabel and I were in the audience in the Caird Hall and Isy remarked on the difference in the amount of cheers for the royal personage compared with the famous actor. Ustinov gave a witty and perceptive address and was then dragged through the town in a carriage and plied with large amounts of whisky. He was later introduced to a line of the great and good at a reception in the University. Later I had a note from the Principal's office apologising for not including me in this line as Editor of the newspaper. I hadn't been expecting an invitation so it didn't concern me.

I continued to be a conscientious student and it soon became apparent that there were some very clever students in the single honours psychology corpus. We decided to revive the Psychological Society whose main function was to invite visiting speakers to the university. At the first meeting I was elected Chairman, whose principal role was to host and introduce the visiting speakers. We also had to elect an honorary president and the committee were unanimous in wanting Ian Gordon for this position. Ian lectured in perception and was easily the most popular member of staff. He had an easy, entertaining lecturing style and would go to a lot of trouble through the use of demonstrations to bring the subject alive. Our first visiting speaker was a famous Clinical Psychologist and I spoke to Ian Gordon to get a little background on the speaker for when I introduced him. In the middle of my introduction I completely dried, a sort of stage fright, and it was an embarrassing experience in front of a full lecture theatre. You can imagine how I felt when I next had to carry out this function! But, fortunately, it never happened again nor throughout my lecturing career.

During the course of Junior Honours, we learned that Ian Gordon was leaving. We were devastated since we assumed that he enjoyed life with us! Because he was easy to talk to, some of us asked him why he was going. We were having a drink with him after one of our meetings. He said it was because of the education system. He couldn't put his children through a system where the teacher had a punishment strap, called a tawse, on the desk at every lesson. In those days teachers were permitted to administer corporal punishment in class. At the time, I think I may have thought that this was something of an overreaction. Much later, as a parent myself, and a child psychologist, I fully supported his stand. Ian obtained an appointment at the other end of the country in the University of Exeter, and I did once visit him in his home in Topsham. When he came to leave, the students collected a lot of money for a leaving present. Some of us were deputed to ask him if he had any preference in the way of a parting gift. Immediately, he said he would like a painting from one of the students at the local college of art. He'd been to a graduation show at the College and knew that there was some good work on view. This was accordingly purchased.

I still played the occasional game of golf – Monifieth was a favourite course. On one occasion I went to St Andrews with John Knight and Hamish and Colin. In those days you could play the Old Course for less than a pound. Like Carnoustie it was a municipal course (and still is) and, in principle, open to anyone. We were unable to get on the Old Course, but did play the almost equally ancient New Course for the princely sum of ten shillings (50p). Hamish did not have a good day and was constantly sticking his ball out of bounds or in thick rough. We had some youths behind us who must have got exasperated by our slow play because eventually, on the seventeenth, a ball was driven that reached us before we had played our second shots. Hamish, who was not in the best of moods, was furious. He picked up the ball and threw it back down in the direction it had come from shouting something like 'Can't you see I'm playing here!' At the end of the round we discovered that the young men behind us were all Scottish internationals.

Vacation

Colin and I planned a major trip to Scandinavia and Russia in the summer vacation. The idea was to take his car and a tent. Visiting the Soviet Union in 1968 was not straightforward and a special visa was required. Tourists were obliged to use the services of Intourist, the official travel agency of the Soviet Union. It had been founded by Stalin himself and used the services of KGB officials. Once we had obtained our visa, because we were camping we somehow escaped the attentions of Intourist and had a remarkable amount of freedom.

It was a memorable trip. Colin collected me from my home in Kent and we drove to Harwich and took the ferry to Esbjerg. From there we drove to Copenhagen and had a couple of days there. This was probably my introduction to Danish pastries. We also visited Elsinore Castle, the setting for Shakespeare's Hamlet.

From Copenhagen we took a ferry the short trip to Helsingborg and drove across Sweden to the capital Stockholm which seemed a sophisticated place. The next leg of the trip was the overnight ferry to Helsinki. The boat was mostly populated by Finns returning home and we discovered that this was a race of serious drinkers. Sleep was eschewed in favour of drinking, dancing and partying. Somehow, we drove off the boat and found a camp site. Helsinki had some striking architecture, delightful parks and a lively waterfront. The land of Sibelius had an attractive, irreverent feel. Being the frontier between the west and its formidable neighbour to the east, they seemed to live for the moment.

The big adventure now began as we set off to the border en route to Leningrad. Although we only spent a week in Russia, as part of a five-week vacation, that week was the one that lived in the memory. It was 1968 and although we didn't realise it, as we spoke no Russian and we were unable to procure any English language papers, our visit coincided with the invasion of Czechoslovakia by USSR forces following the short-lived revolution known as the Prague Spring. There was a railway line at the rear of the campsite where we stayed north of Leningrad. One balmy evening Colin and I were walking by the railway when a huge goods train lumbered past. On it were scores of tanks heading south we knew not where. Subsequently we realised they were probably heading for Prague.

While in Russia we did the sort of things that only foolhardy students would do. We made contact with young Soviets and went back to their homes and sold black-market goods to them. We went on a visit to Novgorod, the ancient Kremlin city some fifty miles from Leningrad and, following a violent storm, we stayed the night with one of the students. None of these activities were allowed and could have got us, and more importantly our Russian friends, in serious trouble. The trip forms the subject of the story, *Seven Days in Russia*.

Because of selling clothes to the Russians, we left the country with more roubles than when we'd entered which we endeavoured to disguise at the border. The Russian guard did not look convinced but he let us leave with a shrug. Our intention now was to drive up to the Arctic Circle. We camped beside a lake in Finland on a beautiful clear night, so clear that we could see the reflections of stars in the water. When we realised how much time we had left, and we still hadn't seen Norway, we abandoned plans to go inside the Circle and drove south into Northern Sweden and on into Norway. The roads were so empty and so straight that we were able to play travel scrabble as we drove along with the driver keeping a rough eye on the road. We stopped at Lillehammer where the winter Olympics had taken place. We stood by the ski jump and marvelled at the bravery of those who leapt off into the air with only a pair of skis between them and a very hard landing.

From Lillehammer we headed to the coast and Kinsarvik which was on the Hardanger fjord. The fjords were a creamy turquoise colour and surrounded by towering mountains. At the campsite we came across another party of young Australian women (we had also encountered some in Leningrad). They had also been to Russia and had bottles of vodka which they seemed anxious to make short work of. Colin and I tucked in with gusto and ended up in tents which weren't our own. Oslo was a next stop. I had the address of a WREN whom I had met in London through John Knight and who was on the staff of the naval attaché in Oslo. She had a nice flat and it was pleasant to sleep in a proper bed once again after five weeks of living under canvas. Olso was a civilised city and we looked round the Parliament and the Kontiki exhibition. Camping was not quite finished. We drove to Goteborg and stayed a night before taking the ferry across to Denmark. From there it was a relatively short drive to Esbjerg and the ferry back to Harwich and the end of a remarkable holiday.

Fourth Year

In our final year Colin and I took a student flat let by the University in Airlie Place which was on the campus. We wanted to be as close to the library and Psychology Department as possible in what we knew was going to be a demanding year. Isabel had moved into 142 Nethergate with Joy Sawkins, a social administration student, and Chris Oddy who was also in final year single honours psychology. It was a stimulating and happy time. I worked hard but also spent much of my spare time with Isy. We went to the theatre, concerts and some union events. Since Isy had a car we were able to drive out to beauty spots like Dunkeld, Pitlochry or Falkland Palace at the weekend.

I did my final year project under Alan Wilkes's supervision and, having abandoned a project with children as being too difficult logistically, I embraced Wilkes and Kennedy's research on the role of pausing in cognitive and linguistic organisation. (The following year Isabel also did her project with Alan and we eventually published a paper – Wilkes, Lloyd and Simpson – in the Quarterly Journal of Experimental Psychology.) I really got absorbed by the project and stayed up in Dundee over the Easter vacation working hard on the analysis and write up of the dissertation.

I was asked to be best man to Nick Tryhorn who was marrying Ruth Glover, whom I'd known for years and probably introduced to Nick. She was one of three daughters and two sons of our family doctor, Dr Glover. Isabel suggested we borrowed their family's large Humber Super Snipe as it could act as a wedding car for delivering Nick to the church. We drove down from Knutsford and I performed my best man duties in Farnborough church and at the reception in Hayes on January 3rd, 1969.

As it was my final year, I was having to give thought to my future. I was confident enough of my progress in psychology to want to make it my career. My initial thought was to aim for educational psychology which required obtaining a teaching qualification and experience before applying for a postgraduate place. Another area I was considering was psychology and media which capitalised on my experience in journalism. Leicester

University was pioneering this area and I attended an interview for a place on their Master's course. Staff in the Dundee Department encouraged me to go for a PhD place and I applied to Bristol. Again I got an interview and was eventually offered a place and an SSRC studentship with Colin Fraser, who had worked with the famous Roger Brown at Harvard. I also had an interview with John and Elizabeth Newsom at Nottingham who ran a famous developmental psychology unit. I was offered a place on their MSc course.

I had more or less decided to accept the Bristol offer when I ran into Terry Lee, one of the senior lecturers in social psychology and soon to take a Chair at the University of Surrey. He told me he'd heard of a Research Associate position going at Edinburgh with Margaret Donaldson and advised me to apply. By now I was in the middle of final exams which consisted of eight papers in ten days. I was working very hard and was almost punch drunk with the amount of information I was trying to absorb and then reproduce coherently under exam conditions. Nevertheless, I found time to write for details about the post in Edinburgh and then made an application.

As Isabel was in her junior honours year, she had no exams and finished her studies early. Her brother Willie, who was studying Spanish at St Andrews, was doing a study year in Colombia and Isabel had arranged to visit him during the summer vacation. She said I was welcome to join her but I didn't really have the resources to make such a trip. Besides, I had to sort out my future and so reluctantly declined. I similarly declined Colin's suggestion that we drive to Turkey as a Balkan complement to our Scandinavian tour. Colin went with another friend and had a memorable trip.

By the time I was taking my eighth exam paper I had reached the point where it was difficult to take anything seriously. As I stared at the paper and then started to write I felt like an automaton. Surely there must be a better way of assessing performance and deciding someone's future. During one of the early exams, Jean

Davidson, a bright, attractive student, went to the front of the room after half an hour looking distressed. She left the room. Later I observed her from the window walking in the quad with Alan Kennedy, one of our lecturers who seemed to be counselling her. She eventually returned to the exam room but I remember thinking she had ruined her chances.

I was wrong. Four of us, Chris Oddy, Jean Davidson, myself and another male student were invited to meet the external examiner, Professor Jonqueere from London University, for a viva. I later learned that the four of us had high enough marks to be considered for a first. Up to that moment, Queen's College/Dundee had never given a first. The viva was a pleasant affair; Jonqueere was convivial, but I suspected he was leading me into traps. In the event no one did enough to get moved into the first category but I had to be happy with an upper second. In the evening we had a party with the Social Administration students, many of whom were mature female students and great fun. Everyone, including the staff and external, got very drunk. I ended up with a woman who had live hens scratching around in her flat, a peculiar experience.

Graduation was in July and my parents came up for the occasion and met with Colin's parents. The ceremony was held in Caird Hall. Our year was entitled to take a St Andrews or Dundee degree and the Principals from both universities in their finery were on the platform. I chose Dundee partly to support the new university and because I felt more of a Dundee student than a St Andrews one. It was probably an unwise choice given that I was anticipating an academic career. In the evening Colin and I and our parents had a delicious lobster meal near Arbroath. Afterwards we went paddling in the sea with phosphorescence glistening in the water.

It was difficult leaving Dundee for the last time since it had been life changing for me and I'd developed enormous affection for the people and the place. On the way home I stopped in Edinburgh to have an interview with Margaret Donaldson and Roger Wales who together ran a research centre called The Cognition Project which was funded by the Social Science Research Council. They met me in Staff House in Chambers Street. Margaret, a slight, dark haired woman in her early forties, made me at home in her quiet way, describing the project and my role in it if I were to get the job. Roger Wales seemed distracted and scarcely bothered to engage with me. To be fair, the position was Research Associate to Margaret but he might have been a little more enthusiastic. I was excited by Margaret's description of the project which was looking at language and thought in preschool children. At the end of the interview, by which time Roger had disappeared, she said she had other people to interview but would let me know in a day or two.

I went down to my parents' house with my life feeling a little empty. No Isabel, no Colin, no Dundee. Even the grainy pictures of men walking on the moon for the first time didn't lift me. But then I got a phone call from Margaret Donaldson offering me the position in Edinburgh. Not only was it exciting work but it carried a handsome salary and allowed me to register for a PhD as well. I was sorry to turn down the opportunity to work with Colin Fraser, and Bristol was a city I'd always liked, but I felt I was making the right decision. Things continued to look up when I was invited to Jean Davidson's 21st in Gloucestershire and I met up with a crowd at Henley during the regatta en route to the party.

Soon my brother returned from South Africa looking tanned and handsome. Allan and I drove to Spain where our parents were on holiday at the Agua Blava Hotel in the Costa Brava, somewhere they went most years. This was one of the rare occasions when we were all on holiday together. It was a gorgeous Mediterranean setting but my thoughts were mostly elsewhere. I needed to adjust to a new life and though I looked forward to the challenge it was a little difficult to leave behind a world where I'd felt so comfortable and had achieved a fair degree of success.

The Edinburgh Years

In the last week of August, I headed for Edinburgh. En route I stopped with Colin in Alderley Edge. He'd recently returned from his trip to Turkey and made me regret that I'd had to turn down his offer. Colin had obtained a place on an MBA course at the prestigious Wharton Business School, at the University of Pennsylvania in Philadelphia. No doubt his parents were content to fund this enterprise as now Colin was properly starting his career, having got psychology out of his system. Isabel had invited me to borrow her car while she was away in Colombia and Colin drove me over to Brook Farm to pick up her Mini. I then drove up to Edinburgh.

There was a vacancy in a flat in Marchmont where a friend of Colin's (and Isabel's) lived. Richard Logan was a medical student and the vacancy meant sharing a room with him in a flat that housed two others. Edward Blandy was the son of the owners of Blandy's, the madeira house established 1811 on the island of Madeira. He had been sent to Edinburgh to do a business course and had an elder brother, also Richard, doing an accountancy course in the city. I never recall seeing Edward doing anything in the way of work while I was there. He was a playboy and spent a fair bit of time in London. He used to drive down as fast as he could, scaring his passenger and doubtless other motorists. The final member of the Thirlestane Road house was David Pike, a rep for Blue Circle Cement Co. Prematurely bald with horn rimmed spectacles, he got called John Concrete behind his back by Logan and his medical student friends. He was friendly enough but a little lacking in self-awareness. He had, however, a beautiful cousin who was a nurse at the Edinburgh Royal Infirmary. At a party we held she came and met one of Richard Logan's medical friends. Some years later, in the classic tradition of doctors and nurses, this couple wed.

I reported for duty at the Cognition Project which was housed in the Epworth Halls, a former Wesleyan meeting house, rented by

the University of Edinburgh in Nicholson Square. The Edinburgh
Festival was in full swing and the children hadn't yet returned to
the nursery which formed part of the complex. The nursery was
a research facility in a large room at one end of the building and
there were a series of offices occupied by Margaret, Roger, and
various research assistants and students as well as secretarial staff. I
was assigned an office and introduced to the few people who were
around. Margaret gave me a number of papers to read including the
original research proposal and a number of research publications
and drafts. I was mostly left to my own devices but met Margaret for
lunch once or twice. A research student called Barbara Rowlands
started at the same time as I and we became good friends. After a
few days Margaret said she had a job for me which was to assist
her to mount an exhibition of her art which would be part of the
Festival Fringe. This episode is covered in *The Talking Doll*.

I soon came to realise that Psychology at Edinburgh was
higher powered than Dundee. Most of the staff had international
reputations and many had large egos to boot. These included
Tom Bower, Brendan McGonigle, Colwyn Trevarthen, John and
Halla Belloff, and Bill McGrew. There were also psychologists and
others involved with the behavioural sciences such as the linguists
John Lyon, Carolus Oldfield and John Marshall and the artificial
intelligence group including Richard Gregory, Christopher
Longuet Higgins and Donald Michie as well as Aubrey and
Margaret Manning from Zoology, Sula Wolf from Psychiatry and
Jess Reid from Education. Managing these stars must have been
difficult but Professor Vowles, who had come from Oxford after
establishing a career in animal behaviour, exuded quiet authority.
An example of this was when I missed one of the weekly research
seminars for visiting speakers. It was quietly made known to me
that the professor had noted my absence.

I was in awe of these luminaries but, because the Cognition
Project was a few hundred yards away from the Psychology
Building, we enjoyed a largely separate existence. Margaret had
offices in both buildings but it was apparent that she preferred to

be at the Cognition Project whenever possible. Once the children had returned to the nursery, I started to develop my skills in working with preschool infants initially by spending time in the nursery observing. Later I worked with the children individually or in small groups. I also learned a lot by watching Margaret talk to small children. She was someone else who had quiet authority and I endeavoured to emulate her ability to use Piaget's clinical method. She was one of the few British psychologists who had actually worked with Piaget in Geneva and was respected accordingly. Her ability to gain children's confidence and draw out their thinking processes without leading them into answers was impressive. Her famous book, *Children's Minds*, which published the findings of the Cognition Project including some of my work, was seen as a critique of Piaget. Indeed it was, but it never denied the huge debt that Developmental Psychology owed to Piaget.

The daily life of the Project consisted of formulating research programmes, trialling new methods, collecting empirical data, analysing results and writing reports. Margaret wrote very well but she was not someone who would choose to go into print unless she knew she'd something to say. This possibly held my career back as we didn't publish as much together as was probably warranted. But, essentially, I respected her integrity. She once said, if you want to get ahead in psychology, and perhaps any science, get one good idea and rework it endlessly, publishing ad nauseam. It was definitely not her practice. Most days I would have lunch with Margaret and often Barbara and other members of the project including the ethologist Penny McGrew, wife of Bill. We would drive in Margaret's car – she hated walking anywhere – and park outside the chosen venue, something impossible in Edinburgh today. Margaret and Roger were film buffs and if there was something on that they wanted to see, particularly an old film, they'd announce that the whole Project was going to a film. Sometimes, to make up time, we were expected to go in on Saturday mornings.

There was a constant stream of famous visitors to the Department in Edinburgh and to the Cognition Project, specifically. This may have been partly because Edinburgh as a city was an attraction but also due to the illustrious nature of the University and its reputation in Psychology. In this way, I didn't need to stir from my place of work to meet and hear plenty of the best-known names in the subject. Roger Brown lectured on the research with 'Talking Chimpanzees'. He gave a spell-binding talk to a huge audience without using a single note. The legendary cognitive psychologist George Miller gave a polished talk on language and communication and his celebrated colleague at Harvard, Jerome Bruner, visited the Project on a number of occasions. He'd moved to Oxford in 1970 and automatically assumed the mantle of leader in the field. He and Margaret were old friends and his enthusiasm and self-deprecatory manner were infectious. I met him on a number of occasions over the years and always found him friendly and charming. We also had a visit from Piaget's celebrated collaborator, Barbel Inhelder, and some of my colleagues said her presentation changed their lives.

On one occasion Margaret mentioned that there were some American visitors to the Department and that they wanted to visit the Project and would probably come to lunch with us. A middle-aged husband and wife team appeared and seemed interested in what we were doing. Over lunch in Leith I was talking to the female visitor and she was describing some research she had been doing on children's verbal memory. I was just on the point of saying: 'Yes, the Kendlers have done interesting work in that area,' when something inhibited me. Later in the conversation I realised we were entertaining Howard and Tracy Kendler.

The over-used word 'groundbreaking' was justified in the case of the research emanating from the Cognition Project. It was able to show that children's grasp of words used by Piaget in tasks to gain insights into their early logical thinking was very insecure but showed a developmental pattern. I refer to words like 'same' and different', 'more', 'less', 'all', 'some', and 'none'. We designed ingenious experiments to investigate early word meaning with children of three and four years. One of the techniques invented by Margaret was a talking doll. This was a life sized toy panda with a voice box inserted in its head. The panda 'lived' in my room and the idea was that children would come to help the panda learn to talk. In playing the role of teacher, they would reveal to us what meanings they found acceptable and those they judged false. It turned out to be a brilliant tool (and produced lots of entertainment) and is described in the story *The Talking Doll*.

Naturally I did my doctoral research at The Cognition Project investigating the growth of speaker and listener skills in preschool children. The talking doll was employed in this work and at other times I had the demanding experience of working with two children at once, one a speaker, one a listener. Margaret was very generous in giving me time, for which I was being paid to work for her, to enable me to complete the empirical data gathering in the three years I was in Edinburgh. The work was later published in a book written with Michael Beveridge: *Information and Meaning in Child Communication.*

My social life in Edinburgh was quiet compared to the lively scene I'd enjoyed in Dundee. The compensation was the richer culture as well as the undeniable truth that Edinburgh was a magnificent city. I never tired of walking round Scotland's capital (aesthetically the most pleasing city in Britain) which was just as well as I didn't have a car. The arts were more than satisfactory with weekly concerts at the Usher Hall, decent repertory at the Lyceum Theatre and visiting opera and commercial companies at the King's Theatre. One memorable production was the National Theatre doing Congreve's *Love for Love*. This starred Lawrence Olivier, Maggie Smith and Albert Finney and, at the time, was the most thrilling evening I'd ever had in the theatre. Edinburgh was also fortunate to have The Traverse Theatre with its contemporary productions at that time directed by Michael Rudman and Max Stafford Clark. The jazz scene, however, was disappointing. Al

Fairweather and Sandy Brown were the local stars but they'd long since left Edinburgh for London.

Best of all, there was the incomparable Edinburgh Festival. At that time the Fringe was a fraction of what it was to become and so it was possible to see most of the 'acts' which *The Scotsman* or word of mouth suggested were worth a visit. This was when the Fringe was genuinely amateur, or at the most semi-professional, with a great many student productions. When it subsequently got overrun with professional stand-up comedians it lost much of its unique status. In addition, there was the official festival which provided the opportunity to see foreign theatre productions and renowned international orchestras and other performers. Among the many marvellous events I saw, the stand-out productions were: *Orlando Furioso* by a visiting Italian company at the Haymarket ice rink ; *Woyzeck* by Georg Buchner performed by a Rumanian company; the Netherlands Dance Theatre; and a wild west adaptation of *The Taming of the Shrew* by a Californian student group. The performance of the latter that I attended was 'graced' by Princess Margaret and the start of the second half was held up for nearly twenty minutes while Margaret and her retinue got back from an extended drinks break.

David Pike was a member of Dalmahoy Golf Club, a championship course outside Edinburgh, and I played a fair amount with him. Sometimes we went down the East Lothian coast to play courses like Gullane, North Berwick and Dunbar. One Spring, a business colleague of Pike was staying and decided to join us for a game of golf at Dalmahoy. It was a cold day and the visitor cut a bizarre figure, the only time I've played with someone wearing a three piece suit. The Open Golf Championship was held at St Andrews in 1970. John Knight's ship was berthed in Rosyth at the time and we arranged to go to the course for the last day which was then a Saturday. We saw Doug Sanders miss a three-foot putt on the last green which would have won him the tournament. He had to play-off over 18 holes the following day against Jack

Nicklaus and we went up again to see it. Sanders never got another chance.

One summer I went on a golfing holiday in the Highlands with my brother and Dave Pike. We played at Blairgowrie, Boat of Garten, Kingussie and Gairloch, staying at B&Bs. One evening we found ourselves in Poolewe but unable to get accommodation in the village. We drove along the Inverasdale peninsula, still finding nothing available. Finally, we found a remote cottage where an elderly lady welcomed us in. She showed us round the house with the following commentary: 'This is where you'll sleep; this is where you'll eat; this is where you'll bathe; and this is where you'll sit.' This last was a severe sitting room with mostly hard chairs. I think she seriously expected us to spend our evening in this room but three red-blooded males in their twenties had other ideas. We asked if we could have a key since we planned to return to Poolewe to get something to eat and see if there was any action. Rather reluctantly she produced a key. In Poolewe the only entertainment was a ceilidh in the village hall. The locals were welcoming but amused at our attempts at Scottish dancing. We returned to our digs at an hour which our landlady would regard as ungodly. Next morning she produced fish which she proudly announced she'd caught herself in the loch that very morning. After an evening of drinking Scottish 'heavy', I fear we didn't do her breakfast justice. I fear we also did little to further Anglo-Scottish relations.

The other sporting event I became fond of was rugby internationals at Murrayfield. Dave Pike played for Edinburgh Wanderers whose ground happened to be Murrayfield so I became reasonably familiar with it. In the early '70s it was possible to walk to the ground from Princes Street, stopping off in hostelries en route, and purchase a ticket when you arrived. The capacity at Murrayfield was enormous with standing terraces round most of the stadium. The atmosphere was fantastic, with bottles being passed around liberally, and the crowd good humoured. Wales were playing outstanding rugby at the time with Gareth Edwards and Barry John at half back. In the 1971 match, with a few minutes to go, Scotland were leading in a match where the lead constantly changed hands. It looked as though Scotland had done it until Gerald Davies scored a late try converted by the flanker John Taylor on the touch line with his left boot. Wales won 19-18 which was a pity for the home crowd but no one cared too much and the two sets of supporters mixed convivially.

In the summer of 1970, Edinburgh hosted the Commonwealth Games. Some of my friends from London, including my brother, came up for the event and we attended a number of athletics events and generally enjoyed the associated festivities. By that time my relationship with Isabel had finished. Initially while in Edinburgh, I had returned to Dundee regularly to see Isy and she stayed with me in Edinburgh. As I mentioned, we wrote a paper together with Alan Wilkes that was published in the Quarterly Journal of Experimental Psychology. Writing that paper with Alan was a happy and illuminating experience and taught me something of the craft of journal writing and submission. But it became apparent that Isabel had feelings for a friend she knew from home and had met again while in America the previous summer. It was a painful separation but it gave completion to my move to Edinburgh and a new stage of my life.

By the time of the Commonwealth Games, Richard Logan and Edward Blandy had left the flat and we recruited a new flatmate. Limiting it to one person meant that we could each have a bedroom. Tim Walker was not unlike Edward whom he replaced. He worked for a shipping company (Ben Line), an old fashioned firm that he constantly lampooned. Bespectacled and boyish looking, with a shock of dark curly hair, he was entertaining company and easy going. He claimed to be a fully qualified ship's master and regaled us with stories of the yachts he had sailed for rich owners in the Caribbean and elsewhere.

By now I knew Edinburgh well and enjoyed the night life in both the Old and New Town. A pub in the New Town called The

Darnaway became a popular venue and a place where the location of Saturday night parties could be reliably sourced. At one party there was a beautiful girl with shoulder length fair hair who was dancing with a group of admiring men. Her name was Virginia Morton and she shared a flat with a group of girls in Darnaway Street. Not long after the party Tim started dating her. I myself had a few dalliances in Edinburgh since it was a city replete with attractive interesting young women. On the occasion that he was visiting Rosyth for a brief visit, John Knight contacted me and invited me to visit the frigate that he was serving on. He had been in the West Indies for some time and among the young officers on board was a certain Midshipman Wales, better known as Prince Charles. Unfortunately, I never got the chance to meet HRH as he had left the ship before it docked in Rosyth. John's invitation included the instruction: 'Bring plenty of women', and I did my best to comply with his request.

I got used to seeing Virginia in Thurlestane Road and also met her other flat mates in Darnaway Street: Anne, Liz and Caroline. They were good company. Virginia contracted glandular fever and spent some time in an isolation hospital since she didn't have any family that she could stay with in Edinburgh. Tim then had a bad case of psoriasis and also had to be hospitalised. Soon after his release from hospital, Tim was posted abroad. He was replaced by Clive Gairn, a friendly, garrulous Irishman who was an expert in something called computers.

My destiny was decided at a rugby international at Murrayfield. I went with a crowd, among whom was Virginia. We hit it off and I was disappointed to have to leave the party to go to a previously arranged dinner with a nurse I'd met. The nurse was having a dinner party in her flat and served, among other things, warm *sake*. This, on top of whatever I had been drinking before, during and after the rugby game, proved too much. I was obliged to leave the party. This actually suited me quite well as I'd spent the evening wishing I was elsewhere, preferably in the vicinity of Miss Morton.

Virginia and I now started to spend a lot of time together and I met her sister Evelyn, who lived in Craiglockhart near the famous hospital that housed Siegfried Sassoon and Wilfred Owen and other victims of shell shock during the First World War. Evelyn was an art teacher and immediately likeable. Her husband, George, was a senior civil servant in the Scottish Office. He was disabled, having had polio as a child, but got about with the aid of callipers and sticks. He was uncomplaining and remarkably mobile thanks to a car with hand controls. At the same time, he was a fairly blunt character and seemed jealous of Evelyn's relationship with Virginia. As a result Virginia's relationship with her brother-in-law was strained. Nevertheless, George and Evelyn were both extremely kind to me and I enjoyed their hospitality on many occasions.

After a whirlwind romance Virginia and I got engaged and were married three months later. The 3rd April, 1972 was Easter Monday and a bright, windy day. The Church of the Good Shepherd in Murrayfield was almost next door to where Virginia grew up and on her wedding day she was able to walk the few yards to the church from her friend Lesley Wallace's house in Murrayfield Avenue. In my singular experience everything is a bit of a blur on your wedding day but it was a wonderful occasion. My Uncle Peter said the singing in the church, by Virginia's own choir, while we were signing the register was the best he'd ever heard. Evelyn was the matron of honour, and friends Jane McFadyen and Lesley Holmes were bridesmaids along with her three little nieces. My best man was my brother, Allan, and I followed the tradition of only having unmarried ushers who were David Green, Colin Williams, David Pike and Graham Bennett, an Australian surgeon studying in Edinburgh whom Virginia and I both liked.

Our reception was held in the Staff Club of the University in Chambers Street. As a member of staff, this was a perk that I was allowed and it proved a delightful (and economical) venue. Apart from amusing speeches by Virginia's show business brother William and my best man, my strongest memory from the reception was counselling Margaret Donaldson. At that time she was seeing a man twelve years younger than her and was entertaining the idea of getting married. Most of us had assumed that marriage and Margaret were an unlikely pairing and she was partly of this view herself. Because of my respect and affection for Margaret, I was happy to help her in any way I could but I felt I was a little underequipped to offer marriage guidance on my wedding day. In the event she did marry that man, Steven Salter, who became famous for his work on tidal energy. It has proved a long and happy marriage.

We honeymooned in St David's and so began our love affair with Pembrokeshire and its wonderful coastal footpath. It is a part of the world that we never tire of. Back in Edinburgh we'd rented a flat in Northumberland Street. We had to lie to secure this since the minimum rental contract we could get was six months and I knew we'd probably have to leave Edinburgh before that. I was looking for a job and had two interviews lined up, one in Bradford and one in Nottingham. Even in 1972 jobs were beginning to be scarce but I was reasonably hopeful of getting a position. The Bradford interview came before the one in Nottingham which was unfortunate. After Edinburgh, Bradford hardly compared favourably (in any respect), and when I was offered the job I asked if I could have twenty-four hours to consider the offer and discuss it with my wife, a word that still sounded a little strange to me. The chair of the appointments committee indicated that if I was uncertain about taking the position, there were candidates in the corridor outside who would be glad of the job. In those circumstances I felt I'd no option. I returned to peerless Edinburgh to tell my new wife that she had to abandon this for the dark satanic mills of Bradford. To her credit, she never complained about the move from her beloved home city but found a teaching job in Otley and simply got down to making the best of our future together which she has always continued to do.

Also by the author

Information and Meaning in Child Communication (with M Beveridge)
Psychology: An Integrated Introduction (with A Mayes, A Manstead, P Meudell, H Wagner)
Piaget and After (with W Swann)
Cognitive and Language Development
Lev Vygotsky: Critical Assessments – 4 vols. (with C Fernyhough)
LIST – The Listening Skills Test (with I Peers and C Foster)